Collects of the
Roman Missals

T&T Clark Studies in **Fundamental Liturgy** offer cutting-edge scholarship from all disciplines related to liturgical study. The books in the series seek to reintegrate biblical, patristic, historical, dogmatic and philosophical questions with liturgical study in ways faithful and sympathetic to classical liturgical enquiry. Volumes in the series include monographs, translations of recent texts and edited collections around very specific themes.

EDITED BY

Laurence Paul Hemming
Susan Frank Parsons

PUBLISHED TITLES IN THE SERIES

The Banished Heart: Origins of Heteropraxis in the Catholic Church
The Call of the Holy: Heidegger – Chauvet – Benedict XVI
The Restoration and Organic Development of the Roman Rite

Collects of the Roman Missals

A Comparative Study of the Sundays in Proper Seasons before and after the Second Vatican Council

Lauren Pristas

BLOOMSBURY

LONDON • NEW DELHI • NEW YORK • SYDNEY

Bloomsbury T&T Clark

An imprint of Bloomsbury Publishing Plc

50 Bedford Square	1385 Broadway
London	New York
WC1B 3DP	NY 10018
UK	USA

www.bloomsbury.com

First published 2013

British Library Cataloguing-in-Publication Data

A catalogue record for this book is available from the British Library.

ISBN: HB: 978–0–567–03383–3
PB: 978–0–567–03384–0

Library of Congress Cataloging-in-Publication Data

Pristas, Lauren

The Collects of the Roman Missals of 1962 and 2002/Lauren Pristas p.cm

Includes bibliographic references and index.

ISBN 978–0–567–03383–3 (hardcover) – ISBN 978–0–567–03384–0 (paperback)

2012045678

Typeset by Fakenham Prepress Solutions, Fakenham, Norfolk NR21 8NN

Printed and bound in Great Britain

In memory of my mother

Nihil Obstat
M. Kathleen Flanagan, S.C., Ph.D.
Censor Librorum

Imprimatur
Most Reverend Arthur J. Serratelli, S.T.D., S.S.L., D.D.
Bishop of Paterson
16 October 2012

CONTENTS

ACKNOWLEDGMENTS

The research for this book was made possible by an appointment to the Pope John Paul II Chair for the Study of Person and Community at the Intercultural Forum of the Pope John Paul II Cultural Center in Washington, D.C., a Research Fellowship in Liturgical Theology from the Society of Saint Catherine of Siena, and both a leave and a sabbatical from Caldwell College. I am especially grateful to Archbishop J. Augustine DiNoia, O.P., Rev Richard Schenk, O.P., and Donald Cardinal Wuerl for the time at the Intercultural Forum, to Dr Laurence Hemming and Mr Ferdinand Knapp for the support of the Society of Saint Catherine of Siena, to Sister Patrice Werner, O.P. and Dr Paul Douillard for the leaves from Caldwell College.

All the *Consilium* schemata quoted or referred to in this article are on file at the offices of the Secretariat of the International Commission on English in the Liturgy in Washington, D.C. I am grateful to Rev Msgr Bruce Harbert and Mr Peter Finn, and more recently to Rev Msgr Andrew Wadsworth and Mr Edmund Yates, for giving me access to the ICEL collection of Consilium documents.

During the time this book has been in preparation, many persons have lent assistance of various kinds. I am very grateful to all and particularly wish to thank the following: Rev Dennis McManus, Dr James LeGrys, Dr Michael Carlin, Dr Denis J. Obermeyer, Dr Laurence Hemming, Mrs Joan Reamer, Sister Sara Butler, M.S.B.T., Rev Gabriel O'Donnell, O.P., Rev Daniel O'Mullane and Ms Kathleen Pluth. Grateful thanks are also due for the generous assistance received from the Latin Mass Society of England and Wales, Mrs Catherine Philomena McDonald, and several others in supporting the Research Fellowship from the Society of St Catherine of Siena that made earlier stages of this research possible.

I am also grateful to Dr Gregory La Nave of *The Thomist*, Ms Katherine G. Quan of *Communio, an International Catholic Review*, Dr Matthew Levering of *Nova et Vetera* and Dr Laurence Hemming of *Usus Antiquior* for permission to use in this study material from essays that I first published in their journals. The respective essays are: "Theological Principles that Guided the Redaction of the Roman Missal (1970)," *The Thomist* 67 (April 2003): 157–95; "The Orations of the Vatican II Missal: Policies for Revision," *Communio: an International Catholic Review*, 30:4 (Winter, 2003) 621–53; "The Collects at Sunday Mass: An Examination of the Revisions of Vatican II," *Nova et Vetera* 3.1 (Winter 2005) 5–38; "Parachuted into Lent: The Suppression of Septuagesima," *Usus Antiquior* 1.2 (July 2010) 95–109. Finally, it is by kind permission of Continuum International Publishing Group that material originally published in "Post Vatican II Revision of the Lenten Collects," in Uwe Michael Lang, ed., *Ever Directed Towards the Lord: The Love of God in the Liturgy of the Eucharist Past, Present, and Hoped for* (London: T&T Clark, 2007) 62–89 is used in this study.

ABBREVIATIONS

CO   Moeller, Eugenio, Jean-Marie Clément, and Bertrandus Coppieters 't. Wallant, *Corpus Orationum, I–IX.* Turnholti [Turnholt, Belgium]: Brepols, 1991–9.

    Tomus I, A–C, Orationes 1–880.

    Tomus II, D, pars prima, Orationes 881–1707.

    Tomus III, D, pars altera, Orationes 1708–2389.

    Tomus IV, E–H, Orationes 2390–3028.

    Tomus V, I–O, Orationes 3029–3699.

    Tomus VI, O–P, Orationes 3700–4334.

    Tomus VII, P–Q, Orationes 4335–4954.

    Tomus VIII, R–S, Orationes 4955–5538.

    Tomus IX, S–V, Orationes 5539–6121.

DACL   Cabrol, Fernand, and Henri Leclercq. *Dictionnaire d'Archéologie Chrétienne et de Liturgie.* Paris: Letouzey et Ané (1913–53).

Engol   Patrick Saint-Roch. *Liber sacramentorum Engolismensis: manuscrit B.N. Lat. 816, Le sacramentaire gélasien d'Angoulême.* Turnholti: Brepols, 1987.

GeV   Leo Eizenhöfer, Leo Cunibert Mohlberg, and Petrus Siffrin. *Liber sacramentorum Romanae Aeclesiae ordinis anni circuli* [= *Gelasianum Vetus*].

Had   Jean Deshusses. *Le sacramentaire grégorien, ses principales formes d'après les plus anciens manuscrits.* Fribourg: Éditions universitaires, 1971.

PL   J. P. Migne, *Patrologia Latina.*

Ver   Cunibert Mohlberg, Petrus Siffrin, and Leo Eizenhöfer. *Sacramentarium Veronense (Cod. Bibl. Capit. Veron. LXXXV [80]).* Roma: Herder, 1956.

AUTHOR'S PREFACE

The study that follows examines the orations and collects assigned to the Sundays of proper seasons in the Roman missals currently in use.

The chapters on Advent, Septuagesima, and Lent each begin with a short account of the development of the season. These historical sections rely on secondary sources and do not break new ground. Their sole purpose is to supply pertinent historical, liturgical, theological and/or spiritual background for the discussion of the Consilium decisions and the examination of the Mass prayers that are the principal concern of the chapter.

Most of the collects examined in this volume have been widely and well-prayed over the course of many centuries. Their venerable character and holy purpose requires that they be received with reverence. The antiquity of the prayers and the wide use they have enjoyed means that there is always something more to be learned about them, always other sources to consult. The rhetorical sophistication, genuine piety, sober beauty, succinct theological precision, and spiritual depth of the collects are such that there is always something more in them to be discovered, savored, and appropriated. The manuscript history of each collect is presented and the literary composition carefully considered, but the aim throughout the study is competent, not comprehensive, treatment. Much more could be said than has been said.

This study was undertaken to address the questions that are set forth in the first chapter and to some extent answered in the last. In the opinion of the author, however, its principal value lies in the extent to which it fosters appreciation of these sacred compositions and the great and varied blessings for which they plead.

1

Introduction and Background

The Second Vatican Council mandated a reform of the Roman Catholic Liturgy, and subsequently new liturgical books were produced. The new books have been very well studied in themselves, but not in relation to the pre-Vatican II books or the other sources from which the revisers drew. This leaves a serious lacuna: the primary work necessary to understand how the new Mass is like and unlike its predecessor, not with respect to the rubrics, language, and orientation of worship, but with respect to the prayers that are prayed, has not yet been done.

This study examines the pre- and post-Vatican II missals in order to discover whether they emphasize the same truths of faith and the same aspects of Christian life, whether Catholics who worship by means of the revised rites are shaped by their worship in the same way that earlier generations were shaped by theirs, and if the answer to either of the preceding questions is no, to determine the nature and significance of the differences.

The aim of the present chapter is to introduce the study and to provide the background necessary for the appreciation of subsequent chapters. It is divided into five sections. The first presents, in the most general terms, the state of the question: what scholars have and have not done since the promulgation of the Vatican II missal. The second specifies the scope, method, and goals of the present study. The third introduces the commission established to carry out the liturgical reform mandated by the Fathers of Vatican II and describes its organizational structure and working methods. The fourth introduces the two Consilium study groups whose work we discuss in subsequent chapters: *Coetus* 1, entrusted with the revision of the liturgical calendar, and *Coetus* 18*bis*, responsible for the revision of the prayers and prefaces. The fifth section discusses the revision policies that were originally agreed upon and the indications that the policies themselves may have been subsequently revised.

The State of the Question

In the decades following the publication of the Vatican II missal, there was much discussion about the character and quality of the vernacular translations, and about the way in which they were produced and approved.[1] After years of examination and reflection, the Church revised her approach and procedures and, as a result, a new English translation of the Roman Missal was published, one that is more faithful and more excellent and, in consequence, better suited to divine worship.[2]

The long preoccupation with translation has, perhaps, kept us from giving deserved attention to the character and quality of the Latin orations in the typical editions of the Vatican II missal, and to the processes by which they were selected, edited, and composed.

The Vatican II books have been very well studied in themselves, and so it may seem that we know all that we need to know to appreciate them fully. This is not the case, however. For the most part, the new liturgical books have not been examined in relation to the pre-Vatican II books or the other sources upon which the revisers drew. This is the case for the missal. The pre- and post-Vatican II missals have both been carefully studied, each in all its various parts, but not in relation, part by part, with the other.

No careful comparative examination of the texts of each missal has been published that shows whether the pre- and post-Vatican II missals assume the same posture before God, express the same convictions and sentiments about him, present the human situation in the same way, beseech God for the same or similar graces – and if they do not, in what specific ways, and to what extent, they differ.

Since we are shaped by our worship, this means we cannot say whether those who worship by means of the revised missal receive essentially the

---

[1] See, for examples, Robert Speaight, "Liturgy and Language," *Theology: Monthly Review* 74 (October, 1971) 444–56; Ralph A. Kiefer, "The Eucharistic Prayer," *Worship* 50 (1976) 316–23; Richard Toporoski, "The Language of Worship," *Communio* 4 (Fall, 1977) 226–60; Ansgar J. Chupungco, "The English Translation of the Latin Liturgy," *Notitiae* 18 (1982) 91–100; Cuthbert Johnson, "Prefaces: Shaping a New Translation," *Pastoral Music* 16 (April–May, 1992) 34–7; Erasmo Leiva-Merikakis, "The Catechetical Role of the Liturgy and the Quality of Liturgical Texts: the Current ICEL Translation," *Communio* 20 (Spring, 1993) 63–83; Eamon Duffy, "Rewriting the Liturgy: the Theological Issues of Translation," *New Blackfriars* 78 (January, 1997) 4–27, reprinted in Stratford Caldecott, ed., *Beyond the Prosaic* (Edinburgh: T&T Clark, 1998) 97–126; Donald Trautman, "Rome and ICEL," *America* 182 (4 March 2000) 7–11 and the Letter to the Editor written in response to Bishop Trautman's article by the Prefect for the Congregation for Divine Worship and the Discipline of the Sacraments entitled "Cardinal Jorge A. Medina on the ICEL Controversy," *America* 182 (14 April 2000) 17–19; Ad Hoc Committee on the Forum on the Principles of Translation, *The Voice of the Church: A Forum on Liturgical Translation* (Washington: United States Catholic Conference, 2001).

[2] *The Roman Missal: Renewed by Decree of the Most Holy Second Ecumenical Council of the Vatican, Promulgated by Authority of Pope Paul VI and Revised at the Direction of Pope John Paul II* (Collegeville, MN: Liturgical Press, 2011).

same doctrinal and spiritual formation as those who worshiped by means of its predecessors.

It is necessary to be clear about what we mean and do not mean when we speak of worship shaping or forming us. We do not mean that the intended purpose, or even that one of the intended purposes, is pedagogical or practical. Indeed, it is unfitting to ascribe any utilitarian purpose to worship, for in true worship the human person adores and honors God for his own sake alone.

The formation of which we speak is not the purpose of worship but its effect, and this in two respects especially. First, because human beings become what they most consistently do, we are formed by the way we habitually worship – by the posture, attitudes, and dispositions we customarily assume before God and the things that we habitually say to him, or seek from him, when we speak from our hearts. Second, at worship the Church beseeches God on behalf of the faithful and seeks from him the things that they need. On the one hand, from the Church's public prayer we can gain great insight into what God wants for us and from us; on the other, by means of these same prayers, the Church begs God on our behalf for the graces and gifts we need to become what he desires.

There are many elements in the Mass and each of these contributes in its own way to the formation of those who worship. A comprehensive answer to the question of whether Catholics who worship by means of the post-Vatican II missal receive substantially the same doctrinal, moral and spiritual formation as do those who worshiped by means of the pre-Vatican II missals must depend upon the collective findings of a great many different studies. Nevertheless, there is one particular study that has the capacity to advance our understanding considerably.

Three proper prayers are assigned to each Mass: the collect, the prayer over the offerings, and the postcommunion. The first of these, the collect, is the true proper prayer of the day. Its Latin text is always but a single sentence.[3]

Because of its brevity, it is easy to dismiss the collect's importance. But the collect praises God in a way that is specific to the day and seeks graces from him that correspond to the feast or day being celebrated. Because the collect typifies the day to which it is assigned, a comparative examination of the collects of the two missals is a fitting place to start an inquiry into whether both missals present and emphasize the same doctrinal, moral, and spiritual truths.

---

[3] Likewise, both the prayer over the offerings and the postcommunion prayer are always only a single sentence.

Scope, Method, and Goal

In this book we compare and contrast the Sunday and feast day collects that are assigned to the proper seasons in pre- and post-Vatican II missals. The proper seasons are Advent, Christmas, Lent, Paschaltide and, in the pre-Vatican missal only, Septuagesima. Our study is confined to collects that belong to privileged times in the Church's Sacred Year and are assigned to days on which Catholics are obliged to worship at Mass.

The method is careful, comparative examination of texts.

The comparative element extends in two directions. Each collect in the Vatican II missal is examined in relation to its counterpart in the 1962 missal. This counterpart may or may not be the source text for the post-Vatican II collect. When it is not, the collect is also compared with its source if one exists. This comparison considers both the text and the use to which the source was put.

The collects of the new missal are drawn from a variety of different sources: some are from the 1962 missal itself;[4] others came from ancient sacramentaries or collections of liturgical formularies; still others are new compositions. Many of the collects that were taken from earlier missals or codices were edited, and many newly composed prayers are woven from threads of two or three ancient orations. In both of these cases we examine the post-Vatican II collect beside the source prayer(s) that the revisers drew upon to produce it. Other new compositions are constructed of phrases from biblical, patristic, or ecclesiastical texts, or composed in their entirety by those who produced the new missal. In such cases there is no source prayer for comparison, and we examine the texts that revisers drew upon.[5]

Our examination of texts uses whatever analytical tools are fitting in the circumstances. These include attention to vocabulary, literary and rhetorical devices, scriptural allusions, and, especially, to the changes editors made to a received text. Careful attention to the literary composition is essential because form and content are inextricably intertwined.

To summarize: The scope of the study is limited to the collects of Masses in proper seasons assigned to days on which the faithful are obliged to worship at Mass. The method is careful comparative textual examination. The goal is twofold. With respect to the prayers, the objective is to understand how the new corpus of Sunday and feast day collects of proper seasons was confected and to appreciate the collects themselves, individually and as a set. With respect to the faithful, the objective is to determine

---

[4] That is, the last edition of the Roman Missal prior to the reforms mandated by Vatican II. The 1962 Missal is the last typical edition of the Missal of Pius V, also called the Tridentine Missal, which was commissioned by the Council of Trent and first appeared in 1570.

[5] Some newly composed collects combine more than one of the methods named in this paragraph. For example, the post-Vatican II collect of the fourth Sunday of Lent combines fragments of an ancient collect and a patristic sermon with text composed by the revisors.

whether those who pray by means of the new set of collects approach God in the same way and seek the same things from him as do those who pray by means of the corresponding collects of the proper seasons in the pre-Vatican II missal, and if they do not, to identify the chief differences.

The Consilium: Organization and Working Methods

The Fathers of Vatican II mandated a reform of the liturgy and outlined its contours in the *Sacrosanctum Concilium* or the *Constitution on the Sacred Liturgy*.[6] On 25 January 1964, Pope Paul VI issued a *motu proprio* in which he announced the establishment of a special commission, the *Consilium ad Exsequendam Constitutionem de Sacra Liturgia*,[7] the principal task of which was to implement the prescriptions of *Sacrosanctum Concilium*.[8] This *ad hoc* body, not the Fathers of Vatican II, did all the editorial work that went into producing the new liturgical books.

The *Consilium* was comprised of members, consultors, and advisors. The members numbered 40, and at the start all but three were bishops.[9] Only members held deliberative vote. It is they who made the policy decisions and approved the work in progress. Final approval was reserved to the Holy See.

The vast work of actually revising the liturgical books was divided among 28 study groups or *coetus*, each of which was assigned a particular

---

[6] Sacrosanctum Oecumenicum Concilium Vaticanum II, *Constitutiones Decreta Declarationes*, vol. 1 (Civitas Vaticana: Vaticanum Typographium, 1967) 3–54. The Fathers of Vatican II approved the final draft of *Sacrosanctum Concilium* on 4 December 1963.

[7] Literally, the "*Consilium* for carrying out the Constitution on the Sacred Liturgy." *Consilium* is Latin for "consultation," "council," or "assembly."

[8] "Sacram Liturgiam," *Acta Apostolicae Sedis* 56 (1964) 140. "... peculiarem condimus Commisionem ... cuius praecipuae erunt partes, ut ipsius Constitutionis de sacra liturgia praecepta sancte perficienda curet" [... we establish a special commission ... whose principal function will be to take care of fulfilling the prescriptions of the *Constitution on Sacred Liturgy* itself].

[9] The list is found in Consilium ad exsequendam Constitutionem de Sacra Liturgia, *Elenchus membrorum – consultorum – consiliariorum coetuum a studiis* (Vatican: Typis Polyglottis Vaticanis, 1964) 9–14. The non-episcopal members are: Benno Gut, Abbot Primate of the Benedictine Order; Ferdinand Antonelli, Promoter General of the Faith; Julius Bevilacqua, pastor. The English translation of the Latin title is: List of Members – Consultors – Advisors of the Study Groups.

task.[10] Each *coetus* was comprised of a *relator*,[11] a secretary, a handful of consultors (usually not more than 5 or 6), and often one or two advisors.[12] The *relator* of each *coetus* organized the group's work and signed its official submissions, called *schemata*, to the members. The *schemata* (outlines) report on the group's progress, identify the questions that were put to the members and their decisions on the same, and include the liturgical texts that the *coetus* had prepared since the last report. The *schemata* bear contemporaneous witness to various stages in the revision work as it progressed.

Consultors did the actual work of revising the texts. Consultors were appointed by Pope Paul VI,[13] and the criteria for appointment were three: specialization, nationality, and availability to meet and work together.[14] The Consilium *Elenchus* lists 134 consultors.[15]

Annibale Bugnini, Consilium secretary, reports that the Consilium also made use of other persons, advisors (*consiliarii*), who were not appointed by the Pope but by the president of the Consilium.[16] Some of these were

---

[10] *Coetus* is the Latin word for "group" or "groups" – the word takes the same form in both the nominative singular and nominative plural. The Consilium *Elenchus*, 39–51, lists 39 *coetus* but 10 of the last 11 have no members save the *relator*. In the case of the eleventh, *De re biblica*, not even a *relator* is named. We note the existence of these 11 other "*coetus a studiis*," but since they do not seem actually to have been "groups" they are not counted above. The *Elenchus* numbers the *coetus* 1 to 38. We count 39 because there is a *Coetus* 18 and a *Coetus* 18*bis*.

In *Res Secretariae*, n. 12 (26 October 1964) Annibale Bugnini states there are 40 *coetus a studiis*. In his tome, *The Reform of the Liturgy (1948–1975)* tr. Matthew J. O'Connell (Collegeville: The Liturgical Press, 1990) 63–5, Bugnini lists 39 *coetus*, 4 of which were subdivided (18 and 18*bis*, 20 and 20*bis*, 23 and 23*bis*, 32 and 32*bis*) making a total of 43. Footnotes (nn. 6–10, on page 64) indicate that five of the *coetus* were established between February of 1965 and sometime in 1970. *The Reform of the Liturgy* is the English translation of Annibale Bugnini, *La Riforma Liturgica (1948–1975)* (Rome: CVL Edizione Liturgiche, 1984).

Bugnini served as the Consilium Secretary from the time of its inception until its work became the responsibility of the Congregation for Divine Worship that Paul VI established in 1969. The new congregation was put in charge of everything pertaining to divine worship in the Latin rite including the revision and preparation of liturgical texts (cf. "Sacra Rituum," *Acta Apostolicae Sedis* 61 (1969) 299–301).

[11] The "*relator*" is the one who relates or reports. The word also means "mover" or "proposer" [Charlton T. Lewis, *A Latin Dictionary* (Oxford: Clarendon Press, 1879) s.v., 1555].

[12] Of the 28 *coetus* listed [*Elenchus* 39–51], 13 had no advisors; 4 had 1; 6 had 2; 3 had 3; 1 had 4. *Coetus* 4, whose responsibility was biblical readings, had 6 advisors.

[13] Annibale Bugnini, *The Reform of the Liturgy*, 66, but see also 950, n. 5 where Bugnini says they were appointed by the Secretary of State.

[14] Annibale Bugnini, *The Reform of the Liturgy*, 66. The first president of the Consilium was Giacomo Cardinal Lacaro (*Elenchus* 7). He was succeeded in January of 1968 by Benno Cardinal Gut (*The Reform of the Liturgy*, 942).

[15] *Elenchus*, 15–31.

[16] Annibale Bugnini, *The Reform of the Liturgy*, 66.

enlisted to advise the president on particular matters, while others became associated with the work of particular *coetus*. The Consilium *Elenchus* lists 62 advisors of the latter sort,[17] and Bugnini 74.[18] In a report issued in October of 1964 Bugnini stated that the number of advisors was increasing daily,[19] but in *The Reform of the Liturgy* he notes that some advisors were engaged only for a single occasion.[20]

Advisors were not expected to take part in Consilium or *coetus* meetings. Rather they were to "make their contribution in writing ... except in rare instances that the president authorized as they arose."[21]

Bugnini describes the working method of the Consilium *Coetus* in this way:

The guidelines, or criteria, for the work of each group were based on the data provided by the liturgical Constitution, the material gathered for the preparatory commission, the desires of the bishops and clergy, and liturgical studies. On the basis of the criteria and the material supplied, each group would compose a first schema for its area. This would be sent for examination to the consultors[22] and to a suitable number of advisors (twenty or thirty) in various parts of the world. The observations that came in from the advisors within a certain period of time and those made by the consultors of the Consilium would serve as the basis for a second draft of the schema, which would in turn be sent to the same persons for examination.[23]

When each schema reached a state of sufficient refinement, it went to the group that was responsible for the overall structure of the books. This group then prepared "a comprehensive schema for the entire book" to be sent to the Consilium members and the Holy Father for examination.[24]

---

[17] *Elenchus*, 32–8. Advisors are listed among the members of particular *coetus*, but have asterisks next to their names.

[18] Annibale Bugnini, *The Reform of the Liturgy*, 950–2. Bugnini states on p. 950, n. 5 that there are other advisors who are not on the list, but whom he names in the chapter of his book which discusses the area of revision to which the advisor contributed.

[19] *Res Secretariae* 12 (26 October 1964), p. 1.

[20] Annibale Bugnini, *The Reform of the Liturgy*, 66.

[21] Annibale Bugnini, *The Reform of the Liturgy*, 66.

[22] Bugnini here means all the Consilium consultors, the 134 mentioned above.

[23] Annibale Bugnini, *The Reform of the Liturgy*, 66. One can only imagine what doing this for every schema of every *coetus* involved in the days before the Internet.

[24] Annibale Bugnini, *The Reform of the Liturgy*, 66.

Two *Coetus: De Calendario* and *De Missali*

The study of the collects in this volume involves consideration of the work of two Consilium study groups: *Coetus* 1, *De Calendario*, responsible for the liturgical calendar, and *Coetus* 18*bis*, *De Missali*, responsible for the Mass orations and prefaces.

Coetus 1: *De Calendario*

The members of *Coetus* 1 were: Rembert Van Doren, O.S.B., Adrian Nocent, O.S.B., Aimé-Georges Martimort, Pierre Jounel, Agostino Amore, O.F.M., and Herman Schmidt, S.J. with Annibale Bugnini, C. M., the Consilium Secretary, serving as *relator* and Ansgar Dirks, O.P., as *coetus* secretary.[25]

Schema 61, *De Calendario* 1, dated 12 February 1965 and titled "*Proprium de Tempore*" [Proper Seasons], consists of 18 questions that the members of *Coetus* 1 were to consider. *Schema* 65, *De Calendario* 2, dated 15 March 1965, also titled "*Proprium de Tempore*," records the answer of each *coetus* member to each question. The questions begin with the Pasch and proceed through the Church's Sacred Year. Each question presents a matter for the *coetus* members to decide. The questions and answers pertaining to particular seasons are discussed below in the appropriate chapters.

Coetus 18*bis*

The original members of *Coetus* 18*bis* were: Placide Bruylants, O.S.B., *relator*; Giovanni Lucchesi, secretary; André Rose, Walter Dürig, and Henry Ashworth, O.S.B., consultors; Juan Antonio Garcia and Antoine Dumas, O.S.B., advisors.[26] Bruylants died suddenly in October 1966, and Dumas

---

[25] The names appear in Schema n. 65, *De Calendario*, 2 (15 March 1965) described below, and Annibale Bugnini, *The Reform of the Liturgy 1948–1975*, trans. Matthew J. O'Connell (Collegeville: The Liturgical Press) 305. In the body of the same page (305), Bugnini, quoting a text he does not identify, explains "Presidency of the group was reserved to the secretariat of the Consilium, at least ... until the final, decisive stages of the work is reached." Jounel was appointed relator of the group in 1967 (305, n. 1).

Consilium, *Elenchus* lists the members of *Coetus* 1, *De Calendario* (using Latin for both the titles and Christian names): *relator*: Secretaria Consilii; *secretatarius*: P. Ansgarius Dirks, O.P.; *Consultores*: Abb. Ramboldus van Doren, O.S.B.; Mons. Johannes Wagner; Sac. A. Georgius Martimort; Sac. Petrus Jounel; P. Augustinus Amore, O.F.M.; P. Hermannus Schmidt, S.J. P. Hannibal Bugnini, C.M. is listed as the *Secretarius*. Bugnini, *The Reform*, 305, n. 1, states that Jounel became relator of *Coetus* 1 in 1967.

[26] Consilium ad exsequendam Constitutionem de Sacra Liturgia, *Elenchus*, 45–6. The *Elenchus*, however, puts their titles and Christian names in Latin: P. Placidus Bruylants, O.S.B., Mons. Joannes Lucchesi, Sac. Andreas Rose, Sac. Walter Dürig, P. Henricus Ashworth, O.S.B., Sac. Joannes Antonius Garcia, and P. Antonius Dumas, O.S.B.

succeeded him as *relator*.[27] It seems that Dumas assumed the position as *relator* while technically still an advisor suggesting that, at least in his case, the roles of advisors and relators were not as distinct as Annibale Bugnini's statement in *The Reform of the Liturgy* suggests.[28]

Revision Policies

Placide Bruylants: Fall of 1966

In the Fall of 1966, Placide Bruylants approached the Consilium members and asked them to approve six principles according to which the orations of the missal would be revised. He accompanied each request with the rationale for proposing it and provided examples where useful for the sake of clarity.[29] The six principles, in the form in which they were finally approved, are as follows:

I. Does it please the Fathers[30] that in revising the Roman Missal the text of orations not be repeated?

II. Does it please the Fathers that, in the way indicated about which we have [already] spoken, corrupt texts be corrected?

III. Does it please the Fathers a) that the commemoration of local or historical events whose significance has been lost to the Church universal of the present day be removed from orations; b) does it please you that orations be accommodated to the rules/customs[31] of Christian life today in cases where there are discrepancies?

IV. Does it please the Fathers that for each oration appearing or inserted into the missal, its own particular [proper] literary genre be preserved or restored?

V. Does it please the Fathers that the orations of the Roman missal, in general, be directed to the Father?

---

[27] Bugnini, *La Riforma*, 394, reports that Bruylants died of a heart attack on 18 October 1966 and footnote 10 on the same page that Antoine Dumas succeeded him as *relator*. The corresponding note in the English translation of Bugnini's book, *The Reform of the Liturgy*, 397, mistakenly reports that André Rose became *relator* upon Bruylants's death.

[28] See p. 7 above and *The Reform of the Liturgy*, 66.

[29] *De Missali* 27, Schema n. 186 (19 September 1966) 1–4.

[30] "Fathers" refers to the Consilium members.

[31] Bruylants uses the word *instituta* which can mean "precepts," "customs," or "regulations." The word has legal overtones. In context it can refer either to the binding precepts, or to the customary observances of Catholic life, or to both.

VI.   Does it please the Fathers that new texts, composed chiefly by
       means of centonization, be inserted into the Roman missal?[32]

The schema in which the policies are proposed, Schema 186, is a 69 page
document.[33] The policy questions with the accompanying rationale are set
out in the first 4 pages. The remaining 65 pages are a draft of the orations
for the Masses of the proper seasons in which the principles Bruylants is
asking the members to approve have already been applied. That is, when
the members voted, they were able to see from the texts that they had in
hand what the implementation of each policy would mean practically.

   A discussion of the policies and the reasons that Bruylants put forth in
support of them follows.

I. Does it please the Fathers that in revising the Roman Missal the text of
orations not be repeated?

Bruylants identifies two situations that, in his view, call for correction.
Some orations appear repeatedly in the 1962 missal, he says, even up to
26 times. Others are used in more than one setting but, additionally, are
appointed without regard for the proper character of the day to which they
are assigned – for example: the secret and postcommunion prayers assigned

---

[32] The list follows *De Missali* 27, Schema n. 186 (19 September 1966), pp. 2–4 and Addendum
I, p. 1:
  I.   Placetne Patribus ut, in missali romano recognito, textus orationum non repetatur?
  II. Placetne Patribus, ut, sensu quo modo de his locuti sumus, textus orationum recogno-
       scatur, vel in casu, emendetur?
  III. Placetne Patribus: a) ut ex orationibus tollatur memoria eventum, localium vel histori-
       corum, quae momentum suum amiserunt pro Ecclesia universali hodierna? b) placetne
       vobis ut, in casu, accommodentur orationes institutis vitae christianae hodierna?
  IV. Placetne Patribus ut unicuique orationi in missali exstanti vel inserandae, servetur vel
       restituatur genus litterarium suum proprium?
  V.   Placetne Patribus ut orationes missalis romani generatim ad Patrem dirigatur.?
  VI. Placetne Patribus, ut inserantur missali romano novi textus, modi praesertim "centonis"
       exarati?
Bugnini, *The Reform of the Liturgy*, 398 presents the principles as follows:
   The criteria to be applied in the revision are these: The number of texts is to be increased
so as to avoid the many unnecessary repetitions found in the present Missal; the texts are
to be revised in the light of the originals in order to restore a fullness of meaning, including
theological meaning, that has sometimes been altered; expressions that have now lost most of
their meaning (for example, the reference exclusively to bodily fasting in the prayers of Lent)
are to be replaced, as opportunity allows, by others more in keeping with modern conditions.
   The number of prayers can be increased not only by taking texts from the sacramentaries
but also by composing new ones through shrewd centonization that uses and combines in
a suitable way elements from various prayers found in the sacramentaries.
[33] The schema is supplemented by a six-page addendum containing corrections that is
identified as *De Missali* 27, Schema n. 186, Addendum I (19 September 1966).

to Sunday within the octave of the Lord's Nativity are also, respectively, the secret and postcommunion prayers of Palm Sunday.

On the analogy of *Sacrosanctum Concilium* 51, the paragraph that calls for "a more representative portion of the holy scriptures" being read to the faithful over a period of years, Bruylants proposes introducing more of the riches of ancient Latin euchology into the Roman Missal.

Describing the work that had already been done, Bruylants explains that, with few exceptions, the revisers had retained [only] the most ancient use of texts that appear numerous times and then selected new prayers to replace repetitive occurrences.[34]

II. Does it please the Fathers that, in the way indicated about which we have [already] spoken, corrupt texts be corrected?

Bruylants presents the example of the collect for Sunday of the Resurrection, the latter part of which he identifies as a corruption.[35] He asks permission to restore it according to an eighth-century manuscript, explaining to the members that he is not advocating "archeologism" – that is, a preference for more ancient texts simply because they are more ancient.[36] And, indeed, Bruylants does not say anything about restoring the texts to their original, or to their most ancient extant, forms. He asks only whether the Fathers desire corrupt texts to be edited or corrected within the limits he has specified.

There is good reason for Bruylants's clear repudiation of archeologism: Pope Pius XII's explicit rejection of the same in his 1947 encyclical, *Mediator Dei*. Pius XII likens a person who would indiscriminately go back to the liturgical rites and practices of antiquity to one who would reject

---

[34] *De Missali* 27, Schema n. 186 (19 September 1966), p. 1. All the information presented in the three paragraphs above comes from page 1 of the schema.

[35] *De Missali* 27, Schema n. 186 (19 September 1966), p. 2. The collect of Easter Sunday, which is discussed in Chapter 7, is one of two examples presented. The other is secret of the third Sunday after the Epiphany: Haec hostia, Domine, quaesumus, emundet nostra delicta: et, *ad* sacrificium celebrandum, subditorum tibi corpora mentesque sanctificet [May this offering, O Lord, we beseech you, cleanse our sins: and may it sanctify the bodies and minds of your servants *for the purpose of celebrating* the sacrifice). According to Bruylants *ad* was added in the tenth century and completely changed the theology of the prayer. He asks the members for permission to omit the *ad*, and to restore other orations that are found to be corrupt. Without *ad* the oration would be translated: May this offering, O Lord, we beseech you, cleanse our sins: and may the sacrifice *which must be [is to be] celebrated* sanctify the bodies and minds of your servants. *Cf. CO* IV, 2811.

[36] *De Missali* 27, Schema n. 186 (19 September 1966), p. 2: "Non agitur hic de aliquo archae-ologismo, quo lectio antiquior, ipso facto melior aestimaretur. Sed quibusdam mutationibus textus antiqui, sub aspectu theologico vel pastorali, reapse imminuti vel corrupti sunt." [It is not a question here of some kind of archeologism, in which the more ancient reading is reckoned better by this fact alone. But of ancient texts [that] have in fact been diminished or corrupted in a theological or pastoral aspect by certain changes].

more recently defined dogmas or more recently promulgated laws in favor of the earliest doctrinal formulations or legal precepts.[37] While Pius XII mentions archeologism only in reference to rites, customs, and ceremonies, everything he says on the subject applies equally well to texts.

The error of archeologism, as Pius XII's analogy demonstrates, is that it makes no distinction between genuine development, and enfeebling or misleading corruptions, as it casts aside every change in an indiscriminate preference for the most ancient forms. In context, Bruylants's phrasing of the policy presupposes that revisers will distinguish texts that have been refined by the wisdom of the tradition from those that have suffered some sort of loss over the course of time.

III. Does it please the Fathers a) that the commemoration of local or historical events whose significance has been lost to the Church universal of the present day be removed from orations; b) does it please you that orations be accommodated to the rules/customs of Christian life today in cases where there are discrepancies?

The third policy has two elements, removing references for which the significance has been lost and accommodating prayers to current practice or discipline. Bruylants offers two examples, one for each type of situation: a) the collect of Thursday after Sunday III in Lent which mentions Cosmas and Damian;[38] b) the majority of Lenten orations because the existing texts do not conform adequately to the prescriptions of *Sacrosanctum Concilium*.[39]

---

[37] "Mediator Dei," *Acta Apostolicae Sedis* 39 (1947) 546–7. Pius XII repeats the condemnation of archeologism made by Pius VI in the 1794 Bull "*Auctorem fidei.*"

[38] *De Missali* 27, Schema n. 186 (19 September 1966), p. 2. The collect in question reads: Magnificet te, Domine, sanctorum tuorum Cosmae et Damiani beata solemnitas: qua et illis gloriam sempiternam, et opem nobis ineffabili providentia contulisti [May the blessed solemnity of your saints Cosmas and Damian, by which you grant everlasting glory to them and aid to us, magnify you]. The Station for the day is the church of Saints Cosmas and Damian.

De Missali 20, Schema n. 156 (30 April 1966) is an earlier draft of *De Missali* 27, Schema n. 186 (19 September 1966). There Bruylants also presents two examples of "commemoration of local or historical events whose significance has been lost to the Church universal of the present day." One is the same Lenten collect named in Schema n. 186. The other is "the character of the orations of the time of Septuagesima" ["... v. gr. character orationum temporis Septuagesimae ...].

[39] *De Missali* 27, Schema n. 186 (19 September 1966), pp. 2–3: "Nam, memoria *et* praeparatio baptismi, quae secundum Constitutionem de sacra Liturgia (n. 109, a) prima indoles sunt huius temporis, fere omnino absunt. Quoad secundam indolem, characterem nempe poenitentialem, patet quod in orationibus fere unice de ieiunio loquitur [in the manuscript which I saw in the archives of the offices of the International Commission on English in the Liturgy in Washington, D.C., 'loquitur' is crossed out and 'sermo fit' hand-written in the margin] et non sufficienter tractatur neque de spiritu poenitentiae in genere, neque de praeparatione mysterii paschalis." [For the memory of *and* preparation for baptism, which according to the Constitution on the Sacred Liturgy (n. 109, a) are the first character (*indoles*) of this

This policy seems to have undergone modification as the revision work progressed and we return to it below.

IV. Does it please the Fathers that for each oration appearing or inserted into the missal, its own particular [proper] literary genre be preserved or restored?

Policy four was voted upon with the wording above, but the question Bruylants originally posed was: "Does it please the Fathers that for each oration appearing or being inserted into the missal, its own particular and original character be restored?"[40] The change replaces "particular and original character" with "particular [proper] literary genre" implying that the original use is not the only proper or authentic use. We revisit the subject of a prayer's literary genre at junctures below.

V. Does it please the Fathers that the orations of the Roman Missal, in general, be directed to the Father?

This is another policy that underwent revision before it was agreed upon. Bruylants's original question had two parts: "Does it please the Fathers a) that all the orations of the Roman Missal be directed to the Father; b) do you desire that even the collects on the Sundays of Advent be revised in this way?"[41] In explanation of his proposal, Bruylants tells the members:

> ... many orations, especially pertaining to saints, ought to be revised [because they are not addressed to the Father]. This is most rarely the case among the orations *de tempore*, except for the collects of the Sundays of Advent. On account of their antiquity and more venerable

---

season, are almost entirely absent. With respect to the second character, namely the penitential character, it is evident almost exclusively in the language of fasting and neither the spirit of penance in general nor preparation for the paschal mystery is sufficiently treated]. Hereafter International Commission on English in the Liturgy is designated ICEL.

De Missali 20, Schema n. 156 (30 April 1966) is an earlier draft of *De Missali* 27, Schema n. 186 (19 September 1966). There no mention is made of Lenten collects as a whole. Rather, on page 2, Bruylants offers the collect of Monday after Sunday III of Lent as an example, calling attention to the phrase "as we abstain from flesh foods" ["... quando in feria II eiusdem hebdomadae Quadragesimae oramus: 'sicut ab escis carnalibus abstinemus.'"]. Bruylants's point in context is that the collect does not conform to present day Church practice for in 1966 the faithful did not abstain from meat on this or any other Monday of Lent.

[40] *De Missali* 27, Schema n. 86 (19 September 1966), p. 3: Placetne Patribus ut unicuique orationi in missali exstanti vel inserendae restituatur, character suus proprium et originalis?

[41] *De Missali* 27, Schema n. 186 (19 September 1966), p. 3: Placetne Patribus a) ut omnes orationes missalis romani ad Patrem dirigantur; b) optatisne ut etiam collectae in diebus dominicis Adventum in hoc sensu recognoscantur?

character, we have not changed them. New orations, however, that have been selected for all the ferial days of this time [of Advent] are all addressed to the Father.[42]

In the context of Bruylants's statement, the revised wording of the principle suggests that the members were willing to have the sanctoral collects revised so that, in the main, they would be addressed to the Father, but were not willing to approve the same revision in the case of the Advent Sunday collects.

VI. Does it please the Fathers that new texts, composed chiefly by means of centonization, be inserted into the Roman Missal?

Here again the original question was modified before it was approved. Bruylants asked whether orations composed by the method called "centonization" could be inserted into the missal. The members granted a wider permission, stipulating that centonization be the principal method of composition, not the only method. The English "centonize" comes from an Indo-European word meaning "patch." It means to compose a new text from the phrases of existing compositions.

Bruylant tells the members that one of the more difficult aspects of the *coetus*'s work is selecting new prayers either to substitute for texts that are repeated in the 1962 missal or to provide orations for the ferial days of Advent and Paschaltide to which, formerly, proper prayers had not been assigned.

The *coetus*'s first recourse was to select suitable prayers from the ancient sacramentaries. Sometimes, however, they found it necessary to draft new orations which they did by the method called "centonization." Bruylants lists three points in favor of centonization: 1) it is a very ancient [*perantiquus*] practice in Latin euchology; 2) it is conducive to preserving the unity of the corpus; 3) it allows for the preservation of beautiful elements that appear in banal contexts. He tells the members that the revisers had centonized from sacramentaries, Sacred Scripture and the works of the Fathers.[43]

---

[42] *De Missali* 27, Schema n. 186 (19 September 1966), pp. 3–4: ... plures orationes, praesertim de sanctis, recognosci deberent. In orationibus de tempore rarissimae sunt, praeter collectas in diebus dominicis Adventus. Propter earum antiquitatem et characterem venerabiliorem, eas non mutavimus. Novas orationes tamen, quas pro omnibus feris huius temporis [the copy in the ICEL archives inserts "Adventus" by hand], omnes ad Patrem diriguntur.

The collects assigned to Sunday I, II, and IV of Advent in Schema n. 186 are the same as those found in the 1962 missal. The collect assigned to Sunday III is a variant of the collect assigned to the same Sunday in the 1962 missal. None of the aforementioned is assigned to Advent Sundays in the Vatican II missals.

[43] *De Missali* 27, Schema n. 186 (19 September 1966), p. 4. All the information summarized in this paragraph and the preceding is found on page 4.

In sum, the principles agreed upon in 1966 require that (1) orations not be repeated; (2) demonstrably corrupt texts be corrected; (3) local or historical references which cannot be understood/appreciated universally be omitted, and orations which do not reflect the present customs or rules governing Christian life be accommodated to what is now the case; (4) the particular genre of orations be respected; (5) orations usually be directed to the Father. In addition, the members approve of (6) new orations being composed by centonization or other means.

These policies allow for modifications to existing orations in only three specific, and narrowly defined, circumstances: (1) when corruptions required correction (policy n. 2); (2) if an oration has been rendered outmoded by changes in practice or incomprehensible because it contains local or historical references incompatible with the universal character of the Church's prayer (policy n. 3); (3) *perhaps*, if an oration is not addressed to the Father, with, it seems, a clear understanding the Advent Sunday collects will continue to address the Son (policy n. 4).

Antoine Dumas: Fall of 1968

In the Fall of 1968 Antoine Dumas, as the *relator* of *Coetus* 18*bis*, re-presented the policies approved in the Fall of 1966 to the Consilium members in this way:

> In the session of the Consilium that we held in the autumn of the year 1966, these principles, which Dom Placide Bruylants proposed to direct the work of revising the Orations of the Missal (Schema n. 186, *De Missali* 27), were approved by the Fathers:
>
> I. Insofar as possible, the texts of the same orations are not to be repeated again and again as happens in the present Missal.
> II. Corrupt texts are to be examined and corrected according to their pristine form.
> III. The mention of local and particular deeds, as well as historical remembrances for which the whole significance and function is lost to the Church of our time, are to be removed from certain prayers. These prayers are to be accommodated to the needs of Christian life today.
> IV. Both the literary genre and proper liturgical function are to be restored to all Orations. Therefore the Collect, prayers over the offerings, after Communion and over the people have their own particular character.
> V. Orations are always directed to God the Father (unless certain reasons persuade otherwise).
> VI. Newly produced/prepared orations, in order to preserve unity of style, are to be composed chiefly by means of centonization – from

biblical texts and, especially, from ancient sacramentaries. New compositions, sober and confected according to Roman custom, are by no means excluded.[44]

Dumas's reference to the 1966 meeting prevents us from supposing that the principles were officially modified at some time after they were initially approved. And, in fact, no such modification is mentioned in any of the intervening *coetus* schemata. The differences between Dumas's articulation of the second and third policies and the form in which they were actually approved are especially important because the different wordings of each policy describe significantly different tasks.

Dumas Policy II: Corrupt texts are to be reviewed and corrected according to their pristine form.
The original phrasing calls only for the correction of corrupt texts. The 1968 wording stipulates the manner in which corrupt texts are to be corrected: according to their "pristine" form. While the Latin word *pristinus* can mean former, previous, earlier, original, or pristine, the context leaves little doubt about the intended meaning: corrupt texts are to be corrected according to the original or most ancient extant text. Further Annibale Bugnini, the Consilium secretary, paraphrases this same policy: "texts are to be revised according to the originals, restoring fullness of meaning, even theological meaning, that has sometimes been altered."[45]

    Thus there is a trajectory of sorts. Bruylants asks permission to correct corrupt texts and explicitly repudiates archeologism. Dumas likewise limits

---

[44] *De Missali* 56, Schema n. 319 (7 October 1968), p. 2:
   In sessione Consilii, quam habuimus autumno anni 1966, haec principia quae Domnus Placidus Bruylants exposuit ad dirigendum opus recognionis Orationum Missalis (Schema n. 186, De Missali 27) a Patribus probabata sunt:
   I.   Pro possibilitate, iidem textus Orationum ne repetantur iterum atque iterum, ut evenit in hodierno Missali;
   II.   Textus corrupti recognoscantur et corrigantur ad pristinam formam;
   III. Ex quibusdam Orationibus tollantur mentiones factorum localium et particularium, necnon memoriae historicae quae omne pondus et officium in Ecclesia nostri temporis amiserunt. Quae Orationes tamen accommodentur necessitatibus hodiernae vitae christianae;
   IV.   Cunctis Orationibus restituantur et genus litterarium et munus liturgicum proprium. Ideo Collecta, Orationes super oblata, post Communionem et super populum habeant suum characterem particularem;
   V.   Orationes ad Deum Patrem (nisi certae rationes aliud suadeant) semper dirigantur;
   VI.   Orationes noviter concinnatae, ad servandam styli unitatem, elaborantur praecipue more centonum, ex textibus biblicis ex maxime antiquis Sacramentariis. Minime excluduntur novae compositiones, sobriae et confectae secundum romanum consuetudinem.
[45] *The Reform of the Liturgy*, 398. Bugnini's Italian text, *La Riforma Liturgica*, 393, has "... di rivedere i testi sugli originali, restituendo la pienezza di significato, anche teologico, qualche volta alterato."

application of the principle to corrupt texts, but does not explicitly reject archeologism. Indeed he chooses language which suggests a preference for the most ancient simply because it is the most ancient. Bugnini stipulates "the original" and does not confine re-pristinization to texts that had suffered loss or corruption. In fact, he seems to assume that any alteration results in loss of meaning. If this is an accurate description of Bugnini's view, he must be suspected of archeologism.

Dumas Policy III. The mention of local and particular deeds, as well as historical remembrances for which the whole significance and function is lost to the Church of our time, are to be removed from certain prayers. These prayers are to be accommodated to the needs of Christian life today.
The "Church universal of the present day" of the original has become the "Church of our time," and "present-day precepts" or "customs" [*instituta*] has become "present-day needs" [*necessitates*]. The movement is from the objective (precepts or customs) to that which is, at least potentially, quite subjective (needs). Bruylants's wording requires only mechanical adjustments to the texts, whereas Dumas's involves the editors in decisions of considerable subtlety.

Further, although the 1968 wording stipulates that only the mention of particular deeds or of historical remembrances whose significance had been lost are to be accommodated to the needs of present-day Christian life, Dumas reports in his 1971 essay on the revisions that every oration was reviewed in the light of modern needs.[46]

Changes in the wording of the remaining principles, while not as far-reaching in their ramifications, are also noteworthy.

Dumas Policy IV: "Both the literary genre and proper liturgical function are to be restored to all orations. Therefore the collect, prayers over the offerings, after communion and over the people have their own particular character."
Dumas adds "liturgical function" to "literary genre" which is gratuitous, but not entirely illogical. From this he draws a conclusion – namely that each of the four types of orations has its "particular character" – reintroducing

---

[46] "Les Oraisons du nouveau Missel Romain," *Liturgiques* 25 (1971) 263–70 passim. After mentioning several principles according to which the revisers made the prayers a) conform to "*aspirations contemporaines*" [contemporary aspirations, p. 263], b) true with respect to "*hommes, à leur relations, à leur besoins*" [men, to their relations, to their needs, p. 263], c) present a "*leçon pratique … aux hommes d'aujourd'hui*" [practical lesson … to men of today, p. 264], d) accommodate "*la mentalité moderne*" [the modern mentality, p. 266], Dumas states: "*Lorsqu'ils ne posaient aucune problème relatif aux principes ci-dessous rappelé, les textes d'ancien Missel ont été maintenus*" [When they posed no problem relative to the principles named above, the texts of the former missal were kept, p. 266]. For an English translation of Dumas's 1971 essay see Lauren Pristas, "The Orations of the Vatican II Missal: Policies for Revision," *Communio: an International Catholic Review*, 30:4 (Winter, 2003) 629–39.

a concept, or at least language, that the members had rejected in 1966. The implications of these adjustments are elusive in the abstract, but become clear when one compares the ways in which particular orations were used in antiquity with their usage in the new missal. The ancient liturgical codices do not support the view that each oration belongs to a particular type and, therefore, has only one liturgical function for, as we shall see below, in antiquity many prayers were used variously.

Dumas Policy V: "Orations are always directed to God the Father (unless certain reasons persuade otherwise)."
Dumas changes "in general" to "always," and his parenthetical addition of "unless certain reasons persuade otherwise" still leaves the principle heavily weighted toward "always." He does not mention the dispensation from this rule which the Advent Sundays collects seemingly enjoyed in 1966.

There is no indication in the schemata that any of the Consilium members took exception to Dumas's re-wording of the revision policies.

Conclusion

In this first chapter we identify the subject of our study as well as its scope, method, and goals. The Sunday collects of proper seasons in the Vatican II missals are to be studied in relation to (1) their counterparts in the *Missale Romanum (1962)*, (2) their individual sources, and (3) the revision policies approved by the Consilium members in 1966.

The object is three-fold: to gain a fuller and deeper appreciation of the collects of our missals, both past and present; to examine and evaluate the editorial work of the revisers; to compare and contrast the two sets of collects with respect to their spiritual and theological import and pastoral effect.

The differences between the policies as they were approved by the Consilium members in 1966 and as they were re-articulated by Dumas in 1968 are significant. We return to them as occasions warrant.

2

Resources

In the previous chapter, we stated that the primary work necessary to determine how the prayers of the new missal are like and unlike the prayers of its predecessor has not yet been done, and further suggested that the long preoccupation with the character and quality of the vernacular translations may have diverted scholarly attention from questions about the character and quality of the Latin texts themselves. But there is another reason also. In the two decades following the publication of the first typical edition of the *Missale Romanum (1970)* the materials needed to do the sort of comparative study undertaken here were not easily obtained.

This chapter discusses the principal resources upon which the study depends, not the collects of the missals. Readers who are not interested in the state of the evidence or the usefulness and limitations of particular resources may prefer to go directly to the next chapter.

The resources fall into two broad categories: (I) materials that pertain directly or indirectly to the revision of the collects; (II) materials that either identify, or make it possible to identify, the sources of particular collects and/or learn how the sources have been used over the course of the centuries.

Materials Pertaining to the Revision of the Collects

Coetus Schemata[1]

Although most of the *coetus* schemata have never been published, they have been preserved and are available for review.[2] Particularly important for our study are the schemata of *Coetus* 1 and *Coetus* 18*bis*.[3]

Coetus 1[4]

Coetus 1 had responsibility for the reform of the liturgical calendar and, in this capacity, proposed both the suppression of feasts and/or seasons and the revisions to a) the arrangement of the Church's Sacred Year as a whole and in its constitutive parts; b) the sequence or order of celebrations; c) the liturgical titles given to particular days.

This study makes use of the calendar schemata when discussions or determinations of *Coetus* 1 shed light on the Consilium's understanding of a particular liturgical season and/or account for changes in the corpus of collects.

Coetus 18*bis*[5]

It is with the work of *Coetus* 18*bis* that we are principally concerned. In point of fact, however, the schemata of this study group do not provide much assistance with respect to the selection, editing, or new composition of texts. In the previous chapter we note that 65 pages of *Coetus* 18*bis*'s *Schema* 186 contains the set of orations *de tempore* that the *coetus* first proposed to the Consilium members.[6] The schema not only gives the text of the collect assigned to each day, but also provides information about the source of the text. This set as a set, however, does not appear in *Missale Romanum (1970)*.[7] Subsequent schemata of *Coetus* 18*bis* do not include a second draft of *orationes de tempore* or tell us why the set that was eventually published differs so greatly from the one originally proposed.

---

[1] See p. 4 for a general description of the *coetus* schemata.

[2] The list of the Consilium schemata is found in Piero Marini, "Elenco Degli 'Schemata' del 'Consilium' e della Congregazione per il Culto Divino (Marzo 1964–Iuglio 1975)" *Notitiae* 18 (1982) 448–539.

[3] The offices of the International Commission on English in the Liturgy (ICEL), in Washington, D.C., have a complete set of the schemata of *Coetus* 18*bis* and some of the schemata of *Coetus* 1.

[4] See p. 8 for the members of *Coetus* 1.

[5] See p. 8–9 for the members of *Coetus* 18*bis*.

[6] *De Missali* 27, Schema n. 186 (19 September 1966), pp. 5–69.

[7] None of the Advent or Paschal Sunday collects is exactly the same, and only two of the Lenten Sunday collects are the same.

Such lacunae are more often the rule than the exception. In their work on the sources of the orations in the *Missale Romanum (1975)*, Anthony Ward and Cuthbert Johnson describe the state of the evidence as follows:

> The material conserved in the Congregation's[8] archive documenting any particular text is uneven, depending on the work methods of a particular group (*coetus*) of revisers, the opportunities offered by distance and commitments to meet in person and so on. It should not be forgotten that all those involved were in some way experts in their field, many having worked for the best part of a lifetime with the texts in question. Accordingly, there was often no need to prepare extensive written explanations, but simply to operate selections, and revisions of texts, the rationale of the details being more or less obvious to fellow specialists once broad policies had been defined. Let all users of this work be therefore assured that personal access to the official archival material would reveal no further information, except of the most incidental variety. Of what is available, the fullest use has been made.[9]

The schemata of *Coetus* 18*bis* are useful principally for the record they provide of the revisions policies as (1) originally proposed, (2) originally approved, and (3) later re-stated.[10] We refer to these policies as occasion warrants.

Ecclesiastical Documents

There are three documents that bear directly or indirectly on the revision of the Lenten collects: (1) *Acta et Documenta Vaticano II Apparando* which presents the solicited responses on questions pertaining to Lenten discipline that were gathered in preparation for Vatican II;[11] (2) Vatican II's *Sacrosanctum Concilium* which stipulates how the Lenten liturgical formularies were to be revised;[12] and (3) Paul VI's *Paenitemini*, the 1966 apostolic constitution that changed the Church's obligatory discipline with respect to

---

[8] The Congregation for Divine Worship and the Discipline of the Sacraments.

[9] Cuthbert Johnson and Anthony Ward, "The Sources of the Roman Missal (1975)" *Notitiae* 22 (1986), 454.

[10] Schema n. 186, *De Missali* 27 (19 September 1966), pp. 1–4 (proposed) and Addendum p. 1 (as approved where changes were made); *De Missali* 56, Schema n. 319 (7 October 1968), p. 2 (as later re-articulated). For a discussion of these documents see above, pp. 9–18.

[11] *Acta et Documenta Concilio Oecumenico Vaticano II Apparando*, series 1, appendix volume II: (Typis Polyglottis Vaticanis, 1961).

[12] *Sacrosanctum Oecumenicum Concilium Vaticanum II, Constitutiones Decreta Declarationes*, vol. 1 (Civitas Vaticana: Vaticanum Typographium, 1967) 3–54.

Lenten observance.[13] The use of ecclesiastical documents is confined to the discussion of the Lenten collects in Chapter 6.

Works Authored by Consilium *Periti*

Because the *coetus* schemata often say little or nothing about particular revision decisions, the works that fall into this category are often quite illuminating. After the new missal appeared, many of those involved in the work of the reform published articles in which they set forth the principles that guided the selection, arrangement, redaction, and creation of texts, and explained how the principles were concretely applied.[14] Frequently they offer examples.

Since ours is a comparative study of select collects of the pre- and post-Vatican II missals and not a history of the revision of the collects or an explanation of what the revisers intended or hoped to achieve, our use of works authored by Consilium *periti* is sparing and reserved to those instances in which they answer questions which naturally arise in the course of our considerations.

Materials Useful for Source Identification

Lists of Sources

Antoine Dumas, relator of *Coetus* 18*bis*, published lists of the sources of the orations of the *Missale Romanum (1970)* shortly after the missal appeared.[15] Cuthbert Johnson, O.S.B. and Anthony Ward, S.M., who worked at the Congregation for Divine Worship and the Discipline of the Sacraments, did likewise after the second typical edition of the post-Vatican II missal was published.[16] These lists cite, rather than present, the sources.

---

[13] *Acta Apostolicae Sedis* 58 (1966) 177–98.

[14] See, for example, Henry Ashworth, "The Prayers for the Dead in the Missal of Pope Paul VI," *Ephemerides Liturgicae* 85 (1971) 3–15; Matias Augé, "Le Colletta del Proprio del Tempo nel Nuovo Messale," *Ephemerides Liturgicae* 84 (1970) 275–98; Carlo Braga, "Il Nuovo Messale Romano," *Ephemerides Liturgicae* 84 (1970) 249–74; Carlo Braga, "Il 'Proprium de Sanctis,'" *Ephemerides Liturgicae* 84 (1970) 401–03; Annibale Bugnini, *The Reform of the Liturgy (1948–1975)* tr. Matthew J. O'Connell (Collegeville: The Liturgical Press, 1990); Antoine Dumas, "Les Oraisons du nouveau Missel Romain," *Questions Liturgiques* 25 (1971) 263–70; Walter Ferretti, "Le Orazioni 'Post Communionem' de Tempore nel Nuovo Messale Romano," *Ephemerides Liturgicae* 84 (1970) 323–41; Vincenzo Raffa, "Le Orazioni Sulle Offerte del Tempo nel Nuovo Messale Romano," *Ephemerides Liturgicae* 84 (1970) 299–322.

[15] See A. Dumas, "Les Sources du Nouveau Missel Romain," *Notitiae* 7 (1971) 37–42, 74–7, 94–5, 134–36, 276–80, 409–10.

[16] See Cuthbert Johnson and Anthony Ward, "The Sources of the Roman Missal (1975)," *Notitiae* 22 (1986) 445–747, and Cuthbert Johnson, "The Sources of the Roman Missal

To see the actual source prayer or text, one must obtain a copy of the work in which it appears.

These lists enable scholars to learn how old, at the least, particular collects are,[17] but not how widely particular prayers were used, for how long, in what liturgical settings or, frequently, whether they appear in the new missal in revised form.

When they first appeared these lists of sources were the only way, short of searching through every extant liturgical codex, of ascertaining the source(s) of the orations not found in the *Missale Romanun (1962)*. Since the publication of the volumes discussed in the next section, this is no longer the case. Nevertheless, these lists remain indispensable in two types of circumstances: (1) when an oration is an adaptation of an ancient prayer in which both the opening and closing words were altered, and (2) when a prayer is a new composition, whether centonized or not. In these cases the lists of Dumas, Johnson and Ward are the only way of reliably identifying the source texts or being certain that the revisers composed the text from scratch. We rely on these lists as need arises.

Corpus Orationum

Between 1992 and 1999 Eugenio Moeller, Joanne Maria Clément and Bertrandus Coppieters 't Wallant published ten volumes of orations as part of *Corpus Christianorum Series Latina* under the title *Corpus Orationum* [Corpus of Orations].[18] These volumes present, in alphabetical order, the full text of all the orations contained in over two hundred extant Latin liturgical codices that dated from before the Tridentine reform – 6,163 different orations in all.[19] The editors list the codices in which each oration appears, identify the way it is used in each manuscript, and cite the textual variants. Separate lists in each volume date the codices. The last volume, CLX-J, contains indices of both first lines and closing words.

From these volumes it is possible to determine how widely a particular prayer was used in antiquity, in which centuries, and in what settings. The

---

(1975)" 32 (1996) 3–161. Johnson and Ward also cite earlier editions of the *Missale Romanum* and the oration numbers assigned by Placide Bruylants, *Les Oraisons du Missel Roman* texte et histoire, vol. 2 (Louvain: Centre de Documentation et d'Information Liturgiques, 1952).

[17] The presence of an oration in a particular ancient codex means only that it is at least as old as that codex. It may be much older.

[18] Eugenio Moeller, Joanne Maria Clément and Bertrandus Coppieters 't Wallant, eds., *Corpus Orationum*, vols. 1–9 and 11, *Corpus Christianorum Series Latina* CLX–CLX-H and J (Turnholt: Brepols, 1992–9).

[19] A few of the codices are earlier than the eighth century. Most date from the eighth century to 1570, when the Tridentine missal first appeared. Some of the codices listed are early reproductions, for example nineteenth century, of pre-Trent liturgical books. The earliest codex, *Rotulus* of Ravenna, is dated fifth/sixth century.

data represents a minimum, the "*at least* during these centuries, in these codices," and so forth, because it is gleaned from the manuscripts that have survived, not necessarily from all that ever existed. Because the *Corpus Orationum* volumes also list the variants, they make it possible to state with confidence whether particular prayers were revised before being incorporated into a modern missal (whether the Tridentine or Vatican II missal). Because the *Corpus Orationum* volumes list the use to which each prayer is put in each codex in which it appears, they also make it possible to state whether there is precedent in the manuscript tradition for the liturgical use to which the Vatican II revisers put it.

As we indicate above, the *Corpus Orationum* volumes are only helpful in those cases in which the revisers adopted or adapted an ancient oration leaving either the first or last words untouched. Otherwise one must have recourse to the lists of sources discussed above.

A particular advantage of the *Corpus Orationum* volumes [hereafter CO] over the lists of sources is that CO lists all the extant codices in which a prayer is found, sometimes as many as 50. Dumas identifies only the specific codex from which the revisers actually took the text. Ward and Johnson identify the principal ancient codices in which a text appears as well as its biblical and patristic background.

The *Corpus Orationum* volumes are the resource without which this study simply would not have been possible. They are used to discover all the things indicated above: the antiquity of texts, the uses to which particular texts have been put over the centuries, whether variants exist and their particular forms, and so forth. There is no prayer considered in this study for which the *Corpus Orationum* volumes were not consulted. The contribution of Eugenio Moeller, Joanne Maria Clément and Bertrandus Coppieters 't Wallant cannot be underestimated.

Liturgia.it

An Italian website[20] has links to the *Missale Romanum* of 1962, 1975 and 2002, the last typical edition of the Tridentine missal and the second and third typical editions of the Vatican II missal respectively. It also has links to the *Gelasianum Vetus*,[21] the Veronense or Leonine Sacramentary,[22] the

---

[20] http://www.liturgia.it.

[21] *Codex Vaticanus Reginensis* 316, which was copied at Chelles *circa* 750 and is usually called the Old Gelasian Sacramentary or *Gelasianum Vetus*. The modern critical edition is: Leo Cunibert Mohlberg, Leo Eizenfoefer, Peter Siffrin, eds., *Liber Sacramentorum Romanae Aeclesiae ordinis anni circuli* (Rome: Herder, 1960). Hereafter *Gelasianum Vetus = GeV*.

[22] Verona, Biblioteca capitolare, *codex* 85 (olim 80). The critical edition Leo Cunibert Mohlberg, Leo Eizenhöfer, and Petrus Siffrin, (eds), *Sacramentarium Veronense* (Rome: Casa Editrice Herder, 1956). The so-called Veronense or Leonine Sacramentary is not a true sacramentary, for it was never used in public worship. Rather, it is a private collection of

Sacramentary of Hildoard of Cambrai (*Hadrianum*),[23] and the Sacramentary of Angoulême (*Engolismensis*).[24] Each missal and sacramentary is accompanied by a concordance that is easy to use.

Using the concordances at this website, it is possible to find particular texts easily, to discover quickly the settings in which a particular oration appears in different missals, and to research many questions that arise concerning vocabulary.

This wonderful website, like the *Corpus Orationum* volumes, has been a constant companion through the execution of this study and has saved countless hours. Since everything posted there is available in print and all references in this volume are to the print editions, Liturgia.it is only cited to assert a negative – for example, that a particular word or phrase does not appear in a particular missal. It is mentioned here for the assistance of those who might find it helpful and to express my gratitude to Alessandro Toniolo who maintains the site.

The present study is based on the Latin texts of the typical editions of the respective missals, not vernacular translations. Therefore the precise issue under consideration is not necessarily the text that the faithful hear, but the text in the typical edition of each missal.

Unless otherwise noted, everything said of the *Missale Romanum (1970)*, the first typical edition of the Vatican II missal, is also true of the second and third typical editions – *Missale Romanum (1975)* and *Missale Romanum (2002)*, respectively. The designation "1970/2002" is used when this is the case and clarification is provided when it is not.

Unless otherwise noted, all Latin scriptural citations are to the *Vulgate*, all English citations are to the *Revised Standard Version*, and all English renderings of non-biblical texts are my own.

Roman formularies. The manuscript dates from the first quarter of the seventh century but the prayers in it are dated variously from 400–560 AD. See Cyrille Vogel, *Medieval Liturgy: An Introduction to the Sources*, revised and translated by William G. Storey and Niels Rasmussen, O.P. (Washington, D.C.: Pastoral Press, 1986) 38–45 for a description of the codex and a survey of scholarly opinions concerning it. Hereafter, Veronense = *Ver*.

[23] Cambrai, Bibliothèque municipale, codex 164 (olim 159). The critical edition is J. Deshusses, ed., *Le sacramentaire grégorien: Ses Principales Formes D'après Les Plus Anciens Manuscrits*, tome I, (= Spicilegium Friburgense, 16, Fribourg en Suisse, 1971). Scholars date the codex, which is also called the *Hadrianum*, to the years 811–12 (Cyrille Vogel, *Medieval Liturgy*, 82). Hereafter, *Hadrianum = Had*.

[24] The codex is Paris, Bibliothèque Nationale, m.s. Latin 816. The modern edition is P. Saint Roche, *Liber Sacramentorum Engolismensis* [= CSSL CLIX C], (Turnhout, 1987). Scholars date the codex c. 800 (Cyrille Vogel, *Medieval Liturgy*, 70). Hereafter, *Sacramentary of Angoulême = Engol*.

3

Advent

Introduction

The Church's Sacred Year begins with Advent. The season opens with I Vespers of the Sunday nearest the feast of Saint Andrew (November 30) and ends with None on the Vigil of the Nativity.[1] While this continues a practice of long duration, the decision to place Advent at the start of the Church year was made only after the revisers considered putting it at the end.

The second schema of the Calendar *coetus* records the initial discussion of its members concerning this question:

> Whether the time of Advent ought to be placed at the beginning of the liturgical year, so that it prepares for the feast of the Lord's Nativity, or be considered the conclusion of the liturgical year so that its eschatological meaning is restored?[2]

Rembert Van Doren, Agostino Amore, and Ansgar Dirks answer that Advent should open the liturgical year, while Pierre Jounel and Herman Schmidt say that Advent should close it.[3] Aimé-Georges Martimort, wanting to preserve both significations, is not satisfied with either alternative.[4] Adrian

---

[1] Cf. Schema n. 75, *De Calendario* 4 (10 April 1965) p. 1; *Res Secretariae*, n. 19 (14 June 1965) p. 1, and the arrangement of both the pre- and post-Vatican II missals. *Res Secretariae*, n. 19 (14 June 1965) p. 1: "Tempus Adventus est initium anni liturgici, et decurrit a primis Vesperis primae dominicae usque ad Nonam vigiliae Nativitatis." [The season of Advent is the beginning of the liturgical year, and runs from first Vespers of the first Sunday until None of the vigil of the Nativity].

[2] Schema n. 65, *de Calendario* 2 (15 March 1965) p. 11, question 14: Utrum tempus Adventus habendum est initium anni liturgici, ita ut sit praeparatio ad festum Nativitatis Domini, an considerandum est conclusio anni liturgici, ita ut sensu exhatologico instaurandum sit?

[3] Schema n. 65, *de Calendario* 2 (15 March 1965) pp. 11–12.

[4] Schema n. 65, *de Calendario* 2 (15 March 1965) p. 11: "Utrumque omnino servetur, neque istam alternativam esse bonam censeo." [That both certainly be preserved; I deem neither alternative good].

Nocent does not answer the question as asked, but rather comments that the two senses of the Lord's coming found in ancient authors are lacking in the present readings of the Mass and Office.[5]

From the phrasing of the question, it is evident that difference of opinion about the placement of Advent is rooted in difference of opinion about Advent's proper character: is it a season of preparation for Christ's coming at Christmas, or his coming at the end of time, or both?

This chapter has two main parts. The first describes the development of the Roman Advent until it attains a settled character – the character that, once attained, remained unaltered for more than thirteen centuries. The second is a comparative examination of the corpus of Advent collects in the pre- and post-Vatican II missals. It has three parts. The first is a quantitative overview that explains both what happened to the Advent collects in the 1962 missal and where the Advent collects of the 1970/2002 missal came from: how many are from the 1962 missal, how many from other sources, and how many of both sorts were edited for inclusion in the new missal. The second is a comparative analysis of the Advent Sunday collects of the two missals. It studies each Advent Sunday collect in relation to its counterpart in the other missal and, in the case of each edited collect, in relation to its ancient source. The third part considers the set of four 1970/2002 Sunday collects in relation to the set in the 1962 missal. A conclusion follows.

The Origins and Development of Advent at Rome

Advent, as a season of preparation for the feast of the Lord's Nativity, was first observed outside of Rome.[6] Its origins are somewhat obscure, and we do not attempt to trace them here. Rather, this introductory section discusses three stages by which the Roman Advent attained its distinctive character. Our presentation relies on the scholarship of Thomas J. Talley and Thierry Maertens who, in their individual works on Advent, respectively examine the December Ember Day sermons of Pope Saint Leo the Great and the early Roman liturgical books.[7]

---

[5] Schema n. 65, de Calendario 2 (15 March 1965) p. 12: "Mihi videtur retinendus duplex sensu[s] Adventus Domini de quo multi et antiqui auctores ... Attamen, in liturgia Adventus desunt lectiones quae, tam in Officio quam in Missa, hunc sensum duplicem ... ostendunt." [It seems to me the two senses of the Coming of the Lord, concerning which many and ancient authors [write]..., are to be retained.....However, in the Advent liturgy, in the Office as in the Mass, the readings lack this two-fold sense].

[6] Thomas J. Talley, The Origins of the Liturgical Year, (New York: Pueblo, 1986), 150.

[7] Thomas J. Talley, The Origins of the Liturgical Year, pp. 149–50; Th. Maertens, "L'Avent: Genèse historique de ses thèmes bibliques et doctrinaux," Mélanges de science religieuse 18 (1961), 47–110. Maertens relies on the textual work and hypotheses of Antoine Chavasse,

Fifth Century: December Ember Days and Pope Saint Leo I

From an earlier time than can be precisely identified, the Church annually observed three, and then four, weeks in which three days were fasted.[8] These weeks commenced the start of each season and came to be called *Quattuor Tempora* (four times) in Latin, *Quatember* in German, and Ember Days in English.[9]

According to Talley, the earliest detailed evidence we have about the character of the December fasts at Rome comes from the surviving tenth month Ember Day sermons preached by Pope Saint Leo I (d. 461).[10] They are pervaded by "an atmosphere of thanksgiving" that is "consistent with the celebration of agricultural bounty," but which also contain "eschatalogical nuances."[11] The last seems natural enough for, at Rome, both the annual agricultural cycle and the civil year came to a close in December.[12] Talley provides an example of Saint Leo's Ember Day preaching on the end times:

> When the Saviour would instruct His disciples about the *Advent* of God's Kingdom and the end of the world's times, and teach His whole Church, in the person of the Apostles, He said, "Take heed lest haply your hearts be overcharged with surfeiting and drunkenness, and care of this life." And assuredly, dearly beloved, we acknowledge that this precept applies more especially to us, to whom undoubtedly the day denounced is near, even though hidden, for the *advent* of which it behooves every man to prepare himself lest it find him given over to gluttony, or entangled in the cares of this life.[13]

The word "advent" appears twice in this short passage from a December sermon that was preached before a season of Advent was known at Rome. Talley comments: "The advent theme is all the more remarkable in that at no point in the sermons for the December fast does Leo refer to the coming

---

"L'Avent Romain, du VIᵉ au VIIIᵉ Siècle," *Ephemerides Liturgicae* (1953), 297–308 for aspects of his study.

[8] Pope Saint Leo I held that the observance was an apostolic institution. Francis Mershman, "Ember Days," *The Catholic Encyclopedia*, vol. 5 (New York: Robert Appleton Company, 1909), p. 399.

[9] Thomas J. Talley, *The Origins of the Liturgical Year*, p. 148.

[10] Thomas J. Talley, *The Origins of the Liturgical Year*, p. 149.

[11] Thomas J. Talley, *The Origins of the Liturgical Year*, p. 149.

[12] From 46 B.C., the Roman empire celebrated New Year's Day on the first of January.

[13] Charles L. Feltoe, *Leo the Great* in Select library of Nicene and post-Nicene Fathers of the Christian Church, Second series, vol. 12 (Grand Rapids, MI.: Eerdmans, 1956) 127. Quoted in Talley, *The Origins of the Liturgical Year*, 149. Emphasis added.

festival of the nativity of Christ."[14] He concludes "the Roman December fast at the time of Leo I is not a preparation for Christmas" but, rather, focusing as it does "on the end time, the consummation of the year ... is ... a liturgical sign of the consummation of history."[15] Preparation for the end times entails avoiding all that impedes either freedom or vigilance: gluttony, drunkenness, and entanglement in the cares of the present life.

In Pope Saint Leo's day, then, Rome knew two distinct December observances: a fast in which the faithful were admonished to prepare for the Lord's coming in glory and a feast in honor of his birth in the flesh.

Sixth Century: Ember Day and Sunday Lessons of the *Comes of Wurzbourg*

Comes of Wurzbourg is a *capitulare* or list of the *pericopes* used at Mass.[16] Thierry Maertens tells us it was composed by an unknown person of the sixth century "to realize a synthesis among different Roman usages."[17]

The *Comes* assigns the following lessons to the December Ember Days:

Wednesday: Isaiah 2.2–5, 7.10–15; Luke 1.26–38
Friday: Isaiah 11.1–5; Luke 1.39–47
Saturday: Isaiah 19.20–22, 35.1–7, 40.9–11, 42.1–9, 45.1–11; 2
   Thessalonians 2.1–8; Luke 3.1–6.[18]

Taken together, these lessons provide an admirably complete mini-catechesis on the Lord's Nativity. The prophetic lessons speak of the coming Messiah and the Gospel lessons present accounts of the Annunciation, Visitation, and the appearance of John who preaches a baptism of repentance for the forgiveness of sins and exhorts his listeners to "prepare the way of the Lord." The Epistle lesson deflects attention from the eschaton inasmuch as it warns the faithful not to give heed to deceptive reports that the day of the Lord's return has arrived.

In the Wurzbourg *Comes* the Ember Days, at least with respect to the scripture lessons, become preparation for the coming feast of the Lord's Nativity. The nature of this preparation is, in the main, historical or catechetical. The historical lessons, however, culminate in John's exhortation to repentance.

---

[14] Thomas J. Talley, *The Origins of the Liturgical Year*, 149.
[15] Thomas J. Talley, *The Origins of the Liturgical Year*, 150.
[16] Cyril Vogel, *Medieval Liturgy*, 316.
[17] Th. Maertens, "L'Avent: Genèse historique de ses thèmes bibliques et doctrinaux," *Mélanges de science religieuse* 18 (1961) 57.
[18] The list comes from Th. Maertens, "L'Avent: Genèse historique de ses thèmes bibliques et doctrinaux," *Mélanges de science religieuse* 18 (1961) 57.

Except for the lesson from Isaiah 42, originally assigned to Ember Saturday, the very same *pericopes* continued in use on the same days in the same order until the revision of the Roman lectionary that followed the Second Vatican Council.

The Wurzbourg *Comes* also presents an Advent of six Sundays and assigns the following Epistle lessons to them:[19]

Sunday 1: Romans 13.11–14. "... Besides this you know what hour it is, how it is full time now for you to wake from sleep. For salvation is nearer to us now than when we first believed; ... Let us then cast off the works of darkness and put on the armor of light ..."

Sunday 2: Jeremiah 23.5–8. "Behold, the days are coming, says the LORD, when I will raise up for David a righteous Branch, and he shall reign as king ..."

Sunday 3: Romans 15.4–13. "May the God of steadfastness and encouragement grant you to live in such harmony with one another, in accord with Christ Jesus ... and further Isaiah says, 'The root of Jesse shall come, he who rises to rule the Gentiles; in him shall the Gentiles hope.' ..."

Sunday 4: 1 Corinthians 4.1–5. "Therefore do not pronounce judgment before the time, before the Lord comes, who will bring to light the things now hidden in darkness and will disclose the purposes of the heart. Then every man will receive his commendation from God."

Sunday 5: Philippians 4.4–7. "Rejoice in the Lord always ... Let all men know your forbearance. The Lord is at hand ..."

Sunday 6: *vacat.*[20]

The Sunday Epistle lessons have three things in common. First, all contain moral exhortation. Second, all refer in some way to the Lord's coming or to a decisive new moment. Third, the language of the lessons is not univocal, but is capable of being variously accommodated to the Lord's different comings: in grace or in feast, in judgment or in glory. The faithful are being reminded of the Lord's final return as they are being urged to prepare themselves for the grace of the coming feast through renewed fidelity to the moral and spiritual demands of Christian life.

At this stage, there is a six-week Advent in which the Sunday Epistle lessons prepare the faithful for the coming feast by moral exhortation and eschatological reminders. These envelop, so to speak, the Ember Day

---

[19] The list comes from Th. Maertens, "L'Avent: Genèse historique de ses thèmes bibliques et doctrinaux," *Mélanges de science religieuse* 18 (1961) 59. The selection of quotations is my own.

[20] No lessons are assigned to this Sunday. The *pericopes* listed above for the first, third, fourth, and fifth Sundays appear in the *Missale Romanum (1962)* as the Epistles for the first, second, fourth, and third Sundays of Advent, respectively.

lessons that provide more proximate preparation of a catechetical nature by recalling the Old Testament prophecies and New Testament events that immediately preceded the Lord's birth and preaching. The lesson from Jeremiah assigned to the second Sunday is messianic prophecy having the same character as the non-Gospel lessons assigned to the December Ember Days. It is the only instance in which the otherwise distinct modes of preparations, one accorded to the Sundays and the other to the Ember Days, overlap.

At the same time the six-week Advent was observed in the presbyteral churches of Rome, in other places, seemingly both inside and outside the city, a four-Sunday Advent was known.[21] The shorter Advent does not appear to have come about through a reduction of the longer one, but was a three-week (four-Sunday) observance from the start.[22]

Late Sixth Century: Contribution of Pope Saint Gregory the Great

During the pontificate of Pope Saint Gregory I (d. 604), the duration of Advent was set at four Sundays;[23] Gospel lessons and formularies were assigned to three Sundays; Epistles assigned to all four; and new, or anyway different, prayers were assigned to the Ember Day Masses. The assignments combined old and new elements. The result was both an integration of earlier aspects and a deepening of the whole. Pope Saint Gregory imprinted a spiritual character upon the season that remained in place until the revision of the missal that followed Vatican II.

The Gregorian Epistolary retains four of the five Wurzbourg *pericopes*, thereby preserving both the moral exhortation and eschatological motif of the earlier Advent:

Sunday 1: Romans 13.11–14.
Sunday 2: Romans 15.4–13.
Sunday 3: 1 Corinthians 4.1–5.
Sunday 4: Philippians 4.4–7.[24]

---

[21] Maertens, "L'Avent: Genèse historique de ses thèmes bibliques et doctrinaux," *Mélanges de science religieuse* 18 (1961) 69. Maertens, p. 69, n. 3 cites Antoine Chavasse, "L'Avent Romain, du VIᵉ au VIIIᵉ Siècle, *Ephemerides Liturgicae* (1953) 297–308.

[22] Maertens, "L'Avent: Genèse historique de ses thèmes bibliques et doctrinaux," *Mélanges de science religieuse* 18 (1961) 69.

[23] Maertens, "L'Avent: Genèse historique de ses thèmes bibliques et doctrinaux," *Mélanges de science religieuse* 18 (1961) 70.

[24] Th. Maertens, "L'Avent: Genèse historique de ses thèmes bibliques et doctrinaux," *Mélanges de science religieuse* 18 (1961) 70. The Sundays are designated: "4ᵉ dimanche av. Noël" [4th Sunday before Christmas], etc. These same lessons are found in the Tridentine missals but with the order of the last two reversed.

From Saint Gregory's *Homelarium* we know that the Advent Gospel *pericopes* of his day are the same as those found in the Tridentine missals:[25]

Sunday 1: Luke 21.25–33.
Sunday 2: Matthew 11.2–10.
Sunday 3: John 1.19–28.

The first Gospel *pericope* speaks of the end times; in the second John bears witness to Jesus; in the last, Jesus bears witness to John.

Saint Gregory assigned three sets of formularies, nine proper prayers in all, to the three Sundays of Advent.[26] Early in the seventh century each set was advanced one Sunday, so that the formularies of the first Sunday of Advent in the Gregorian Sacramentary of 595 were later assigned to the twenty-fourth Sunday after Pentecost, those of the second Sunday of Advent to the first, and those of the third Sunday to the second. The Gregorian prayers that were moved to the twenty-fourth Sunday after Pentecost are not included in the Tridentine missals, but those moved to the first and second Sundays of Advent are. These latter continued in use on the same days until the post-Vatican II revision of the Sacred Liturgy.

The collect that was moved to the first Sunday of Advent, Maertens tells us, was confected by Gregory himself.[27] It is a centonized composition which combines a phrase that appears in several pre-*Gelasian* Advent prayers, "Excita, quaesumus, Domine, potentiam tuam et veni" [Rouse, we beseech you, O Lord, your power and come], and the latter portion of a December Ember Day prayer in the same codex. Saint Gregory's confection appears below with its sources which are preserved in the eighth century *Gelasianum Vetus*. The words in boldface type were introduced by the pope himself.

---

[25] The list comes from Maertens, "L'Avent: Genèse historique de ses thèmes bibliques et doctrinaux," *Mélanges de science religieuse* 18 (1961) 70. He cites *PL* 1077. [*PL* =*Patrologia Latina*].

[26] Maertens, "L'Avent: Genèse historique de ses thèmes bibliques et doctrinaux," *Mélanges de science religieuse* 18 (1961) 71. The Gregorian Sacramentary was compiled in 595.

[27] Maertens, "L'Avent: Genèse historique de ses thèmes bibliques et doctrinaux," *Mélanges de science religieuse* 18 (1961) 72.

GeV 1120, 1141, 1149	GeV 1158	595 Advent Sunday II
EXCITA, QUAESUMUS, DOMINE, POTENCIAM TUAM ET UENI ... 1120: et quod aecclesiae tuae usque in finem saeculi promisisti, clementer operare. 1141: UT hii qui in tua pietate confidunt, ab omni cicius aduersitatebus liberentur. 1149: UT tua propiciacione saluemur.	*Subueniat nobis, domine, misericordia tua, et ab inminentibus peccatorum nostrorum periculis te mereamur uenienti saluari.*	EXCITA, QUAESUMUS, DOMINE, POTENTIAM TUAM, ET VENI: UT *ab imminentibus peccatorum nostrorum periculis, te mereamur* protegente eripi, te liberante *salvari.*
ROUSE, WE BESEECH YOU, O LORD, YOUR POWER AND COME ... 1120: and graciously work unto the end of the ages that which you have promised to your church. 1141: THAT those who trust in your mercy may more quickly be freed from every adversity. 1149: THAT we may be saved by your mercy.	*May your mercy assist us, O Lord, and from the imminent dangers of our sins may we be able to be saved by your coming.*	ROUSE, O LORD, YOUR POWER AND COME, THAT *from the threatening dangers of our sins, we may be deemed worthy to be* delivered by you protecting, *saved by you* freeing.

Saint Gregory adopts a clause that opens several orations and, in consequence, has several different endings. All are Advent orations. He uses this opening clause to replace the opening clause of a December Ember Day oration (same season). The adopted and replaced clauses are similar – both call for the Lord to come, the one with his power using imperative verbs and the other to our aid with his mercy using a subjunctive verb. Since the difference in the two opening clauses lies not so much in the desire expressed as in the intensity with which it is expressed, the second clause of the second prayer is a natural thematic fit with its new opening. Saint Gregory's then heightens the expression of need in the adopted second clause giving the collect an intensity that is sustained throughout. In the resulting prayer we do not ask simply to be saved from the threatening dangers of our sins by the Lord's coming in power but, having demanded (the imperative verbs) that he come, we beg to be delivered by his protecting and saved by his freeing.

Here Saint Gregory introduces, Maertens observes, new elements: a "penitential resonance"[28] and "the echo of the theology of grace":

> The coming of the Lord in grace is the corollary of the primacy of God in the work of salvation. Left to ourselves we are able only to hasten to sin and to evil. The *veni* of this prayer thus expresses quite a new note, an echo of the theology of grace: man is able to do nothing and relies completely on the initiative of God.[29]

The prayer eventually assigned to the second Sunday is "Excita, Domine, corda nostra ad praeparandas Unigeniti tui vias: ut per eius adventum, purificatis tibi mentibus servire mereamur" [Rouse, O Lord, our hearts to prepare the ways of your Only-begotten Son, that through his coming, we may be deemed worthy to serve you with minds made pure]. The same themes are present in this prayer as in the preceding: God's work is primary; we can do nothing without his assistance.

Further, both prayers speak of the Lord's coming, and both express great confidence in his mercy and saving power.

Saint Gregory also assigned formularies to the December Ember Days.[30] He selected eight of the nine collects from a pre-Gelasian sacramentary and made editorial changes to many in service, Maertens states, of greater clarity or a more pleasing rhythm.[31] Unlike the earlier prayers which focused on the fast in the manner customary for Ember Day formularies, the prayers which Saint Gregory chose look to the Lord's coming. As a group, they also exhibit the theology of grace, intense human need, awareness of sin and impotence, and confidence in God's mercy and power present in the Advent

---

[28] Maertens, "L'Avent: Genèse historique de ses thèmes bibliques et doctrinaux," *Mélanges de science religieuse* 18 (1961) 72: "résonance pénitentielle."

[29] Maertens, "L'Avent: Genèse historique de ses thèmes bibliques et doctrinaux," *Mélanges de science religieuse* 18 (1961) 72: "La venue du Seigneur est corollaire de la primauté de Dieu dans l'œuvre du salut. Livrés à nous-mêmes nous ne pouvons que courir au péché et au maleur. Le *veni* de cette oraison rend ainsi un son très nouveau, écho de la théologie de la grâce: l'homme ne peut rien et tout relève de l'initiative de Dieu."

[30] While it is true that formularies for the third and fourth Sundays and the Gospel for the fourth Sunday were yet to be appointed, the later compilers assigned texts which were thematically consistent with Gregory's work.

[31] Maertens, "L'Avent: Genèse historique de ses thèmes bibliques et doctrinaux," *Mélanges de science religieuse* 18 (1961) 75, n. 4. Maertens relies on the work of Antoine Chavasse, *Le Sacramentaire Gélasien Du VIIe Siècle: Ses Deux Principales Formes* (s.l.: s.n.: 1959) to identify the pre-Gelasian texts which Saint Gregrory adopted or adapted (Cf. Maertens, p. 57, n. 2).

Sunday prayers considered above. The way in which each collect mentions the Lord's coming and expresses human need or confidence is presented below.

Prayer	The Lord's coming	Human need, awareness of sin, or confidence in God's mercy
Or 2 Ember Wednesday	adventus tui consolationibus subleventur	qui in tua pietate confidunt
	may be lifted up by the consolations of your coming	who trust in your mercy
Ember Friday	excita … potentiam tuam et veni	ut hi qui in tua pietate confidunt ab omni citius adversitate liberentur
	rouse your power and come	that those who trust in your mercy may be more speedily set free from every adversity
Or 1, Ember Saturday	ex tua uisitatione consolemur	ex nostra pravitate affligimur
	may we be consoled by your visitation	we are afflicted by our depravity
Or 2, Ember Saturday	expectata unigeniti Filii tui nova nativitate liberemur	qui sub peccati iugo ex vetusta servitute deprimimur
	may we be set free by the awaited new birth of your only-begotten Son	we who are weighed down under the yoke of sin
Or 3 Ember Saturday	unigeniti Filii tui adventu laetifica	Indignos nos … famulos tuos, quos actionis propriae culpa contristat
	make [us] joyful at the coming of your only-begotten Son	us, your unworthy servants who are saddened by the guilt of their own actions
Or 4 Ember Saturday	ut Filii tui ventura solemnitas	et praesentis nobis vitae remedia conferat et praemia aeterna concedat
	that the coming solemnity of your Son ….	grant both remedies in present life and eternal rewards

Or 5 Ember Saturday	pietatis tuae visitatione consolemur	qui iuste pro peccatis nostris affligimur
	may be consoled by the visitation of your mercy	justly afflicted on account of our sins

The ways in which the Lord's coming is named are varied and sometimes open to more than one interpretation. As a set, the Ember Day collects include mention of all the ways the Lord comes: in grace (as consolation, as a visit of mercy); in glory (a coming that sets free from every adversity); in the feast or in grace (awaited new birth); in the feast (coming solemnity).

Elements of the first (*oratio* 1 of Wednesday) and ninth (*oratio* 6 of Saturday) Ember Day collects are not presented in the table above. The ninth prayer is not unique to Advent, but is the sixth oration assigned to every Ember Saturday Mass in the Tridentine missals.[32] Maertens tells us the remaining prayer, that assigned to Ember Wednesday, was composed by Saint Gregory.[33] Placed as it is before the first reading, it introduces the mini-catechesis first presented in Wurzbourg and preserved by Saint Gregory and the Tridentine reformers. The prayer looks forward to the coming feast and begs for its efficacy:

Praesta, quaesumus, omnipotens Deus: ut redemptionis nostrae ventura solemnitas, et praesentis nobis vitae subsidia conferat, et aeternae beatitudinis praemia largiatur.	Grant, we beseech you, almighty God: that the coming solemnity of our redemption may both bring us helps of the present life and bestow the rewards of eternal blessedness.

Although the formularies for the last two Sundays of Advent and the Gospel lesson for the last Sunday were added after 600 A.D., by that year the Roman Advent had essentially become what it would remain for the next thirteen centuries.

Saint Gregory retained the elements of the earlier tradition: from Wurzbourg, the lessons; from neighboring custom, the four-Sunday Advent. He then assigned Gospel lessons to Sundays and orations to Sundays and Ember Days. The orations imprint upon the season a distinctive spiritual character that resides not, *per se*, in waiting for the Lord, but in the posture

---

[32] In all, it follows the reading of Daniel 3.47–51, the account of the three young men in the fiery furnace, and is thematically related to it: Deus, qui tribus pueris mitigasti flammas ignium: concede propitius; ut nos famulos tuos non exurat flamma vitiorum. [O God, who tamed the flames of the fires for the three boys, mercifully grant that we, your servants, may not be consumed by the flame of vices.]

[33] Th. Maertens, "L'Avent: Genèse historique de ses thèmes bibliques et doctrinaux," *Mélanges de science religieuse* 18 (1961) 76.

of our waiting – ever conscious of our need and utterly confident in the Lord's power, goodness, and mercy.

With Gregory's contribution Advent attains new depth, breadth, and unity. The collects, both individually and as a group, give eloquent expression to the Church's theology of grace, but do so without undermining the emphasis on moral and spiritual vigilance urged in the Epistle lessons. And the advents named in the lessons and prayers, both implicitly and explicitly, include all the ways Christ comes: in history, in the feast of his Nativity, in grace, and in glory.

The Collects

Quantitative Overview

The 1962 missal has thirteen Advent collects: those of the four Sundays and the three Ember Days. The post-Vatican II missals have twenty-nine collects: four assigned to Sundays, and twenty-five to ferial days. A different collect is provided for each day of Advent.[34]

The Disposition of the 1962 Advent Collects

Of the thirteen 1962 collects, seven were retained in the Advent corpus of the 1970/2002 missal.[35] Five of the seven were revised, and none appears on the same day in both missals.

The six 1962 Advent collects not retained in the Advent corpus of the 1970/2002 missals were omitted from the new missals entirely. The omitted prayers are the collect of Sunday III, the collect of Ember Friday and the first, second, fifth, and sixth collects of Ember Saturday. Matias Augé tells us that the third of these was omitted because its content is quite

---

[34] There is a proper collect for each day from Monday of the first week through Friday of the third week (seventeen) and for each day from December 17 through the morning Mass of December 24 (eight).

[35] These are the collects of Sundays I, II, and IV, the second collect of Ember Wednesday and the second, third, and fourth collects of Ember Saturday. Matias Augé, "Le Colletta del Proprio del Tempo nel Nuovo Messale," *Ephemerides Liturgicae* 84 (1970) 275–98 at 278 counts eight retained collects, but he includes the 1962 collect of Sunday III which was replaced by a similar prayer. The two may even be variants of the same prayer, but the opening words of each are different. See the discussion on p. 39, n. 39 below.

generic,[36] the next two because they were alike and too negative,[37] and the last because it is a prayer that is proper to the preceding scripture lesson.[38] Augé does not mention the omission of the collect of the third Sunday of Advent, perhaps because a similar prayer was substituted in its stead,[39] or that of Ember Wednesday, perhaps because it is very like the fourth collect of Ember Saturday which was retained.[40]

---

[36] Matias Augé, "Le Colletta del Proprio del Tempo nel Nuovo Messale," *Ephemerides Liturgicae* 84 (1970) 275–98 at 278. The collect reads: *Excita, quaesumus, Domine, potentiam tuam, et veni: ut hi, qui in tua pietate confidunt, ab omni citius adversitate liberentur* [Rouse, we beseech you, O Lord, your power, and come: that those who trust in your mercy may be the more speedily freed from every adversity]. Augé writes: *"... la colletta ... ha un contenuto assai generico e la sua scomparsa non è da rimpiangere, se si tiene poi anche presente che la tipica espressione 'Excita, quaesumus, Domine, potentiam tuam, et veni" appare tuttora in altre collette e testi dell'Avvento"* ["... the collect has quite generic content and its disappearance is not to be lamented if one considers that the typical expression which it also presents 'Rouse, we beseech you, O Lord, your power, and come' still appears in other collects and texts of Advent."]

[37] *Ibid.* The first of the two is: *Concede, quaesumus, omnipotens Deus, ut, qui peccati iugo ex vetusta servitute deprimimur: exspectata unigeniti Filii tui nova navitate liberemur* [Grant, we beseech you, almighty God, that we who are weighed down by the yoke of sin from age-old servitude may be set free by the eagerly awaited new birth of your only begotten Son]. The second is: *Preces populi tui, quaesumus Domine, clementer exaudi: ut, qui iuste pro peccatis nostris affligimur, pietatis tuae visitatione consolemur* [Graciously hear the prayers of your people, we beseech you, O Lord: that we who are justly afflicted on account of our sins, may be comforted by a visitation of your mercy].

Concerning these two orations, Augé writes: *"... sono di contenuto molto simile ed esprimono lo stato d'animo dell'assemblea in termini troppo negativi, vale a dire come situazione di profunda afflizione"* ["They are very similar in content and express the assembly's state of soul in terms which are too negative, that is to say in a situation of profound affliction."]

[38] *Ibid.*, Daniel 3.47–51, the account of the three young men in the fiery furnace. The lesson and collect are common to all the Saturdays in Ember weeks in the Tridentine missal.

[39] Compare the omitted 1962 collect of the third Sunday of Advent (CO 358): *Aurem tuam, quaesumus, Domine, precibus nostris accommoda: et mentis nostrae tenebras, gratia tuae visitationis illustra* [Fit your ear, we beseech you, O Lord, to our prayers: and illumine the darkness of our mind with the grace of your visitation], with the 1970/2002 collect of Monday of the third week of Advent: *Voci nostrae, quaesumus, Domine, aures tuae pietatis accommoda, et cordis nostri tenebras gratia Filii tui nos visitantis illustra.* [Fit the ears of your mercy to our voice, O Lord, and illumine the darkness of our heart with the grace of your Son visiting us].

The 1962 collect is exactly the same as CO I, 358. The 1970/2002 collect, however, is an edited version of CO IX, 6105 which closes: *"... et cordis nostris tenebras lumine tuae visitationis illumina"* [illumine the darkness of our heart with the light of your visitation]. The original prayer addresses the Son. The revisers changed it to address the Father.

[40] Compare Ember Wednesday: *Praesta, quaesumus, omnipotens Deus: ut redemptionis nostrae ventura solemnitas, et praesentis nobis vitae subsidia conferat, et aeternae beatitudinis praemia largiatur* [Grant, we beseech you, almighty God: that the coming solemnity of our redemption may both bring us helps of the present life and bestow the rewards of eternal beatitude]. Ember Saturday: *Praesta, quaesumus, omnipotens Deus: ut filii tui ventura solemnitas et praesentis nobis vitae remedia conferat, et praemia aeterne concedat* [Grant, we

The three 1962 Advent Sunday collects that were retained in the revised missal were moved to ferial days.[41]

The Sources of the 1970/2002 Advent Collects

Three of the four 1970/2002 Sunday collects were adapted from ancient liturgical codices. The fourth Sunday collect, that of the last Sunday in Advent, is the 1962 postcommunion of the Annunciation of the Blessed Virgin Mary (March 25). It was incorporated into the new missal without emendation.

The twenty-two ferial collects in the 1970/2002 missal that were not taken from the 1962 Advent corpus came principally from two sources: the sixth-century *Rotulus of Ravenna*[42] and the mid-eighth-century *Gelasianum Vetus* or the Old Gelasian Sacramentary. These two ancient liturgical manuscripts, along with the 1962 missal, account for all but two of the 1970/2002 Advent collects.[43]

Of the twenty-five ferial collects appearing in the 1970/2002 missal, all but the two 1962 Sunday collects mentioned above were revised for inclusion in the new missal. These changes vary from simply modifying the word order to substantially revising the text.

Lastly, the collects assigned to December 20 and 23 in the first and second typical editions appear in slightly modified form in the third typical edition, *Missale Romanun (2002)*.

---

beseech you, almighty God, that the coming solemnity of your Son may both bring us remedies of the present life and grant eternal rewards]. 1970/2002 Wednesday of the third week of Advent: *Praesta, quaesumus, omnipotens Deus, ut Filii tui ventura solemnitas et praesentis nobis vitae remedia largiatur, et praemia aeterna concedat* [Grant, we beseech you, almighty God, that the coming solemnity of your Son may both bestow upon us remedies of the present life and grant eternal rewards].

[41] The collect of the first, second, and fourth Sundays were transferred to Friday of the first week, Thursday of the second week, and Thursday of the first week, respectively. Only the last was edited.

[42] *Rotulus* means "scroll." A critical edition of the scroll of Ravenna is found in Leo Cunibert Mohlberg, Leo Eizenhöfer, Petrus Siffrin, (eds), *Sacramentarium Veronense* (Rerum Ecclesiasticorum Documenta, Series maior, Fonte, I (Rome: Casa Editrice Herder, 1956), 173–78 and 202–03.

[43] The remaining two, the collects of Tuesday of the third week and December 22, were taken from the Bergomese Sacramentary which dates from the second half of the ninth century. A modern critical edition is available in Angelo Paredi, *Sacramentarium Bergomense: Manoscritto del secolo IX della Biblioteca di S. Alessandro in Colonna in Bergamo*, VI (Bergamo: Edizioni "Monumenta Bergomense," 1962). The Bergomese Sacramentary is an Ambrosian or Milanese rite text – that is, it is a Western, non-Roman sacramentary. The manuscript is cited as Bergamo, S. Alessandro in Colonna, *Codex* 242 [Cf. Vogel, *Medieval Liturgy* 109, 437].

Comparative Examination of the Pre- and Post-Vatican II Sunday Collects

The discussion of each collect includes a brief account of its manuscript history and a detailed examination of the text. Of particular interest is the way in which the source prayers of the 1970/2002 collects were edited by the modern revisers. Following the discussion of each individual Sunday collect, the two sets of Sunday collects are considered in relation to one another.

The First Sunday of Advent

1962: Sunday I of Advent	1970/2002: Sunday I of Advent
Excita, quaesumus, Domine, potentiam tuam, et veni: ut ab imminentibus peccatorum nostrorum periculis, te mereamur protegente eripi, te liberante salvari.	Da, quaesumus, omnipotens Deus, hanc tuis fidelibus voluntatem, ut, Christo tuo venienti iustis operibus occurrentes, eius dexterae sociati, regnum mereantur possidere caeleste.
Rouse, O Lord, your power and come, that from the threatening dangers of our sins, we may be deemed worthy to be delivered by you protecting, saved by you freeing.	Grant, we beseech you, almighty God, this will to your faithful, that, hastening with righteous deeds to meet your coming Christ, joined to his right, they may be worthy to possess the heavenly kingdom.

Manuscript History

The 1962 collect appears as the collect for the first Sunday of Advent (or the fourth Sunday before the Nativity of the Lord) in numerous extant ancient codices dating from the eighth through the sixteenth century, after which it took its place as the collect of the same day in the Tridentine missal.[44] The centonized character of the prayer, its sources and Pope Gregory's original contribution are discussed above.[45] The collect was retained unchanged in the post-Vatican II missals where it appears as the collect of Friday of the first week of Advent. While no ancient codex specifically assigns the collect to this day, the custom of praying the Sunday collect on the ferial days of the week following means this collect was also assigned to Friday of the first week of Advent in the Tridentine missals.

---

[44] *CO* IV, 2554 list forty-one codices dating from the eighth through the sixteenth centuries. The order of the words *quaesumus* and *Domine* found in the 1962 missal follows a variant that dates from the ninth century.

[45] See pp. 33–5 above.

Antoine Dumas and Cuthbert Johnson cite *Gelasianum Vetus* 1139, a postcommunion oration for the first Sunday of Advent, as the source of the 1970 collect.[46] The prayer also appears in twelve other codices dating from the eighth to the tenth century where it always serves as an Advent postcommunion or *super populum*.[47] The oration was edited for inclusion in the Paul VI missal. The changes which the revisers made to the text of the oration and the use to which they put it in the new missal are without precedent in the manuscript tradition.

1962 Collect

Insofar as the collect is *the* prayer of the day or, in the 1962 missal, the week, the liturgical year of the pre-Vatican missal begins on the same note with which it ends: "Rouse, we beseech you, O Lord," for the collect of the twenty-fourth and last Sunday after Pentecost begins with the same words and then asks God to rouse the wills of his faithful.[48] This Sunday's collect begs Christ to rouse his power and come – "come" being so much the theme and entreaty of the season that it takes its name from the word. In neither collect is the intensity of the invocation broken by a statement of fact. That is, there is no *qui* clause, a construction found in the invocation of many collects that simultaneously praises God for particular attributes and provides the motive for the petition which follows. Rather, this collect consists entirely of petition. The "*quaesumus,*" which follows immediately upon the imperative "*excita,*" adds to the intensity of the need being expressed.

The collect is addressed to Christ. It develops through a succession of verbs: two imperatives and two active participles whose subject, explicitly or implicitly, is Christ; and two passive infinitives whose implied subject is "we."

The prayer begs that Christ rouse his power and come that, literally, by covering before or over (*pro-tegente*) he may set free, that by setting free he may save us from the threatening dangers of our sins. The presence of verb forms even where one might expect to encounter nouns – for example, *te protegente* instead of *protectione tua* – emphasizes both the personal presence of Christ (*te*/you) and his activity (protecting and freeing). The step parallelism of the petition describes Christ's coming, removing us from the dangers of our sins and bringing us to salvation through two successive

---

[46] A. Dumas, "Les Sources du Nouveau Missel Romain," *Notitiae* 7 (1971) 409; Cuthbert Johnson, "The Sources of the Roman Missal (1975)," *Notitiae* 32 (1996) 17.

[47] CO II, 1006. The "super populum" is a blessing prayed over the people [*super populum*] at the end of a Mass.

[48] ... that carrying out more willingly/readily/intently the effects of divine action [in our souls], we may receive the greater cures of his mercy: *Excita, quaesumus, Domine, tuorum fidelium voluntates: ut divini operis fructum propensius exsequentes; pietatis tuae remedia maiora percipiant.*

yet continuing acts (the active participles). In this way, the prayer not only expresses awareness of our constant need of Christ's active intervention at every moment until salvation is finally and irrevocably received but, more importantly, that Christ's presence in power suffices to save us.

Even for a Roman oration, the collect is exceedingly compressed: there is no laudatory clause; *mereamur* governs two infinitive clauses, unusual in itself and the more so because no conjunction links them. The first part of the collect builds to *veni*, the word upon which both the prayer and the season pivot, and then rushes to the end with rapid effect – the economy of language mirroring the economy of Christ's acts which are swift, sure, and sufficient. The request that Christ free us from the *dangers* of our sins extends beyond our actual transgressions to include all their deleterious effects: harmful attachments, weakened wills and so forth.

It is noteworthy that the petition does not ask that we be able *to do* anything, only that Christ do all this for us. The power of the prayer lies in its directness, its simplicity, its confidence – and in the starkness of our need.

1970/2002 Collect

As we noted above, the prayer chosen from the Gelasian sacramentary to be the collect of the first Sunday of Advent in the new missal was edited. The original and redacted versions follow with the differences italicized:

GeV 1139: Advent Postcommunion	1970/2002: Sunday I of Advent
Da, quaesumus, omnipotens Deus, *cunctae familiae tuae* hanc voluntatem *in Christo filio tuo domino nostro venienti: in* operibus iustis *aptos occurrere, et* eius dexterae sociati regnum mereantur possidere *caelesti.*	Da, quaesumus, omnipotens Deus, hanc *tuis fidelibus* voluntatem, *ut, Christo tuo venienti* iustis operibus *occurrentes,* eius dexterae sociati, regnum mereantur possidere *caeleste.*
Grant, we beseech you, almighty God, to your *whole family* this will *in Christ your Son our coming Lord: to present themselves made fit* in righteous deeds, and may they, assigned to his *glorious* right, be worthy to possess the kingdom.	Grant, we beseech you, almighty God, this will to your *faithful,* that, *hastening* in righteous deeds *to meet your coming Christ,* assigned to his right, they may be worthy to possess the *heavenly* kingdom.

Source Text

Several aspects of the *GeV* 1139 require comment.

First is the matter of grammatical agreement. The recipient of the graces sought by the prayer is God's *familia*, a feminine singular noun. The words which follow do not agree with *familia. Mereantur* is a third person plural verb, and *aptos* and *sociati* are masculine or neuter plural participles.[49] The prayer moves from the collective noun, family, to its members who act individually.

Second, the reflexive and medieval use of *occurro*, which more usually means "to meet," is unexpected. But a direct object is not to be found without introducing a break in *in Christo filio tuo domino nostro venienti*. This requires, at the very least, that the word Christ, and possibly some of his titles, be read in the ablative because they are governed by the preposition *in*, and that other titles or, at the very least, the participle *venienti* be read as the dative direct object of *occurro*. There is no indication in the Latin that the author intended such a break. The case endings are ambiguous, however, for each of these words is in a form that can be either dative or ablative. Many ancient orations use all the titles needed to name Christ's relationship both to us and to the Father – that is, "Christ your Son our Lord," and the addition of *venienti* in an Advent oration is not unexpected.

Third, the phrase "heavenly kingdom" is so common that we expect *caelesti* to modify *regnum* but it does not – as this would require *caeleste*. Either it modifies *dexterae* so that "(eius) dexterae" and "caelesti" form an inclusion, suggesting that worthiness is supported by the Lord's glorious right hand, or, more likely, it is a spelling error.

Lastly, the primary meaning of *sociati*, the perfect participle passive of *socio*, seems here to have the medieval meaning of "to assign" rather than the more frequently encountered sense of "to unite" or "join together." But a strong case can be made for either meaning, and it may be best to keep both in mind.

The scriptural background of the oration is Matthew's parable of the sheep and the goats which depicts the general judgment that is to take place upon Christ's coming in glory.[50] The liturgical setting is a postcommunion prayer: the faithful have just received the Lord in Holy Communion. In context, then, *venienti* refers to Christ coming both in sacrament and at the end of time.

Upon reception of Christ's sacramental presence, the Church beseeches God to give his whole family the will in Christ to present themselves made fit in righteous deeds *and* to be worthy to possess the kingdom (which is given to those assigned to his heavenly right). A great deal is compressed into this deceptively simple petition.

---

[49] A similar grammatical breakdown is frequently seen in popular English usage as one begins with a collective noun that requires a singular pronoun – for example, committee or team – and lapses into plural pronouns because one's thoughts have moved from the committee or team to its members.

[50] Matthew 25.31–46. Forms *dextera*, *regnum*, and *possidere* appear in Matthew 25.34 of the Vulgate. Matthew 25.31–46 is the Gospel *pericope* in Year A for the last Sunday *per annum*, the Solemnity of Christ the King.

First, the movement from the singular to the plural and back to the singular has theological weight. God is asked to give one will in Christ to his whole family, a will that renders many, indeed all the family members, able to present themselves made fit by just works *and* to become worthy to possess the kingdom of Christ's right (singular again). Unless we belong to the Father in the Son – that is, unless we are members of Christ and therefore belong to the unit which the oration identifies as God's family – we cannot receive "this will" or merit. And, indeed, we have just become one in the reception of the sacrament of Christ's body.

Second, the primacy of grace is deftly expressed. God gives the will in Christ without which neither righteous deeds nor fitness is possible. The will, the meeting or presenting of oneself to Christ, and the just deeds are all *in Christ*. The effect is that we are made ready, or made fit, in the just deeds that we do in Christ as a result of the will in Christ that God graciously grants to us in Christ. Because we have been made fit, we, like the sheep of Matthew 25.33–46, are assigned to Christ's right and given possession of the heavenly kingdom. Moreover the *et* underscores that in the first place it is neither righteousness, nor fitness, nor the combination of the two, but the God-given will in Christ that makes it possible for the members of God's family to merit heaven.

Third, in addition to the relationships already named between familial unity and individual responsibility and between divine grace and human effort, there is one other that increases the dynamism of the oration: that of Christ's comings in history, in sacrament, and at the end of time. These are respectively manifest in the liturgical season, the liturgical setting of the oration and the eschatological imagery. The Eucharistic banquet is a foretaste of and preparation for the eschatological banquet. The food of Christ's risen body nourishes us now spiritually giving vigor to virtue and making us capable of righteous deeds that in turn fit us for the kingdom of God.

This oration is a theological advance over the scriptural parable which, taken by itself, can be understood simply to teach that those who serve Christ in the least of his brethren by practicing the corporal works of mercy will be rewarded in the life to come, and, of course, the opposite also: those who fail to serve Christ in this way will suffer eternal punishment. The theological advance has two aspects. First, God gives the will in Christ to serve Christ in his needy brethren. We do not muster it up ourselves. Second, heaven is not simply a reward for just deeds. It is something for which we are prepared by graced living and willing in Christ (the *aptos*). Heaven is for the Christified.

The 1970/2002 Collect

The revisers changed the setting of the oration. It is now a collect, not a postcommunion prayer. As a result the implicit reference to Christ's sacramental coming and its power to draw us into the eschaton are gone from the text.

Also, everything that made the Gelasian text difficult has been edited:

1. *Cunctae familiae tuae* is changed to *tuis fidelibus,* a plural noun that agrees grammatically with *sociati* and *mereantur,* as well as the also-revised *occurrentes.*

2. *Hanc voluntatem* is splayed to enclose *tuis fidelibus* so that the faithful are visually and poetically girded with "this will."

3. *In Christo ... venienti* is removed – the will sought is not identified as a will in Christ.

4. *Ut* is inserted so that it follows *voluntatem.*

5. Several changes are made to the clause containing the verb *occurro*: the infinitive becomes a present participle agreeing with *fidelibus,* modifying the understood subject of *mereantur,* taking *Christo tuo venienti* as its direct object (the *in* preceding Christ is omitted); *aptos* is removed and no functional equivalent supplied.

6. The *et* is removed.

7. *Caelesti* becomes *caeleste* so that it modifies *regnum.*

Besides repairing the breakdown of strict grammatical agreement in the original text, the substitution of *fidelibus* for *familiae* gives greater emphasis to the moral dimension of Christian existence. To be faithful is different from being family.

The Latin construction which wraps the faithful in the God-given will is evocative and visually striking, but the reconstruction of this and the following phrase contains lamentable losses as well. Unlike the source oration, the will sought is not specifically a will in Christ, nor is it a will to *do* anything that is named. In the original a double accusative follows the will and each accusative involves an infinitive: *occurrere* and *mereantur possidere.* That is, the original seeks for the family a will to present themselves in a particular way, made fit in righteous deeds and worthy to possess the kingdom. Here the *ut* clause, following as it does upon *voluntatem,* names the result or effect of the will. But it does not explicitly name its content or, more importantly, the intention it bestows on those who receive it. The one who reads the collect quickly is not likely to notice this, and the person who does notice is likely to supply what is missing intuitively. Nevertheless, the theological anthropology of the original text is attenuated in the new wording and then undone by the omission of *aptos.*

The will sought is not explicitly in Christ nor are we made ready/fit for heaven. The theological advance over the parable that we observe in the source prayer is forfeited in the revision. Since the new oration makes no mention of the transformation that takes place in Christ, the synergy of divine grace and human freedom which drives the original oration gives way to a more transactional depiction of relations between God and man.

The Second Sunday of Advent

1962: Sunday II	1970/2002 Sunday II
Excita, Domine, corda nostra ad praeparandas Unigeniti tui vias: ut, per eius adventum, purificatis tibi mentibus servire mereamur.	Omnipotens et misericors Deus, in tui occursum Filii festinantes nulla opera terreni actus impediant, sed sapientiae caelestis eruditio nos faciat eius esse consortes.
Rouse, O Lord, our hearts in order to prepare the ways of your only-begotten Son: that, through his coming, we may be able to serve you with minds made pure.	Almighty and merciful God, may no deeds of earthly impulse impede us as we hasten to meet your Son, but may the instruction of heavenly wisdom make us to be co-heirs with him.

Manuscript History

The 1962 collect was in constant use as the collect of this day (the second Sunday of Advent or the third Sunday before the Nativity of the Lord) from the eighth century until the twentieth.[51] It appears without change in the new missal as the collect of Thursday of the second week of Advent.

Dumas and Johnson identify *Gelasianum Vetus* 1153 as the source of the 1970/2002 collect.[52] Eight manuscripts dating from the eighth through the eleventh centuries witness to the use of the prayer as an Advent *oratio*.[53] The revisers modified it slightly for use in the post-Vatican II missal. There is no precedent in the manuscript tradition for the changes they made.

1962 Collect

Having one imperative instead of two, the 1962 collect for this day is less intense than that of the preceding Sunday. Still it opens with the same plea: *Excita*. Last Sunday the faithful asked Christ to rouse his power and come; this week they ask God the Father to rouse their hearts for the purpose of preparing the way for Christ's coming. Sister Mary Gonzaga Haessly comments on the relationship between the two collects:

> The Petition in this Collect is the counterpart of that in last Sunday's, the two requests setting forth two aspects of the coming of the '*Unigenitus tuus.*' The Petition '*Excita potentiam tuam*' (I Adv.) refers to God's part in the operations of grace in our hearts, His '*divinum opus,*' whereas the

---

[51] CO VI, 2553.
[52] A. Dumas, "Les Sources du Nouveau Missel Romain," *Notitiae* 7 (1971) 409; Cuthbert Johnson, "The Sources of the Roman Missal (1975)," *Notitiae* 32 (1996) 476 [36].
[53] CO IV, 2669.

Petition '*Excita corda nostra*' is concerned with our part: 'Stir up our hearts' to receive the proffered grace.[54]

The collect asks God to rouse our hearts for a specific purpose that consists of three interdependent ends. The first is for our hearts "to prepare the ways of your Son." Here the collect echoes, but does not quote, John the Baptist's role as prophesied by Isaiah,[55] as well as the verse from Malachi which Jesus quotes in reference to John in the Gospel *pericope* of this Sunday's Mass.[56] We ask God to rouse our hearts to prepare the ways for his Son's liturgical and spiritual coming at Christmas. And in echoing John, the oration points out the way in which we are to prepare: by repenting.

The second end is the God-given result of the first: that our reception of the Son's coming is such that our minds will be made pure (*purificatis ... mentis*). The use of the preposition *per* together with the passive perfect participle indicates a hope that our mind will have undergone a process of purification and that the Son's coming will have effected it. We do not purify ourselves.

The third end is that we will be able to serve God with purified minds, and indeed do so.

The collect seeks these graces from God: that he stir up our hearts so that they will prepare the ways of his Son, and that our preparations be such that our minds (hearts, souls) will be purified as a result of Christ's coming, and that we will serve God in our purified state.

1970/2002 Collect
The collect and its source are below.

Gelasianum Vetus 1153	1970/2002: Sunday II
Festinantes, omnipotens Deus, in occursum Filii tui *Domini nostri* nulla impediant opera actus terreni sed caelestis sapientiae eruditio faciat nos eius esse consortes.	Omnipotens *et misericors* Deus, in tui occursum Filii *festinantes* nulla opera terreni actus impediant, sed sapientiae caelestis eruditio nos faciat eius esse consortes.

---

[54] Sister Mary Gonzaga Haessly, *Rhetoric in the Sunday Collects of the Roman Missal: with Introduction, Text, Commentary and Translation* (Saint Louis: Manufacturers Printery, 1938) 26. Translation of the Latin phrases in the quotation: *Unigenitus tuus* = your only-begotten Son; *excita potentiam tuam* = rouse your power; *divinum opus* = divine work; *excita corda nostra* = rouse our hearts.

[55] Cf. Isaiah 40.3; Mark 1.2; Matthew 3.3; Luke 3.4.

[56] Matthew 11.2–10; Malachi 3.1.

As we hasten, almighty God, to meet your Son our Lord may no deeds of earthly impulse impede us but may the instruction of heavenly wisdom make us to be sharers with him.	Almighty and merciful God, may no deeds of earthly impulse impede us as we hasten to meet your Son, but may the instruction of heavenly wisdom make us to be sharers with him.

The changes made to the original text are printed in italics. There are three:

1. The opening words are rearranged. The principal effect of this is to place the direct address at the beginning of the prayer.

2. *Et misericors* is added so that God is praised for his mercy as well as his omnipotence.

3. The title which describes the Son's relationship to us, *Domini nostri*, is omitted.

Putting the direct address at the head of the collect makes the prayer more reverent inasmuch as we speak of God before we speak of ourselves. But it also decreases the intensity, for *festinantes*, hastening, loses some of its force in being, as it were, delayed. The addition of the attribute "merciful" acknowledges that the freedom from worldly impediments and schooling in heavenly wisdom that enable us to be sharers of Christ are the fruit not only of God's omnipotence but also of his gracious clemency.

The Third Sunday of Advent

The third Sunday of Advent is traditionally known as *Gaudete* Sunday.[57] The name comes from the first word of the Introit.[58] The day retains this name, for the Introit antiphon of the new missal begins with the same scripture verse. Further, both the Philippians lessons from which the verse comes and the theme of rejoicing are prominent in the Offices of the day.[59]

The old and new collects follow:

---

[57] "Gaudete" is a Latin plural imperative verb which means "rejoice."

[58] Philippians 4.4–6: Gaudete in Domino semper; iterum dico gaudete. Modestia vestra nota sit omnibus hominibus. Dominus prope. Nihil solliciti sitis sed in omni oratione et obsecratione cum gratiarum actione petitiones vestrae innotescant apud Deum. [Rejoice in the Lord always; again I say, Rejoice. Let all men know your forbearance. The Lord is at hand. Have no anxiety about anything, but in everything by prayer and supplication with thanksgiving let your requests be made known to God.]

[59] The *Antiphon ad introitum* of the post-Vatican II missals is Philippians 4.4, 5: Gaudete in Domino semper: iterum dico, gaudete. Dominus enim prope est [Rejoice in the Lord always: again I say rejoice. For the Lord is near].

1962: Sunday III	1970/2002: Sunday III
Aurem tuam quaesumus Domine precibus nostris accommoda, et mentis nostrae tenebras gratia tuae visitationis illustra.	Deus, qui conspicis populum tuum nativitatis dominicae festivitatem fideliter exspectare, praesta, quaesumus, ut valeamus ad tantae salutis gaudia pervenire, et ea votis sollemnibus alacri semper laetitia celebrare.
Fit your ear, we beseech you, O Lord, to our prayers and illumine the darkness of our mind with the grace of your visitation.	O God, who see your people faithfully awaiting the feast of the Lord's nativity, grant, we beseech you, that we may be able to arrive at the joys of such a great salvation, and ever to celebrate them [joys/ *gaudia*] with solemn prayers and eager/glad/ready rejoicing.

Manuscript History

The 1962 collect served as the collect of the third Sunday of Advent from the eighth century until the sixteenth when it was adopted for use on the same day in the reform of the liturgy that followed the Council of Trent.[60] It does not appear in the Paul VI missal, but a prayer very like it does.[61]

Dumas and Johnson identify *Rotulus* of Ravenna 25 as the source of the 1970/2002 collect.[62] The source prayer was edited for inclusion in the new missal.

1962 Collect

The 1962 collect of this Sunday is the only Advent Sunday collect in the pre-Vatican missal that does not begin with the imperative "*Excita.*" It is the third Sunday collect in a row that has no statement of fact and, like the 1962 collect of the first Sunday of Advent, the prayer contains two imperative verbs.

Here, however, the first word of the collect is not the imperative, but rather its direct object: *aurem tuam*. The imperative occupies the last place in the clause. The reversal is a rhetorical device that serves to heighten the intensity of both words. The petitioner is so anxious to gain a hearing with Christ (the prayer is addressed to the Son) that he says "ear" first. A similar

---

[60] CO I, 358.

[61] See the discussion of *Aurem tuam* and *Voci nostri* on p. 39, n. 39 above.

[62] A. Dumas, "Les Sources du Nouveau Missel Romain," *Notitiae* 7 (1971) 409; Cuthbert Johnson, "The Sources of the Roman Missal (1975)," *Notitiae* 32 (1996) 484 [44]. The oration appears in no other codex. *Cf. CO* XI, 6798.

reversal is found at the end of the collect where *tenebras* precedes *illustra* so that the collect ends on the cry, indeed the command, that Christ grant us light.

The typographical arrangement makes the artistry of the collect easier to see:

Aurem tuam	quaesumus Domine	precibus nostris	accommoda:
et mentis nostrae tenebras		gratia tuae visitationis	illustra.

The two independent clauses, both petitions, are structurally parallel. The first, which seeks an audience with Christ, introduces the second, the plea that he illumine the darkness of our minds with the grace of his visitation. In the first clause, "your ear" [*aurem tuam*] is separated from "our prayers" [*precibus nostris*] by *quaesumus* [we beseech you]. The arrangement suggests a certain distance exists between God's ear and our prayers. In the second clause, nothing separates "mentis nostrae tenebras" [of our minds the darknesses] and "gratia tuae visitationis" [with the grace of your visitation]. Indeed, Christ's grace is placed next to the darkness – poised, as it were, to pierce it.

The collect is supported by both the Introit antiphon and the Epistle lesson of the same Mass, both of which contain the verse from Saint Paul: "Have no anxiety about anything, but in everything by prayer and supplication with thanksgiving let your requests be made known to God."[63] Prayer is a prominent theme in the liturgical texts of the day, and the collect's request that God bend his ear to our prayers is but one aspect of it.

1970/2002 Collect

The collect of the third Sunday of Advent, together with its source, are shown below with the differences between them italicized:

Rotulus 25 = Ver 1356 = CO XI, 6798	1970/2002: Sunday III
Deus, qui conspicis populum tuum *incarnationem dominicam* fideliter exspectare, praesta, quaesumus, ut valeamus ad tantae salutis gaudia pervenire, et votis sollemnibus alacri semper laetitia celebrare.	Deus, qui conspicis populum tuum *nativitatis dominicae festivitatem* fideliter exspectare, praesta, quaesumus, ut valeamus ad tantae salutis gaudia pervenire, et *ea* votis sollemnibus alacri semper laetitia celebrare.

---

[63] Philippians 4.6 (RSV). The Introit antiphon for this day in the post-Vatican II missals omits this verse.

O God, who see your people faithfully to await *the Lord's incarnation*, grant, we beseech you, that we may be able to attain unto the joys of such a great salvation, and to celebrate always in solemn prayers with glad jubilation.	O God, who see your people faithfully to await *the feast of the Lord's nativity*, grant, we beseech you, that we may be able to attain unto the joys of such a great salvation, and to celebrate *them* always in solemn prayers with glad jubilation.

This is the first Advent collect in which there is a *qui* clause. It describes God as seeing his people faithfully await – and here we come to the first difference between the two texts. The ancient oration describes the people as awaiting the "Lord's incarnation" and the post-Vatican II collect the "feast of the Lord's nativity."

The emendation has two aspects: (1) "feast" replaces "incarnation" – both are accusatives or direct objects; (2) the birth, not the incarnation, is named. The second aspect of the revision gives the prayer greater literal or historical accuracy without changing its meaning in any significant way – for Christmas does celebrates the Lord's birth. The first change is a bit more striking, for "*festivitatem*" takes the grammatical position held by "*incarnationem*." Whereas the *Rotulus* oration associates "great salvation" with the incarnation of the Lord, the revised prayer associates it not with his nativity, but with the *feast* of his nativity.

The last change to the collect is the insertion of the pronoun *ea* into the petition. *Ea* is a neuter plural pronoun in the objective case and supplies a direct object for *celebrare* – something the original prayer does not have. The only possible grammatical antecedent for *ea* is *gaudia* (joys). It seems that the revised petition asks not that we celebrate the salvation, but the joys of it. The meaning of the distinction is not entirely clear nor is the revisers' purpose in making it.

The Fourth Sunday of Advent

1962: Sunday IV	1970/2002 Sunday IV
Excita, quaesumus, Domine, potentiam tuam, et veni: et magna nobis virtute succurre; ut per auxilium gratiae tuae, quod nostra peccata praepediunt, indulgentia tuae propitiationis acceleret.	Gratiam tuam, quaesumus, Domine, mentibus nostris infunde, ut qui, Angelo nuntiante, Christi Filii tui incarnationem cognovimus, per passionem eius et crucem ad resurrectionis gloriam perducamur.

Rouse, we beseech you, O Lord, your power and come, and hasten to assist us with your great might; that, through the help of your grace, what our sins impede the remission of your mercy may speed.	Pour forth, we beseech thee, O Lord, thy grace into our hearts, that we to whom the incarnation of Christ, thy Son, was made known by the message of an angel, may, by his passion and cross, be brought to the glory of [his] resurrection.[64]

Manuscript History

The 1962 collect was used as the collect on this day, often designated the first Sunday before the Nativity of the Lord in ancient codices, from the eighth/ninth century through the sixteenth when it became the collect for this day in the Tridentine missal.[65] It appears in edited form as the collect of Thursday of the first week of Advent in the revised missal.

The 1970/2002 collect is the postcommunion prayer for the feast of the Annunciation in the 1962 missal. *CO* IV, 2748 A and B name 60 codices in which the prayer appears. In 48 it is used on the feast of the Annunciation and, in 36 of these, it is the postcommunion prayer for the Mass of that day (*CO* IV, 2748A). This use goes back to the eighth century (one witness), but the extant manuscript evidence suggests that it only became widespread in the eleventh century. Most of the earliest codices, those of the eighth through the tenth century, witness to the prayer being "the collect," "another collect," or "another oration" assigned to the Annunciation.[66]

The remaining twelve codices witness to uses in the Hours of the Divine Office or in Masses which commemorate the Blessed Virgin (*CO* IV, 2748B). In seven of these latter the oration is used during Advent, the rubric reading: *De beata Maria virgine in adventu, postcommunionem* [Masses of Blessed Virgin Mary in Advent, postcommunion]. The earliest two of these seven codices are eleventh century, but four belong to the fifteenth or sixteenth century. Placide Bruylants tells us that the Roman Missals of 1471 (the first printed edition of the *Missale Romanum*), 1570 (the first typical edition of the Tridentine missal) and 1604 (the second typical edition of the Tridentine missal) present this same prayer as an oration *"pro diversitate temporum"* [for a variety of occasions] to be used from the first Sunday of Advent to December 23.[67]

---

[64] The translation given here is the traditional English rendering of the Angelus prayer.

[65] *CO* IV, 2550.

[66] The use of *Gratiam tuam* (*CO* IV, 2784A) as the postcommunion prayer on the feast of the Annunciation corresponds to the adoption of another prayer as the collect of the feast. Beginning in the ninth century, and expanding greatly in the eleventh, the collect of the Annunciation found in the 1962 missal came to be used as the collect for the feast. *CO* II, 1518 identifies 37 witnesses to this parallel development.

[67] Placide Bruylants, *Les Oraisons Du Missel Romain: Texte Et Histoire* (Louvain: Centre de documentation et d'information liturgiques, 1952) vol. 2, p. 156, #575. This Advent usage is in addition to its being the postcommunion prayer of the Mass of the Annunciation.

The evidence is not conclusive, but strongly suggests that the oration was first used as a collect of the feast of the Annunciation. Soon, however, it came to be used instead as the postcommunion of that feast and, around the same time, to be used also as the postcommunion for Masses of the Blessed Virgin celebrated during Advent. Immediately before and after the Council of Trent, it was also used as an oration "*pro diversitate temporum*" during Advent up to and including December 23. There is no record of it ever having served as the collect of the fourth Sunday of Advent prior to its inclusion in the post-Vatican II missal.

1962 Collect

Like the collect of Sundays I and II, this collect begins with the imperative that characterizes Advent in this missal: *Excita*. Again, as in Sunday I, we ask Christ to rouse his power and come. This time we beg him to hasten to help us with his great might. The 1962 collect of the first Sunday of Advent has two imperative verbs; that of the second Sunday, one; that of the third, two again. But here we find three imperative verbs.[68] The intensity and the longing expressed in the prayer of the Church grows as the awaited time approaches.

Not only are there three imperative verbs, but there are three petitions: that Christ rouse his power and come, that he assist us with his great might, and that his grace bring the pardon of his mercy to bear on the impediments caused by our sins. The *quod* of the *ut* clause is general and all encompassing – in effect, embracing whatever and however the grace of Christ is hindered by the particular sins of all the individuals on behalf of whom the prayer is prayed. The hope of the prayer, which progresses by causally successive petitions made to Christ, is that we do not lose any of the graces he brought us through his birth. Grace, as Haessly points out,

> ... is one of the most important words in the Collect. It is through grace that the first Advent of the Savior is perpetuated. The phrase '*per auxilium gratiae tuae*' implies our dependence on God.[69]

This dependence, in the view of the collect, is absolute – for we need the grace of Christ to receive the grace of Christ. As paradoxical as this may seem, it accurately expresses the Catholic doctrine of grace.

1970/2002 Missal

The rhetorical arrangement of the opening clause of this collect is precisely that of the 1962 collect of the third Sunday in Advent. In both the usual

---

[68] Haessly, *Rhetoric in the Sunday Collects of the Roman Missal*, 29 notes that this is the only Sunday collect in the entire missal that has three imperative verbs.
[69] Haessly, *Rhetoric in the Sunday Collects of the Roman Missal*, 30.

order of the imperative verb and its object is reversed. Here again the effect is to heighten the rhetorical force of both words. The Church is so focused on the need for grace that she says that first, putting off the plea or, more literally, the command, "pour forth" to the end of the clause. The grace sought is not simply the grace that attaches in a limited way to the incarnation and, in context, to the birth of the divine Son, but for the full redemption that flows from these initial mysteries: that we may be brought through the passion and cross of Christ to the glory of resurrection – not to the Pasch but to the vision of the resurrected Christ and, ultimately, to the resurrection of our own bodies.

The collect has but one imperative. When the revisers exchanged the 1962 collect for this one, they selected another prayer in which the petition for grace is central. And what the 1970/2002 collect, comparatively speaking, lacks in intensity and longing, it makes up for in comprehensiveness – for it situates the mystery of Christ's incarnation and birth in the context of his saving death and its full effect: our resurrection to glory.

In Milanese usage, the Annunciation is celebrated on the last Sunday of Advent.[70] The March 25 date of the feast of the Annunciation, however, is ancient. The oldest extant mention comes from 656 when the Council of Toledo established a feast called "Mother Mary of the Lord" to be celebrated on December 18 because Mary is prevented from receiving the honor she deserves on March 25 which always falls during Lent or the Paschal Octave.[71]

The post-Vatican II revisers appropriated the Milanese custom in their own fashion by choosing *Gratiam tuam* to be the collect of the fourth Sunday of Advent. The Mass collect is accompanied by the Gospel lesson of the Matthean annunciation to Joseph, the Lucan annunciation to Mary, and Luke's account of Mary's visit to Elizabeth in Lectionary Cycles A, B, and C respectively.

The Two Sets of Advent Sunday Collects: Comparative Analysis

As we indicate in Chapter one, the task of identifying the substantive differences between two sets of collects that have not one prayer, nor even one source prayer, in common presents methodological difficulties. The principal problem is that we are not approaching the sets with specific questions like "how are the Advent Sunday collects of missal alike and different with respect to x?" where x is any particular spiritual theme,

---

[70] Holweck, Frederick, "The Feast of the Annunciation," *The Catholic Encyclopedia*, vol. 1 (New York: Robert Appleton Company, 1907), 543.

[71] F. Cabrol, "Annonciation (fête de L')," *DACL* vol. 1.2 (Paris: Letouzey et Ané, 1913–53), col. 2244: "die decimo quinto kalendarum Januarium."

doctrinal truth, posture before God, or whatever else may pertain. Rather we want to discover the differences whatever they may be.

We need an approach that has a large enough net, so to speak, to catch whatever is there, and yet is sufficiently well-defined that characteristic differences are identifiable. It is imperative that we avoid the very real danger of ending up with a great mound of detailed information that is meaningless because it is formless.

In the examination that follows we take a two-pronged approach. First we examine the verbs of the respective sets, and then the logical assumption that undergirds each collect.

Analysis of the Verbs

The examination of verbs does not consider the formulaic "quaesumus" [we beseech you], and the various forms of *mereo* [to merit, be worthy] are considered only in the context of the verbs which they govern.[72] The verbs of the Advent collects in the respective missals appear in Table 1 below and are arranged according to type.

The eight strong imperatives in the 1962 missal set its Advent tone. We cry out to Christ, and our need and eagerness are so intense that we beseech him with imperative verbs to rouse his power and come, to bend ear to our prayers and illumine the darkness of our minds with the grace of his visitation, to hasten to help us with his great might. In the one collect not addressed to Christ, we cry to God to stir up our hearts to prepare the way for his Son. The eagerness expressed in imperative verbs intensifies as Advent progresses. The two imperatives in the collect of the first Sunday give way to the single imperative in the collect of the second Sunday (the only collect of the four addressed to the Father), but then we find two imperatives again in the collect of the third Sunday, and three in the collect of the Sunday immediately preceding the Lord's birth.

The active participles and indicative verbs describe either Christ's activity (protecting and freeing), or the agency of a harm that besets us (dangers threatening, sins impeding). The passive participle describes what we hope will be done through Christ's coming – that our minds will be made pure. The subjunctive verbs express particular petitions: that Christ's pardon may speed what our sins impede and that we may be worthy to serve God.

Except for what is implicit in the act of praying itself, there are only two agents in the 1962 prayers. On the one side, the divine persons who bend ear to prayers, rouse, come, illumine, succor, protect, deliver, purify, and speed; and, on the other side, our sins and the dangers that attach to them

---

[72] *Mereo/mereor*: to be worthy; to be made worthy, to be deemed worthy, to merit. The grace of Christ makes us worthy; it also makes us able to merit. In liturgical usage *mereo* in the passive sometimes means "to be able." As such, it insists upon a capacity in the human person to receive graces and gifts from God without implying that the graces or gifts are deserved.

Table 1: The Verbs of the Advent Sunday Collects

Verb form	1962 Advent collects	1970/2002 Advent
imperative	8: excita (3), veni (2), succure (1), accommoda (1), illustra (1)	3: da, praesta, infunda
	8: stir up (3), come (2), hasten to aid (1), bend (1), illumine (1)	3: grant, grant, pour forth
present active participles	3: imminentibus (modifying the dangers of our sins), protegente and liberante (both modifying you = Christ)	3: venienti (modifying Christ), occurentes and festinantes (both modifying us)
	3: threatening (modifying the dangers of our sins), protecting and freeing (both modifying you = Christ)	3: coming (modifying Christ), hastening to meet and hastening (both modifying us)
past passive participles	1: purificatibus (modifying our minds)	0
	1: having been made pure	
present indicative active	1: nostra peccata praepediunt	2: conspicis, cognovimus
	1: our sins impede	2: you see (you = God); we know
present subjunctive active	1: indulgentia … acceleret	2: nulla opera impediant, eruditio faciat
	1: may pardon speed	2: may no works impede, may training make
present subjunctive passive	0	1: perducamur
		1: may we be led.
active infinitives	1: mereamur … servire	5: mereantur possidere regnum, [faciat nos] esse consortes, exspectare festivitatem, valeamus pervenire ad gaudia et … celebrare ea (gaudia)
	1: may we be worthy to serve	5: worthy to possess the kingdom [make us] to be co-heirs to await the feast we may be able to arrive at the joys and to celebrate them. (subject is variously the faithful, we, your people)

passive infinitives	2: mereamur ... eripi, salvari	0
	2: may we be able to be delivered, saved	

which both threaten and impede. We are situated between Christ who saves and the perils from which we need saving.

The dangers named are interior to us: our sins, darkness, and impurity. The theology of grace at work in the aggregate of 1962 Advent Sunday collects is manifest most clearly, perhaps, in the collect of the second Sunday. We ask God to rouse our hearts to prepare the way for his Son, implying that unless he rouses us we will not be able to prepare for the Son. But unless we prepare the Son's way, our minds will not be made pure through his coming; and unless they are made pure through him we will not be able to serve God. Everything pertinent to salvation comes forth from God, catches us up and transforms us, and then returns us to himself with our own human willingness fully engaged.

The picture painted by the verbs in the 1970 collects is quite different. It is not simply that the imperatives are far fewer (three) and weaker (grant and pour out); but that the human subjects, however they are named (variously the faithful, we, your people) are far more active; indeed, they are the subject of the five active infinitives. In one collect God is described as seeing their activity (they are faithfully awaiting), and in other places he is asked to make their activity fruitful: to grant that they may be deemed worthy to inherit the kingdom, may be made partakers of Christ through training in heavenly wisdom, may be able to attain the joys of salvation and celebrate the joys with solemn prayers in glad rejoicing. Moreover, the motion verbs of the two sets describe exactly opposite movements: in the 1962 collect Christ comes to meet us; in the 1970 collect we go to meet Christ, arrive, are brought to, and so forth. In the 1970 set, Christ is described as coming only in the collect of the first Sunday.

A second difference is that the 1970 collects name no overwhelming obstacles. In contrast to the 1962 collect in which we ask God to rouse our hearts in order that we may prepare for the coming of his Son, in the 1970 collects we are twice described as already hastening to meet him and once as faithfully awaiting the feast of his birth. The only suggestion in the 1970 collects that there are things that could cause us to stumble is the prayer that God let no works of earthly deed impede us as we hasten – where the works can be understood as either our own or those of others. In other words, the collect does not insist upon the existence of interior impediments. In fact, the 1970 prayers contain no reference to sin or its dangers; to darkness or impurity of mind; to human weakness or need for mercy, forgiveness, protection, deliverance, purification; nor to the fact that any or all of us require a divine jump start to begin preparations for Christ's coming. Also, the idea that we must undergo a transformation in order to enter heaven is intimated only by the word *eruditio*, instruction or training, in the collect of the second Sunday.

A third difference is that those who pray the 1970 collects do not seek divine assistance to survive perils or to begin to do good things. Indeed they express no need for such helps. Rather they ask to enter heaven at the last. In contrast, those who pray the 1962 collects do not explicitly seek heaven, but demand – the imperative verbs – immediate and personal daily help on the way.

In these three differences we come to something very delicate. Put simply, Catholic faith holds that every good deed which advances us toward salvation depends upon divine grace. This doctrine is formally defined and is not susceptible to modification that would reverse its import.[73] Every nuance of the 1962 Advent collects expresses this Catholic doctrine of grace unambiguously in the somewhat subtle, non-expository manner proper to orations. While the 1970 Advent collects do not explicitly contradict the Catholic teaching on grace, they neither articulate it nor, more worrisomely, seem to assume it. The delicate bit is how to sum this up fairly for while the 1970 Advent collects may not legitimately be understood or interpreted in a way that is inconsistent with Catholic truth, it must also be acknowledged that they are susceptible to being misunderstood by those who are inadequately schooled in Catholic truth.

In conclusion, when we examine the verbs of the Advent collects in the respective missals, we find not two different spiritualities of Advent, but two different presentations of our spiritual situation and the way in which God responds to it. Our next step is to see whether the impressions gleaned from our study of the verbs are verified or controverted by the logical analysis which comprises our second approach to the same collects.

Analysis of Logical Statements

Each collect rests implicitly upon a logical statement. We believe certain things about God and pray according to the logic of our faith convictions. Roman collects, always a single sentence, generally contain an independent and a dependent clause. Most usually the subordinate clause begins with "*ut*" ("so that"), and the *ut* clause describes a causal relationship between God's gift and what we understand in faith to be its effect.

The assertion that each collect rests implicitly upon a logical statement does not mean that each prayer reduces to a logical proposition. Rather, it recognizes that our prayers reflect what God has revealed to be true and

---

[73] See the canons of the Second Council of Orange (529), especially can. 5, 6, 7, 9–11, 13, 16–20, 22, 24–5 and the conclusion in H. Denzinger and Peter Hünermann, *Enchiridion Symbolorum* 2nd edn. (Bologna: Edizioni Dehoniane, 1966) in nos. 375, 376, 379–81, 383, 386–90, 392, 394–95 and 396. See also *Summa Theologiae* II-I, Q. 109, art. 10.

Table 2: Logical Statements Underlying the Advent Sunday Collects

Sun.	*Missale Romanum (1962)*	*Missale Romanum (1970/2002)*	**Source Oration for *Missale Romanum (1970)***
1	If Christ rouses his power and comes, then we will be delivered from the threatening dangers of our sins and will be saved. <u>Missing premise</u>: Christ's presence protects, delivers, and saves.	If God grants this will to the faithful, they will meet Christ in just deeds. If they meet Christ in just deeds, they will merit ... to possess the heavenly kingdom.	*GeV* 1139: If God grants this will in Christ to his whole family, they will be made fit in just deeds to meet Christ. If the members of the family are made fit in just deeds to meet Christ, they will merit ... to possess the heavenly kingdom.
2	If God rouses our hearts to prepare for his Son, then through his Son's coming our hearts will be purified. If our hearts are made pure, we will be able to serve God.	If God permits no work to impede us as we hasten to meet Christ, and grants heavenly wisdom to instruct us, then we will be sharers of Christ. <u>Missing premise</u>: the prevention of impediments and instruction in heavenly wisdom are necessary for us to be sharers of Christ.	*GeV* 1153: Same as MR 1970
3	If Christ bends his ear to our prayer, the darkness of our minds will be illumined by the grace of his visitation. <u>Missing premise</u>: if Christ hears, he acts.	If God grants it, we will be able to arrive at the joys of such a great salvation and to celebrate these joys in solemn prayers, with glad rejoicing. <u>Missing premise</u>: feast = joys of salvation.	*Rot* 25: If God grants it, we will be able to arrive at the joys of such a great salvation and to celebrate always in solemn prayers with glad rejoicing. <u>Missing premise</u>: incarnation = salvation.

4	If Christ rouses his power and comes, and hastens to help with his great might, we will have the help of his grace. If we have the aid of his grace, then what our sins impede the pardon of his mercy will speed.	If God pours his grace into our hearts, then we will be brought through Christ's passion and cross to the glory of his resurrection. Missing premise: grace suffices.	MR 1962, Annunciation, post communion. Same as MR 1970

that the facts of revealed reality, as well as the causal relationships within it, are as amenable to propositional expression as any other truths.

The logical statements undergirding the collects can be expressed in various ways. They are expressed here as if/then statements, although in several instances the minor premise is lacking. Table 2 presents an attempt to identify the logical statements underlying each Advent Sunday collect, together with the missing premises.

What is attempted here may be clearer if we take the collect of the first Sunday of Advent in the 1962 missal as an example. The logical core, the logical heart of "Rouse, we beseech you, O Lord, your power and come, that from the threatening dangers of our sins we may be able to be delivered by you protecting, saved by you delivering" is "If Christ rouses his power and comes, then we will be delivered from the threatening dangers of our sins and saved." Why? Because the request turns on an unstated premise, or more precisely the unstated faith conviction, that Christ's presence delivers and saves.

As it turns out, all the 1962 Advent Sunday collects rest upon the logical assumption or, more accurately, the firm belief that divine assistance *is* the actual presence of Christ. Christ *comes* and thereby frees, saves, purifies, acts, and overturns the effects of our sins. His presence and action toward us is personal, intimate, interior, and effective: we are protected, delivered, and saved; our minds are purified; the effects of our personal sins are reversed. Collectively these collects impart considerable, even breathtaking, force to what "Advent," that is "the Coming," signifies.

If there is a single assumption or faith conviction that underlies all of the 1970/2002 Advent Sunday collects, it is not so easily detected. The various gifts sought by these collects do not reduce, as it were, to the simple presence of Christ or of God himself. And, although God confers a will, instructs or trains in heavenly wisdom, and grants us to arrive at the joys of salvation – great goods, wondrous goods in themselves – their recipients, in the nature of things, arguably enjoy a less intimate relationship with God than those whose hearts he rouses, whose minds he illumines with the grace of his visitation, and whose sins he reverses the effects of with his pardon. The Advent Sunday collects of the 1970/2002 missal, then, portray God as standing further off and acting toward us in a less personal and more extrinsic manner than the corresponding collects in the 1962 missal.

Conclusion

The answer to the question at the start of the chapter, whether the Roman Advent prepares the faithful for the feast of the Lord's Nativity or for his eschatalogical return, is that it prepares for both. Moreover, it has always done so. The Advent lessons of the *Comes* of Wurzbourg combine moral exhortation and eschatological reminders with texts that look forward to the Lord's first coming in flesh. Pope Saint Gregory retains all this, integrating the two streams and deepening the whole with the addition of Gospel lessons and prayers. One Gospel lesson speaks of the eschaton; the other two look forward to Christ's public ministry. Saint Gregory's prayers await Christ's coming, variously, in the feast, in grace, in judgment, and in glory. The Advent Sunday collects of the Vatican II missal do likewise. The first two speak of Christ's eschatological return, the third of his coming in the feast of his birth, and the last of his coming in grace – begging that his incarnation may have its full intended effect: that through his passion and cross we, with our resurrected bodies, may be brought into his glory.

The manuscript evidence indicates that the post-Trent revisers adopted a set of Advent Sunday collects which had been in wide use for 800 years and that the post-Vatican II revisers did not follow the same approach. Instead of appropriating a prior tradition with its own rationale, they confected a new one by drawing from a variety of ancient traditions. The four Sunday collects come from three different sources. Three, at least, do not have a history of being used as Advent Sunday collects. And one is unique – that is, it appears in only one extant codex.[74]

The new set of Advent Sunday collects does not approach God in the same way, seek the same things from him, exhibit the same preoccupations, or depict the same relationship between God and human beings as the earlier set. The principal differences are discussed in the preceding sections.[75]

---

[74] The 1970/2002 collect of Sunday III.
[75] See p. 58–9 and 61 above.

4

Christmas

The post-Vatican II revision of Christmastide differs from that of Advent principally in two respects. First, while no changes were made to the Advent calendar, that of Christmastide was revised so that neither the feasts of the season nor the order in which they are celebrated is the same in both missals. Second, while all of the 1962 Advent Sunday collects were replaced, more than half of the Christmas Sunday and major feast day collects, five of nine, were retained.

Our study begins with the post-Vatican II calendar revisions. The examination of the collects that follows considers those assigned to the Sundays and major feasts of the season.[1] It has two parts. The first discusses the disposition of the 1962 collects and the origins of the 1970/2002 collects. The second is a careful examination of each prayer that includes comparison to its counterpart in the other missal. A summary of findings closes the chapter.

The Calendar

Table 1 presents the sequence of Sundays and major feasts in the respective calendars of the two missals. Italic type-face indicates the differences.

The Consilium study group responsible for the calendar revisions considered five questions pertaining to Christmastide:

1. Whether the Octave Day of the Nativity is to be dedicated to the memory of Mary Mother of God or to celebration of the Name of Jesus so that the civil year may begin in the name of the Lord?[2]

---

[1] The feasts are: the Nativity of the Lord, the Octave of the Nativity, and the Epiphany. In some regions, however, the Epiphany is celebrated on Sunday.
[2] Schema n. 65, *de Calendario* 2 (15 March 1965), p. 8, n. 9: *Utrum dies octava Nativitatis Domini dedicanda sit memoriae Matris Dei, an celebrationi Nominis Iesu, ita ut annus civilis incipiantur in nomine Domini?*

Table 1

1962	1970/2002
Vigil of the Nativity (*morning Mass*)	Vigil of the Nativity (*evening Mass*)
Nativity of the Lord (Masses for night, dawn, and day)	Nativity of the Lord (Masses for night, dawn, and day)
Sunday within the Octave of the Nativity	Sunday within the Octave of the Nativity: *Holy Family*
Octave Day of the Nativity	Octave Day of the Nativity: *Solemnity of Mary, Holy Mother of God*
Sunday between Octave and Epiphany: *Most Holy Name of Jesus*	*Second Sunday of the Nativity* (not celebrated where the Epiphany transferred to Sunday)
Epiphany – 6 January	Epiphany – *6 January, but transferred to the Second Sunday of the Nativity in some regions.*
Sunday within the Octave of the Epiphany: Holy Family	*Baptism of the Lord (Sunday after Epiphany)*
Commemoration of the Baptism of Our Lord: 13 January, Octave Day of the Epiphany	See preceding entry
Christmas season is followed by *Sundays after the Epiphany which continue until Septuagesima*	Christmas season is followed by *Sundays per annum [through the year] which continue until the first Sunday of Lent*

2. Whether the feast of the Holy Family is to be suppressed?[3]
3. Whether commemoration of the Lord's Baptism is to be assigned to the Sunday after the Epiphany or be retained on January 13?[4]

In the first typical edition of the Tridentine missal (1570), the title of January 1 is *In die Circumcisionis et in Octava Nativitatis Domini* [On the day of Circumcision and on the Octave of the Nativity]. By the twenty-eighth typical edition (1952), the title has become *In Circumcisione Domini et Octava Nativitatis* [On the Circumcision and Octave of the Nativity]. The last typical edition (1962) has only *In Octava Nativitatis Domini.* The feast of the Circumcision was suppressed without, however, any change in the Mass texts of the day.

[3] Schema n. 65, *de Calendario* 2 (15 March 1965), p. 9, n. 10: *Placetne festum S. Familiae supprimi?* [Literally, "is it pleasing that the feast of the Holy Family be suppressed?"]

[4] Schema n. 65, *de Calendario* 2 (15 March 1965), p. 10, n. 11: *Utrum commemoratio Baptismatis Domini assignanda est dominicae primae post Epiphaniam, an retinenda est die 13 ianuarii?*

4. Whether power is to be granted to the competent ecclesiastical authorities to assign the feast of the Epiphany to the following Sunday if local conditions warrant, except in the case of the sixth of January falling on a Sunday?[5]

5. Whether Christmastide is to close after Vespers (Compline) of the Sunday following the Epiphany or after the same hour on January 13?[6]

Rembert Van Doren, Aimé-Georges Martimort, Pierre Jounel, Herman Schmidt, Ansgar Dirks and Adrian Nocent prefer that the Octave Day of the Nativity become the feast of the Mother of God. The main reason given is that the Maternity of Mary is the most ancient Marian feast known at Rome. Agostino Amore alone prefers that the day celebrate the name of the Lord for "historical and theological reasons" which he does not name.[7] Amore suggests that Mary's divine maternity be celebrated during the Octave.[8]

With respect to the feast of the Holy Family, all but Amore favored suppression. Two *periti* thought the Mass should be retained among the votive Masses; others desired that the Gospel *pericope* be retained, thereby keeping the day as Holy Family Sunday in some sense.[9] Amore's stated reason for retaining the feast is: "Pastoral reasons recommend that the feast be retained particularly because lamentably in our days the holiness of families is being lost!"[10]

As to the third question, all the *coetus* members save one favored assigning the Baptism of the Lord to the Sunday after the Epiphany.[11] Also, all save one, agreed that competent authority should be given permission to assign the celebration of the Epiphany either to the Sunday following

---

[5] Schema n. 65, *de Calendario* 2 (15 March 1965), p. 10, n. 12: *Utrum competentibus auctoritatibus ecclesiasticis concedenda est facultas, pro locorum condicionibus, festus Epiphaniae dominicae insequenti assignandi, exceptu casu quo dies sextus ianuarii in dominicam cadit?*

[6] Schema n. 65, *de Calendario* 2 (15 March 1965), p. 11, n. 13: *Utrum tempus natalicium claudendum est post Vesperes (Completorium) dominicae quiae sequitur Epiphaniam, an post Vesperes (Completorium) diei 13 ianuarii?*

[7] Schema n. 65, *de Calendario* 2 (15 March 1965), pp. 8–9. Amore, p. 9: "Rationibus historicis et theologicis ..."

[8] Schema n. 65, *de Calendario* 2 (15 March 1965), p. 9.

[9] Schema n. 65, *de Calendario* 2 (15 March 1965), p. 9, n. 10: A-G Martimort, Schmidt, and Dirks, voted for suppression; Van Doren and Nocent voted for suppression, but desired to see the devotion preserved in a votive Mass; Amore opposed suppression.

[10] Schema n. 65, *de Calendario* 2 (15 March 1965), p. 9: "Rationes pastorales suadent ut festum retineatur praesertim quia nostris temporibus sanctitas familiarum miserrime dilabitur!"

[11] Schema n. 65, *de Calendario* 2 (15 March 1965), p. 10, n. 11: Dirks did not disagree, but thought this question depended on the decisions about the Holy Family and the close of Christmastide.

6 January or, in the view of one *peritus*, it could also be assigned to the Sunday before.[12]

With respect to the close of the season, the responses were mixed. Several thought the answer depended on the still unresolved question of whether the Lord's Baptism would be moved to a Sunday: one favored closing the season on the Baptism of the Lord; two preferred it close on a Sunday, but which Sunday depended on whether the Baptism were moved to a Sunday; one preferred that Christmastide close on the Epiphany; the last said only that it depended upon when the Baptism is celebrated.[13]

Table 1 above shows how matters were eventually resolved. The Octave Day is dedicated to Mary, Holy Mother of God. The feast of the Lord's Baptism is transferred to the Sunday after the Epiphany and closes Christmastide.[14] The assignment of the Lord's Baptism to a Sunday displaces the feast of the Holy Family which is now assigned to Sunday within the Octave of the Nativity. Epiphany is celebrated on 6 January in regions where the day is a holy day of obligation and on the Sunday following 1 January where it is not.[15] The feast of the Holy Name of Jesus was suppressed.

The decision to place Holy Family Sunday before the Epiphany[16] occasioned some discussion about the order of Christmastide Gospel

---

[12] Schema n. 65, *de Calendario* 2 (15 March 1965), p. 9, n. 12: Van Doren said either the Sunday before or after Epiphany; Martimort allowed for the possibility of a dual feast: Epiphany and Baptism.

[13] Schema n. 65, *de Calendario* 2 (15 March 1965), p. 10, n. 13: Van Doren: after Vespers on the feast of the Lord's Baptism on whichever day it is celebrated; Martimort, Jounel, and Amore, and Nocent: on the Sunday following the Epiphany; Schmit: on the Epiphany or, that failing, the Sunday after the Epiphany; Dirks refers the others to his answer to the question of whether the Baptism is to be celebrated on a Sunday or 13 January.

[14] Schema n. 45, *de Calendario recognoscendo* 4 (10 April 1965), p. 1: Propter rationes pastorales omnino optandum est ut Baptismus Domini die Dominica celebretur. Nisi commemoratio Baptismi Domini die Dominica fiat plurimi fideles hoc factum salutis ignorare pergent. [For pastoral reasons it is altogether preferable that the Baptism of the Lord be celebrated on a Sunday. If the commemoration of the Lord's Baptism is not on Sunday very many of the faithful will continue to be unacquainted with this deed of salvation].

[15] Schema n. 45, *de Calendario recognoscendo* 4 (10 April 1965), p. 2: In multis regionibus Epiphania non est festum civile, ideoque festum Epiphaniae ibi sine praecepto celebratur. Concedenda proinde videtur auctoritatibus ecclesiasticis territorialibus facultas festum Epiph[an]iae dominicae insequenti assignandi excepto sextus die ianuarii in dominicam cadit. [In many regions the Epiphany is not a civil holiday, therefore the feast of the Epiphany is celebrated there without precept. Accordingly it seems good that power of assigning the feast of the Epiphany to the following Sunday be granted to territorial ecclesiastical authority except when the sixth of January falls on a Sunday]. See also *Normae Universales de Anno Liturgico et de Calendario*, 36: Epiphania Domini celebratur die 6 ianuarii, nisi, ubi non est de praecepto servando, assignata sit dominicae a die 2 ad diem 8 ianuarii occurrenti [The Epiphany of the Lord is celebrated on the sixth day of January unless, where it is not kept by precept, it is assigned to the Sunday which falls between the second and eighth of January].

[16] The original plan was to celebrate the feast of the Holy Family on the Sunday between January first and fifth. Cf. Schema n. 93, *de Calendario* 5 (10 May 1965), p. 2.

lessons. From at least the Middle Ages, the Gospel *pericope* assigned to Sunday within the Octave of Epiphany is the account of Jesus being found in the temple and then returning to Nazareth with his parents where he is subject to them (Luke 2.42–52).[17] When the feast of the Holy Family was placed on the universal calendar in 1921, it was assigned to the Sunday in the Epiphany Octave, the day to which this Gospel was already assigned. At this time new orations were assigned to the feast as well as a different Epistle lesson, but the Gospel of the day – the *pericope* which reports Jesus' filial subjection to his parents – was left in place. In the sequence of Christmastide lessons, this *pericope* was read after the Magi adore the infant Jesus (Epiphany)[18] and before John the Baptist identifies the adult Jesus as the one who baptizes with the Holy Spirit (Octave Day of Epiphany).[19]

It is not surprising, then, that the proposal that Holy Family Sunday be celebrated before the Epiphany encountered an objection: namely, that the change in the order of the feasts results in the Gospel lesson about Jesus at age 12 being read before the account of the Magi presenting gifts to him as an infant. The initial response was that an alteration in the sequence of the lessons does not occasion a problem "because an exact chronology of the Lord's life is not preserved in the liturgy."[20] When the Consilium members met in late April of 1965, they were unable to reach a consensus about the feast of the Holy Family and referred the matter for further study.[21] The next report of the *Calendar coetus* notes that there would be no difficulty with the sequence of feasts if another suitable *pericope* could be substituted for the account of the finding in the temple and states:

The Calendar *coetus* will also consider the possibility of assigning

---

[17] Luke 2.42–52 is the Gospel assigned to the Sunday within the octave of the Epiphany in the first typical edition of the Tridentine missal, *Missale Romanum (1570)*. In the reform of the liturgy that followed the Council of Trent, the cycle of readings in the eighth century manuscript known as the *Comes of Murbach* became that of the Roman rite. *Murbach* assigns Luke 2.42ff. to this same day which it titles "*Dom. prima post thephania*" [first Sunday after the Theophany = Epiphany]. See A. Wilmart, "Le *Comes* de Murbach," *Revue Bénédictine* 30 (1913) 25–69 at 36. *Murbach* presents a Romano-Frankish arrangement of texts that dates from the Carolingian era. Cf. Cyrille Vogel, *Medieval Liturgy*, 354.

Further, the *Missale Romanum* of 1570 "hardly differs at all" from the missal that was produced at Milan almost a hundred years earlier, in 1474, and, except for the addition of some new feasts, the 1474 Milanese missal reproduces the missal used in the papal chapel at the end of the thirteenth century [Cyrille Vogel, *Medieval Liturgy*, 132, n. 273].

[18] Matthew 2.1–12.

[19] John 1.29–34.

[20] Schema n. 75, *de Calendario* 4 (10 April 1965), p. 2: *Non habetur magnum incommodum in eo quod Evangelium Pueri Jesu in templo legitur ante festum Epiphania, quia chronologia exacta vitae Domini non semper in liturgia servatur.*

[21] *Res Secretariae* n. 19 (14 June 1965) p. 2.

a commemoration of Holy Family Sunday within the octave of the Nativity and it will offer an example of another formulary.[22]

The revised lectionary offers three pericopes for the feast: Year A: Matthew 2.13–15, 19–23 (the flight into, and summons to return from, Egypt); Year B: Luke 2.22–40 (the Purification); Year C: Luke 2.41–52 (the finding of the Child Jesus in the temple – the 1962 *pericope* with an additional verse).

The feast of the Holy Name of Jesus, added to the universal calendar by Innocent XIII in the eighteenth century, was initially suppressed in the post-Vatican II revisions. It is restored in the third typical edition with new formularies and assigned to 3 January.[23]

Of the Tridentine missals, only the 1962 missal has a feast of the Lord's Baptism (titled "*in commmemoratione baptismatis D.N.I.C.*"). It is celebrated on the Octave Day of the Epiphany, 13 January. No changes were made to the lessons or formularies of the Mass when the title was added in the 1962 edition of the Roman missal.

Collects

Quantitative Overview

Table 2 shows what happened to each of the 1962 collects considered in this chapter:

Table 3 presents a general summary of the sources and the extent of editorial activity for the collects of both Advent and Christmastide.

Table 4 shows the source by type for each collect in the 1970/2002 missals and indicates whether or not it was edited.

---

[22] Schema n. 93, *de Calendario* 5 (10 May 1965), p. 2: *Nulla difficultas haberet … si huic Evangelio [Inventionis Pueri Iesu in templo] aliud aptum substitui posset.*

Coetus de Calendario considerabit etiam possibilitatem commemorationem S. Familiae dominicae infra octavam Nativitatis assignandi, et specimen alicuius formularii offeret.

[23] *Missale Romanum: Ex Decreto Sacrosancti Oecumenici Concilii Vaticani II Instauratum : Auctoritate Pauli Pp. VI Promulgatum: Ioannis Pauli Pp. II Cura Recognitum.* (Vatican City: Typis Vaticanis, 2002), 710. It is found in the *Proprium de Sanctis* [Proper of Saints], not in the *Tempus Nativitatis* [Time of Nativity].

Table 2

1962 Collect	Disposition
Nativity, Mass at Night	Retained in place; edited
Nativity, Mass at Dawn	Retained in place; edited
Nativity, Mass during Day	Moved to 30 Dec or 6th day in the octave; no change
Sunday in Octave of Nativity	Moved to Sun III *per annum*; no change
Octave of Nativity	Retained in place, edited and then restored in 2008
Sun. between 1 Jan. and 6 Jan. Holy Name of Jesus	Omitted from the missal
Epiphany	Retained in place; no change
Holy Family	Omitted from missal
Baptism of the Lord	Retained as the alternate collect for Baptism; no change

Table 3

	Total	1962 Missal without change	1962 Missal with changes	Other Missal[24] without change	Other Missal with change	New Compositions
Advent	4	0/1[25]	0	0	3	0
Christmas	11	3	3	0	3	2

[24] That is, other Mass books or liturgical collections.
[25] The Collect of Sunday IV is found in the 1962 missal but not among the Advent Sunday collects. As such, it does not fit into any of the listed descriptions.

Table 4

1970 collect	Source
Vigil of Nativity	1962, edited
Nativity Mass at Night	1962, edited
Nativity Mass at Dawn	1962, edited
Nativity Mass during Day	Early codex; word order changed
Holy Family Sunday	New composition
Octave of Nativity	1962, edited and then restored in 2008
Sunday II after the Nativity	Early codex; edited
Vigil of the Epiphany (2002 only)	Early codex; edited
Epiphany	1962 missal, no change
Baptism: collect alternate collect	Collect: new composition Alternate collect: 1962, no change

Examination of Collects

The Nativity of the Lord (Four Masses)

Vigil Mass

1962: Vigil Mass (morning Mass)	1970/2002: Vigil Mass (evening Mass)
Deus, qui nos redemptionis nostrae annua exspectatione laetificas: praesta; ut Unigenitum tuum, quem *Redemptorem laeti suscipimus,* venientem quoque iudicem securi *videamus, Dominum nostrum Iesum Christum Filium tuum.*	Deus, qui nos redemptionis nostrae annua exspectatione laetificas, praesta, ut Unigenitum tuum, quem *laeti suscipimus Redemptorem,* venientem quoque Iudicem securi *videre mereamur*
O God, who make us joyful in the yearly anticipation of our redemption: grant that your Only-begotten, whom we joyfully receive as our redeemer, we may also *see* without fear when he comes as our judge: *our Lord, Jesus Christ, your Son.*	O God, who make us joyful in the yearly anticipation of our redemption, grant that your Only-begotten, whom we joyfully receive as our redeemer, we also may be *deemed worthy to see* without fear when he comes as our judge.

Manuscript History

The 1962 form of the prayer is found in numerous codices going back to the eighth century. The most usual use is as the collect for the Vigil of the Lord's Nativity.[26] The post-Vatican II revisers edited the prayer. There are no variants in the manuscript tradition that correspond to the change in the word order or the insertion of *mereamur*. The omission of Christ's titles at the end follows the *Gelesianum Vetus*.[27]

The Text

Three changes were made to the text: (1) the order of the words "*Redemptorem laeti suscipimus*" becomes "*laeti suscipimus Redemptorem*"; (2) "*videamus*" becomes "*videre mereamur*"; (3) the titles "*Dominum nostrum Iesum Christum Filium tuum*" were omitted. Notwithstanding, the essential meaning of the prayer was not altered.

The *qui* clause praises God for making us joyful in the "yearly expectation of our redemption," identifying the feast of the Nativity with its saving effect: redemption. In a manner appropriate to vigils, the clause anticipates rather than celebrates redemption. The change in the word order may have been for the sake of the rhythm of the clause.[28]

The original *ut* clause has a chiastic structure in which "Only-begotten" and "Our Lord, Jesus Christ, your Son," titles that identify the Second Person of the Trinity in relation to the Father or to us, enclose two contrasting descriptions of the Son's roles in salvation history: he is the Redeemer whom we receive (present tense) joyfully, and he is the Judge who is to come and whom we ask to meet fearlessly. The revised prayer does not retain the chiastic structure.

The change from *videamus* to *videre mereamur* increases the reverence of the prayer. Rather than simply asking to see the judge without fear, the

---

[26] CO III, 1915.

[27] Cf. CO III, 1915 and *GeV* 1156. The latter reads: *Deus, qui nos redempcionis nostrae annua expectacione laetificas, praesta, ut unigenitum filium tuum quem redemptorem laeti suscipimus, uenientem quoque iudicem securi uideamus.* The revisers did not follow *GeV* 1156 with respect to "*filium.*"

CO III, 1915 lists no variants, but calls attention to a similar prayer, CO II, 1133, generally assigned to the feast of the Purification: *Deus cui hodierna die unigenitus tuus in nostra carne quam adsumpsit pro nobis in templo est praesentatus, praesta, ut quem redemptorem nostrum laeti suscipimus, uenientem quoque iudicem securi uideamus* [O God, to whom on this day your Only-begotten Son was presented in the temple in our flesh which he assumed for our sakes, grant that he whom we joyfully receive as our redeemer, we may also see without fear when he comes as our judge].

[28] The Church's *orationes* are comprised of a short series of metrical units which close, generally, in a specific arrangement of stressed and unstressed syllables of Latin *cursus*. There are three main forms: 1) *cursus planus* in which the accents are on the 2nd and 5th syllables from the end, 2) *cursus tardus* in which the accents are on the 3rd and 6th from the end, and 3) *cursus velox* in which the accents are on the 2nd and 7th from the end. *Laeti suscipimus Redemptorem* is *cursus tardus*.

revised prayer asks that we may be worthy of seeing him without fear. The word "*mereamur*" appears frequently in the orations of the missal and has great, two-fold importance.

Merit is owed compensation, one's just deserts. On the one hand, we can do nothing to merit the initial gift of God's grace in Christ. God always acts first ("prevenient" grace) in bringing about our justification. On the other, God's justifying ("sanctifying" grace) creates in us a capacity for goodness. It is an undeserved gift; but having been received, it belongs to the recipient like any gift. God's gift of grace makes us good, holy, friends of God. It enables us to respond in faith and good works. Things we cannot do of ourselves, we can do in the grace of Christ. The good deeds we do in his grace, then, are our own; it is in this latter sense that we can truly merit an increase of grace, eternal life, and glory. Nevertheless, as Augustine says, when God crowns us, he is not crowning our merits but his own gifts.[29] The frequent use of the verb *mereamur* gives constant witness in the Church's prayer to the human capacity for goodness, for heaven, for eternal life that the gift of God's grace creates in us.

The most significant aspect of the revision is not in the text of the prayer, but in the setting. With the assignment of this collect to a Mass that fulfills the Christmas obligation, the two comings of Christ that Advent places before the faithful receive new prominence in the feast of the Lord's Nativity.

Mass at Night

1962: Nativity of the Lord: Mass at night	1970/2002: Nativity of the Lord: Mass at night
Deus, qui hanc sacratissimam noctem veri luminis fecisti illustratione clarescere, da, quaesumus, ut cuius in terra mysteria lucis *cognovimus*, eius quoque gaudiis perfruamur in caelo.	Deus, qui hanc sacratissimam noctem veri luminis fecisti illustratione clarescere, da, quaesumus, ut cuius in terra mysteria lucis *agnovimus*, eius quoque gaudiis perfruamur in caelo.
O God, who have made this most holy night grow bright with the splendor of true light, grant, we beseech you, that we who have *known* the mysteries of his light on earth may also enjoy fully the gladness of him in heaven.	O God, who have made this most holy night grow bright with the splendor of true light, grant that we who have *recognized* the mysteries of his light on earth may also enjoy fully the gladness of him in heaven.

---

[29] Saint Augustine, *En. in Ps.* 102,7: *Qui in nobis victi sumus, in illo vicimus. Ergo coronat te, quia dona sua coronat, non merita tua* [We who are conquered in/by ourselves, conquer in/by him. Therefore he crowns you because he crowns his own gifts, not your merits]. [*PL* 37, 1321].

Manuscript History

The prayer is found in manuscripts going back to the mid-eighth century, and its exclusive use is in the Mass of the Lord's Nativity celebrated during the night.[30]

The Text

The collect draws on the language and imagery of the Prologue of John's Gospel which speaks of the Word's coming into the world as the true light shining in a darkness that does not grasp it – *non comprehenderunt* in the Vulgate.[31] The main difference between John's Prologue and the collect is that the former says the world did not know him (*eum non cognovit*) who came as the true light that enlightens every man, and the latter that we have known/recognized (1962: *cognovimus*, 1970/2002: *agnovimus*) the mysteries of his light. We are those who have received the Son and have been given power to become children of God, those who have believed in his name and have been born of God.[32]

The number of synonyms makes the prayer difficult to translate. In the first clause after "most holy night," we find "*luminis,*" " *illustratione,*" and "*clarescere*" – all words that have to do with light, brightness, and making something clear. In the second clause, light/brightness is mentioned once again and here the phrase "the mysteries of whose light" is splayed so that it envelops the earth (*in terra*). There is a paradox in the phrase "mysteries of light": the mystery of Christ is light, not darkness like other mysteries. In the second clause we have a second set of synonyms: "gaudiis," inward joys, as opposed to the joys that show outwardly, and the verb "perfruamur," which means enjoy fully or completely.

In consequence, the night which is "most holy" is a "night" abounding in radiant, clarifying light. The petition asks that we who have known the mystery of his light in this life may enjoy forever the happiness his light reveals.

The single word change from *cognovimus* to *agnovimus* is striking for four reasons. First, there is no precedent in the manuscript tradition – that is, no extant manuscript has *agnovimus.*[33] Second, *agnosco* is a thinner word than *cognosco*. *Agnosco* means to recognize, identify, or perceive; *cognosco* means to know, understand, and be thoroughly acquainted as well as perceive, recognize, and identify.[34] That is, *cognosco* includes every-

---

[30] CO II, 1653.

[31] *Comprehendo* includes grasps both physical and mental: seize, grasp, lay hold of, apprehend, comprehend, understand.

[32] Cf. John 1.9–14.

[33] Cf. CO II, 1653.

[34] When Genesis speaks of the eyes of Adam and Eve being opened so that they knew they were naked and of Adam knowing his wife in sexual union, the Vulgate uses the verb *cognosco* (Gen. 3.7 and 4.1, respectively). *Cognosco* is also found in the verse of Isaiah in which God

thing signified by *agnosco* and much more besides. The more that pertains here is that *cognosco* conveys a depth of personal encounter that *agnosco* does not suggest. The change from *cognovimus* to *agnovimus* produces a collect that claims less about our grasp of the mystery of Christ's light, and therefore, seemingly, credits less revelatory effect to the light which the Father has made to shine. Third, the Prologue of John's Gospel contains the verb *cognosco* but not *agnosco* so the allusion to the Gospel is weakened. Fourth, other collects containing *cognovimus* were not similarly altered.[35]

The second and third reasons cited in the preceding paragraph demonstrate that important features of the original were forfeited by the change of just one word. The first and last reasons show us that this particular change was neither warranted by the manuscript tradition nor, it seems, consistently applied in the work of revision. It is difficult to see what the editors intended to accomplish by the change they made to this prayer.

---

complains that the ox knew its owner and the ass the crib of its lord, but Israel did not know him (Isa. 1.3). In contrast, when the brothers brought Joseph's bloodied robe to their father and Jacob recognized it as Joseph's own, the Vulgate uses *agnosco* (Gen. 37.3). When the brothers arrive in Egypt to buy grain both words are used: Joseph recognized [*agnovisset*] his brothers; but he, while knowing [*cognoscens*] them, is not recognized by them [*non est agnitus ab eis*] (Gen. 42.7–8). Similarly, both words appear in the Lucan passage that tells of the two disciples who encounter Christ on the road to Emmaus. They did not recognize [*ne ... agnoscerent*] the risen Christ on the way (Lk. 24.16), but later knew [*cognoverunt*] him in the breaking of the bread (Lk. 24.35). The disciples' words about their hearts burning within them as the Lord opened the scriptures to them tells us that, in the end, the disciples arrived at real, experiential knowledge, not mere recognition. Revelation imparts true knowledge, and so it is not surprising that *cognosco* in its various forms appears 375 times in the Vulgate while *agnosco* appears only 31 times.

[35] See the collects of Sunday IV of Advent (considered in the last chapter), of the Epiphany (considered later in this chapter) and the Exaltation of the Holy Cross (September 14) below. The last is particularly significant for it contains nearly the same phrase. Compare *"cuius in terra mysteria lucis cognovimus"* of the night Mass of Christmas in the 1962 missal with *"ut cuius mysteria in terra cognovimus"* of the feast of the Exaltation of the Cross in both the 1962 and 1970/2002 missals. The retention of *cognovimus* in the cited phrase is all the more striking because the 1962 collect for the Exaltation was otherwise quite radically revised, a fact which indicates that the editors made all the changes they deemed fitting. The respective collects follow 1962:

1962: Exaltation of the Holy Cross	1970/2002: Exaltation of the Holy Cross
Deus, qui nos hodierna die Exaltationis sanctae Crucis annua solemnitate laetificas: praesta, quaesumus, ut, cuius mysterium in terra cognovimus, eius redemptionis praemia in caelo mereamur.	Deus, qui Unigenitum tuum crucem subire voluisti, ut salvum faceret genus humanum, praesta, quaesumus, ut, cuius mysterium in terra cognovimus, eius redemptionis praemia in caelo consequi mereamur.
O God, who on this day make us joyful in the annual solemnity of the exaltation of the holy Cross, grant, we beseech you, that we may merit in heaven the rewards of his redemption whose mystery we have known on earth.	O God, who willed your Only-Begotten Son to undergo the cross that he might save the human race, grant, we beseech you, that we may merit to attain the rewards of his redemption in heaven whose mystery we have known on earth.

Mass at Dawn

1962 Second Mass at Dawn, the Nativity of the Lord	1970 Second Mass at Dawn, the Nativity of the Lord
Da, quaesumus, omnipotens Deus, ut, *qui* nova incarnati Verbi tui luce perfundimur, hoc in nostro resplendeat opere, quod per fidem fulget in mente.	Da, quaesumus, omnipotens Deus, ut *dum* nova incarnati Verbi tui luce perfundimur, hoc in nostro resplendeat opere, quod per fidem fulget in mente.
Grant, we beseech you, Almighty God, that, we who are filled with (suffused/bathed in) the new light of your incarnate Word may reflect in our action that which through faith shines in our mind.	Grant, we beseech you almighty God, that as we are filled with (suffused/bathed in) the new light of your incarnate Word, that may be reflected in our action which through faith shines in the mind.

Manuscript History
Extant codices indicate that this oration dates from at least the eighth century. It is used exclusively on the feast of the Lord's Nativity.[36] There is no warrant in the manuscript tradition for the change made by the post-Vatican II revisers.

The Text
The original prayer begins with the imperative, "give," the abruptness of which is immediately softened by "we beseech you, Almighty God." The *qui* clause that follows does not describe God, but the faithful: we who are filled with new light. The verbs in the first clause are first person plural, *quaesumus, perfundimur*, while those in the second are the third person singular with neuter pronoun subjects, "hoc ... resplendeat" // quod ... fulget" where *hoc* and *quod* refer to the same reality but not the light, for *lux* is a feminine noun. Rather, the pronouns *quod* and *hoc* are general words that denote all that faith-knowledge of Christ bestows upon the mind. A literal translation is "may this be reflected/shine in our action // which through faith shines in the mind."[37]

The only difference between the original and revised collects is that the modern editors replaced *qui* (who) with *dum* ("as" or "while"). *Dum* is a conjunction that denotes a temporal relationship, either of contemporaneous

---

[36] CO II, 1029.

[37] The new English translation of the *Roman Missal* avoids the awkwardness by identifying the reality to which *hoc* and *quod* refer as "the light of faith" and so has "that ... the light of faith, which illumines our mind, may also shine through in our deeds." See Catholic Church, *The Roman Missal: Renewed by Decree of the Most Holy Second Ecumenical Council of the Vatican, Promulgated by Authority of Pope Paul VI and Revised at the Direction of Pope John Paul II* (Collegeville: Liturgical Press, 2011) 174.

duration or immediate succession. Possible meanings are "now that we are filled with the new light of your incarnate Word," "while, or during the time in which, we are filled/being filled …," or "as we are filled/being filled …" – where "as" denotes time, not manner. It is not clear what the revisers intended this change to accomplish. Possibly they thought the substitution would somehow make the text less difficult. Possibly they introduced the time note to emphasize the efficacy of the feast – that, in the celebration of the Lord's nativity, we are filled with the new light of the Incarnate Word. Both explanations are conjectures, and neither is particularly compelling.

Mass during the Day

1962: Third Mass of the Nativity of the Lord	1970/2002: Third Mass of the Nativity of the Lord
Concede, quaesumus, omnipotens Deus: ut nos Unigeniti tui nova per carnem Nativitas liberet: quos sub peccati iugo vetusta servitus tenet.	Deus, qui humanae substantiae dignitatem et mirabiliter condidisti, et mirabilius reformasti, da, quaesumus, nobis eius divinitatis esse consortes, qui humanitatis nostrae fieri dignatus est particeps.
Grant, we beseech you, almighty God, that the new birth through flesh of your only-begotten Son may set us free, whom age-old bondage holds under the yoke of sin.	O God, who has both wondrously created the dignity of human nature and more wondrously restored it, grant us, we beseech you, to be sharers of the divinity of him who deigned to become a partaker of our humanity.

Manuscript History

The 1962 collect appears in codices that date from the eighth century until the sixteenth when it was incorporated into the Tridentine missal.[38] It was retained in the revised missal as the collect of 30 December.

The 1970/2002 prayer is ancient. It is found in four forms with variants in extant codices dating from the sixth or seventh through, principally, the eleventh century. In these it is used at Mass or Office on the vigil or day of the Lord's Nativity or during the Epiphany Octave.[39]

In the fourteenth century, the words "*per huius aquae et vini mysterium*" [through the mystery of this water and wine] were inserted and the prayer

---

[38] CO I,778 a, b. The prayer is found in the Gelasian and Gregorian Sacramentaries, *GeV* 6, *Had* 49 and *Engol* 21.

[39] CO II, 1692 a, b, c, d. Variant d is also found in a late sixteenth-century (1571) codex, an Ambrosian rite missal where it is the *super sidonem* of a Christmas morning Mass.

Noteworthy early appearances are *Ver* 1239, *GeV* 27 and *Had* 59. Cf. also Pope Saint Leo I, *Sermo XXI, In Nativitate Domini Nostri Jesu Christi*, I.II PL 54 191–92 B.

was added to the ordinary of the Mass (*Ordo Missae*) to be prayed during the offertory rites as water is added to the wine.[40] The prayer passed into the Tridentine missal in this form and context. The post-Vatican II revisers responsible for the *Ordo Missae* kept only part of the prayer and modified it.[41]

Coetus 18*bis* adopted the ancient prayer in its entirety and assigned it to the third Mass of Christmas. The only change they made was to transpose *quaesumus* and *nobis*.

The 1962 collect

Like the collect for the dawn Mass, this prayer begins with an imperative verb. But where the imperative of that collect is immediately softened by the formulaic "quaesumus, omnipotens Deus" and a *qui* clause that describes the faithful as bathed in light, the imperative of this collect builds to a plea for freedom that is followed by self-description of a different sort entirely: we are in servitude to sin.

The second clause of the prayer is typographically arranged below to show the antithetical parallelism:

ut nos	Unigeniti tui		nova per carnem Nativitas	liberet:
that us	of your only begotten son		new birth through flesh	may free
quos		sub peccati iugo	vetusta servitus	tenet.
whom		under the yoke of sin	age-old slavery	holds

The center of the clause is the *new* birth through flesh, a birth that frees. Its antithesis is the *age-old* slavery that holds fast. The allusion is to Adam's sin and the slavery it inaugurated. Christ is the new Adam. *Libero* is to set free and *teneo* is to have or hold in one's power or possession. A second somewhat overlapping contrast is between the "Only-begotten Son" whose birth frees and "us" who are slaves held "under the yoke of sin." The petition seems a response to these words of Jesus:

> Truly, truly, I say to you, every one who commits sin is a slave to sin. The slave does not continue in the house for ever; the son continues for ever. So if the Son makes you free, you will be free indeed.[42]

1970/2002

The *qui* clause of the 1970/2002 collect praises God for the wondrous work of creation and the even more wondrous work of redemption. The latter is

---

[40] CO II, 1692 c.

[41] *Coetus* 10 retained only the latter part of the prayer. They also adopted an ancient variant in which *efficiamur* replaces *esse*. In consequence, the *Novus Ordo* prayer at the preparation of the gifts is: *Per huius aquae et vini mysterium eius efficiamur divinitas consortes, qui humanitatis nostrae fieri dignatus est particeps* [Through the mystery of this water and wine may we be made sharers of his divinity who deigned to become a partaker of our humanity].

[42] John 8.34–6.

the subject of the petition which begs for the fruitfulness in our own case of the *admirabile commercium*: the wondrous exchange at the beginning and heart of redemption by which the very Son of God assumed our humanity in order to share his divinity with us.

One cannot fault the revisers for wanting to include the whole of this beautiful prayer among the proper prayers of the new books.

In sequence, the three collects of Christmas in the 1962 missal ask that the light of Christ might bring us to heaven, that the light of Christ might shine in our deeds, and that the new birth of Christ in the flesh might free us from the yoke of sin.

In sequence, the four collects of Christmas in the 1970/2002 missal ask that we might meet Christ without fear when he comes as Judge, that the light of Christ might bring us to heaven, that the light of Christ might shine in our deeds, and that the incarnation of the Son might effect our deification. There are two new elements: petitions that we meet Christ's eschatological coming as judge without fear and that Christ make us partakers of his divinity. The latter replaces the older set's request that the Son free us from sin.

1962: Sunday within the Octave of the Nativity of the Lord; 1970/2002: Feast of the Holy Family

Because the feast of the Holy Family in the Vatican II books displaces the Sunday within the Octave of the Nativity of the Tridentine missals and a different collect is assigned to the Holy Family in each missal, there are three collects to consider. First we examine the old and new collects appointed for this Sunday, and then the collects assigned to the feast of the Holy Family in each missal.

The collects of Sunday within the Octave of the Nativity are below:

1962: Sunday within the Octave of the Nativity	1970/2002: Feast of the Holy Family
Omnipotens sempiterne Deus, dirige actus nostros in beneplacito tuo: ut in nomine dilecti Filii tui mereamur bonis operibus abundare.	Deus, qui praeclara nobis sanctae Familiae dignatus es exempla praebere, concede propitius, ut, domesticis virtutibus caritatisque vinculis illam sectantes, in laetitia domus tuae praemiis fruamur aeternis.
Almighty, everlasting God, direct our actions in your good pleasure: so that in the name of your beloved Son, we may be able to abound in good works.	O God, who deigned to offer us the splendid examples of the Holy Family, mercifully grant that imitating it [the holy family] in domestic virtues and the bonds of charity, we may enjoy eternal happiness in the joy of your house.

Manuscript History

The 1962 collect of Sunday in the Nativity Octave is ancient and appears in 51 codices dating from the eighth through the sixteenth century when it was incorporated into the Tridentine missal. Its almost exclusive use is on a Sunday in Christmastide: either that within or after the Nativity Octave or within the Epiphany Octave.[43] In the Vatican II missals it is assigned to the third Sunday *per annum*.

The 1970/2002 collect for the feast of the Holy Family is a new composition.[44] The 1962 collect does not appear in ancient codices and may have been composed when the feast was placed on the universal calendar in 1921. Both are below.

1962: Feast of the Holy Family (celebrated on the Sunday after the Epiphany)	1970/2002: Feast of the Holy Family (celebrated on Sunday in the Nativity Octave)
Domine Iesu Christe, qui Mariae et Ioseph subditus, domesticam vitam ineffabilibus virtutibus consecrasti: fac nos, utriusque auxilio, Familiae sanctae tuae exemplis instrui; et consortium consequi sempiternum.	Deus, qui praeclara nobis sanctae Familiae dignatus es exempla praebere, concede propitius, ut, domesticis virtutibus caritatisque vinculis illam sectantes, in laetitia domus tuae praemiis fruamur aeternis.
Lord Jesus Christ, who, subject to Mary and Joseph, sanctified home life with ineffable virtues, grant us, with the help of both, to be instructed by the examples of your holy Family and to attain unto everlasting fellowship.	O God, who deigned to offer us the splendid examples of the Holy Family, mercifully grant that imitating it [the holy Family] in domestic virtues and the bonds of charity, we may enjoy eternal happiness in the joy of your house.

The Texts

1962: Sunday within the Octave.

The prayer, addressed to "Almighty, everlasting God," is a confident request for divine assistance which recognizes our radical need for grace. For unless God directs our wills and unless we do good deeds in union with Christ ("in the name of his Son"), we can neither abound in good works nor merit heaven through the good we do. While the collect has no clear connection

---

[43] Cf. *CO* V, 3830. The exceptions are two: in one missal the prayer serves as the collect for the fifth Sunday after Pentecost and, in another, as the first *oratio* to follow the litany in assembly (*post litaniam in conventu*).

[44] Antoine Dumas, "Les oraisons du nouveau Missel," *Questions Liturgiques* 25 (1971) 263–70 at 269.

to the Lord's birth, its use in Christmastide, and more particularly during the Octave of the Nativity, reminds us that it is only because of the Lord's gracious coming in our flesh and dwelling among us that we are able to be directed in God's good pleasure, act in union with Christ, abound in good works, or merit because of good deeds.

1962: Holy Family

The collect is addressed to Christ who is praised for submitting to his human parents and thereby consecrating family life with "ineffable" virtue. The petition asks that through the help of Mary and Joseph (the "both") we may be fitted out, prepared, built up, equipped, or instructed (*instruo* has all these meanings) by the example of the Holy Family and attain everlasting *consortium*. *Consors* is sharing in common goods or property in the manner of family members. The petition asks that we may share family life with the Holy Family in eternity because, enabled by their assistance, we have followed their example and become like them.

1970: Holy Family

Antoine Dumas identifies this as a new prayer, composed because the 1962 prayer was "particularly weak and because there was no equivalent in the old sacramentaries."[45] In their works on the sources, both Dumas and Cuthbert Johnson list the 1962 collect as the source of the new prayer.[46] The analysis which follows assumes that the 1962 collect was, in some way, the point from which the revisers began their confection of the new text.

In 1966 the *Consilium* members decided that, in general, prayers were to be addressed to the Father.[47] This accounts for the change from the "Lord Jesus Christ" to "God" in the address. This change then necessitates a revision in the relative clause because its subject is now the Father. The revisers supply one which praises the Father for providing us with the example of the Holy Family. The foregoing modifications require at least a minor alteration in the original petition; two, in fact, are made. The petition for the heavenly assistance or intercession of the Lord's parents is omitted, and the request that we may be fitted out, prepared, built up, equipped for, or instructed unto the attainment of heaven becomes a request that we may attain heaven by imitating the Holy Family in charity and the domestic virtues. The *qui* clause and the petition are parallel. The former praises God for providing the example; the latter asks that we may follow it.

---

[45] Antoine Dumas, "Les oraisons du nouveau Missel," *Questions Liturgiques* 25 (1971) 263–70 at 269: "... texte, dans l'ancien missel, était particulièrement faible et qui n'avaient pas d'équivalents dans les vieux sacramentaires (Saint Famille ...)."
[46] Antoine Dumas, "Les Sources du Nouveau Missel Romain," *Notitiae* 7 (1971) 410; Cuthbert Johnson, "The Sources of the Roman Missal (1975)," *Notitiae* 32 (1996) 29.
[47] See discussion on pp. 13–4 above.

The revised prayer is more general and does not highlight, as does the original, the human childhood and attendant submission of the divine Son. One reason for the latter is, most certainly, the decision to address prayer to the Father. The decisions to move the feast to the Sunday immediately following Christmas and to adopt other Gospel lessons for the feast in Years A and B, may explain why the revised prayer does not speak of Jesus's boyhood.

However well reasoned the revisions may have been, the omission of the two intrinsically connected mysteries mentioned in the *qui* clause of the original prayer is a lamentable loss: the divine Son was subject to his human parents and sanctified domestic life by living it.

1 January: Octave of the Nativity and Solemnity of Mary, Holy Mother of God.

1962: Octave of the Nativity[48]	1970/2002: Solemnity of Mary Holy Mother of God on the Octave of the Nativity of the Lord
Deus, qui salutis aeternae, beatae Mariae virginitate foecunda, humano generi praemia praestitisti: tribue, quaesumus; ut ipsam pro nobis intercedere sentiamus, per quam meruimus auctorem vitae suscipere, *Dominum nostrum Iesum Christum Filium tuum.*	Deus, qui salutis aeternae, beatae Mariae virginitate fecunda, humano generi praemia praestitisti, tribue, quaesumus, ut ipsam pro nobis intercedere sentiamus, per quam meruimus *Filium tuum* auctorem vitae suscipere.
O God, who have bestowed the rewards of eternal salvation upon the human race through the fruitful virginity of blessed Mary: grant, we beseech you, that we may experience her interceding on our behalf – she, through whom we have been deemed worthy to receive the author of life, our Lord Jesus Christ, your Son.	O God, who have bestowed the rewards of eternal salvation upon the human race through the fruitful virginity of blessed Mary: grant, we beseech you, that we may experience her interceding on our behalf – she, through whom we have been deemed worthy to receive your Son, the author of life.

Manuscript History

There are two eighth-century witnesses to a variant of this prayer being used on the feast of the Assumption of the Blessed Virgin. The first line is

---

[48] Cf. CO III, 2113 a, b, c.

slightly different: "O God who have granted hope of eternal salvation to the human race ..."[49]

A slightly different form of the collect is assigned to 1 January in numerous codices dating from the eighth to the sixteenth century.[50] They lack the final words: *Dominum nostrum Iesum Christum Filium tuum* [our Lord Jesus Christ your Son]. It seems that the post-Trent revisers added *Dominum nostrum Iesum Christum Filium tuum* when they included the prayer in the first typical edition of the Tridentine missal.

The post-Vatican II revisers retained the prayer in the re-titled feast of the Maternity of Mary, but made two changes. They removed the words *Dominum nostrum Iesum Christum* and placed the *Filium tuum* [your Son] immediately before *auctorem vitae* [author of life]. No known variant has the arrangement which appears in the first three typical editions of the Vatican II missal. The 2008 re-impression of the third typical edition restores the collect to the form found in the 1962 missal.

The Text

The prayer has two relative clauses. The first, in the salutation, praises God for granting "the rewards of eternal life to the human race through the fruitful virginity of the blessed Mary." The second, in the petition, describes Mary as the one "through whom we have been deemed worthy to receive the author of life." The first is a statement of fact about what God has done. The second is a statement of fact about what we have received. Mary is the one through whom God acted; through her we have received the author of life.

Through Mary God undoes what the serpent accomplished through Eve. Eve is the virgin through whom the human race became subject to death. She is also, as her name indicates, mother of all the living. Mary is the virgin mother of the author of life and the one through whom eternal life is granted to the human race. The petition is simply that we may perceive, experience, feel (*sentiamus*) the effects of Mary interceding on our behalf.

The pre-Trent version of the prayer speaks only indirectly of Christ: fruitful virginity becomes the source of the rewards of eternal life, the author of life. One can see why the post-Trent revisers made what is implicit explicit by adding "our Lord Jesus Christ, your Son" to the end of the

---

[49] "Deus, qui spe[m] salutis aeternae, beatae Mariae virginitate foecunda, humano generi praemia praestitisti ..." The codices are the *Gelasianum Vetus* (c. 750) and the *Sacramentaire de Gellon* (end of the eighth century). The codex of the latter is Paris, Bibliothèque Nationale, lat. 12.048 and the modern critical edition is Antoine Dumas and Jean Deshusses, *Liber Sacramentorum Gellonensis* (Corpus Christianorum Series Latina, CLIX), Turnhout: Brepols, 1981.

[50] CO III, 2113b, A. The day on which this prayer is used is titled either Octave of the Nativity or the Circumcision of the Lord.

prayer, and why the post-Vatican II revisers were unwilling to return the prayer to its pre-Trent state.

The prayer is a fitting collect for the feast of Mary's maternity.

The Holy Name of Jesus or the second Sunday of the Nativity

1962: Holy Name of Jesus	1970/2002: Second Sunday of the Nativity	Source text for 1970/2002: CO VI, 3838
Deus, qui unigenitum Filium tuum constituisti humani generis Salvatorem, et Iesum vocari iussisti: concede propitius; ut, cuius sanctum nomen veneramur in terris, eius quoque aspectu perfruamur in caelis.	Omnipotens sempiterne Deus, fidelium splendor animarum, dignare mundum gloria tua *implere benignus,* et *cunctis populis* appare per tui luminis claritatem.	Omnipotens sempiterne Deus, fidelium splendor animarum *qui hanc sollemnitatem electionis gentium primitiis consecrasti, imple* mundum gloria tua *et subditis tibi populis* per luminis tui appare claritatem.
O God, who established your Son as Savior of the human race and commanded that he be called Jesus: mercifully grant that we may enjoy the vision of him in heaven whose holy name we venerate on earth.	O God, splendor of the souls of the faithful, *kindly deign* to fill the world with your glory and reveal yourself *to all peoples.*	O God, splendor of the souls of the faithful, who have consecrated this solemnity with first fruits of the election of the Gentiles, fill the world with your glory and through the splendor of your light reveal yourself *to the peoples who have been made subject to you.*

Manuscript History

The 1962 collect of the feast of the Holy Name does not appear in any extant ancient codex and is not retained in the post-Vatican II missals. It may have been composed when the feast was put on the universal calendar in 1721, or it may be earlier since the feast had been celebrated in local churches and religious orders before it was promulgated for the whole Church.[51]

---

[51] Antoine, Dumas "Les oraisons du nouveau Missel," *Questions Liturgiques* 25 (1971) 269, tells us that the collect assigned to the votive Mass of the Most Holy Name of Jesus in the Vatican II missals is a new composition: Sanctissimum Iesu nomen venerantibus, nobis,

The source prayer for the 1970/2002 collect of Sunday after the Nativity Octave (or the second Sunday of the Nativity) is ancient.[52] It appears in numerous extant codices that date from the eighth to the thirteenth century. It is not seen after the thirteenth century until it was adapted for use in the Paul VI missal. In one ancient codex it is an *oratio* for the Nativity of the Lord. Otherwise its exclusive use is in connection with the Epiphany.[53]

None of the changes made by the post-Vatican II editors has a warrant in the manuscript tradition. These are discussed below.

The Texts

The source of the 1970/2002 collect for this day is CO VI, 3838. Its amplified opening clause addresses God as (1) almighty, everlasting; (2) the splendor of the souls of the faithful; (3) the one who has consecrated this solemnity with the first fruits of the election of the Gentiles. The last of these identifies the text as an Epiphany prayer.

The petition is twofold, and each aspect is governed by an imperative verb. The Lord is asked first to fill the world with his glory, and second, through the brightness of his light to appear, attend, manifest himself to the people who have been made (or who are) subject to him – to those who have acknowledged his Lordship in self-surrender.[54]

Domine, concede propitius, ut, eius in hac vita dulcedine perfruentes, sempiterno gaudia in patria repleamur [Mercifully grant to us who venerate the Most Holy Name of Jesus that we who enjoy his sweetness in this life may be filled with joy in the homeland that lasts forever].

The third typical edition adds a feast of the Most Holy Name of Jesus to be celebrated on 3 January with new formularies. The collect of this Mass is adapted from a Vespers prayer of the Vigil of the Nativity of the Lord found in three extant ninth–eleventh century codices:

CO XI, 6822	MR (2002): January 3. Most Holy Name of Jesus
Deus, qui salutem humani generis in Verbi tui incarnatione fundasti, da populis tuis misericordiam quam deposcunt, ut sciant omnes nationes non esse aliud sanctum quam nomen Unigeniti tui sub caelo, quod debeant invocare.	Deus, qui salutem humani generis in Verbi tui incarnatione fundasti, da populis tuis misericordiam quam deposcunt, ut sciant omnes non esse, quam Unigeniti tui, nomen aliud invocandum.
O God, who have founded the salvation of the human race upon the incarnation of your Word, grant to your people the mercy which they beg, that all nations may know that there is no other [name] under heaven upon which they must call than the holy name of your Beloved Son.	O God, who have founded the salvation of the human race upon the incarnation of your Word, grant to your people the mercy which they beg, that all may know there is no other [name] to be called upon than the name of your Only-begotten Son.

[52] CO VI, 3838.

[53] CO VI, 3838. On the day, at Matins or Vespers; on the Octave Day as collect; on the vigil, as a prayer after the genealogy.

[54] *Appareo*, to appear or become visible, shares its root with the noun *apparitio* which came to be used as the Latin equivalent of *epiphania* [= epiphany or manifestation]. The secret or prayer over the gifts assigned to the Epiphany in three eighth century codices and to the octave day of the Epiphany in thirty others spanning the ninth to the sixteenth centuries uses the word *apparitio* in this way:

1970/2002

The revisers assigned the collect to the Sunday which falls between 1 January and 6 January, a Sunday that is only celebrated where the Epiphany is celebrated on 6 January. It is then understandable that they omitted the clause which distinguishes the original as an Epiphany prayer.[55]

The second change, by which the bare imperative *imple* or "fill" becomes *dignare ... implere benignus* "kindly deign to fill," increases the deference of the prayer.

The last revision changes *subditis tibi populis*, the people subject to you, to *cunctis populis*, all people. The favor reserved in the original to those who are subject to the Lord is requested in the revision for all. The desire for the salvation of all accords with the will of God expressed in the scriptures and is therefore laudable.[56] What captures attention, however, is that the moral requirement stipulated in the original has been eliminated in the revision. It is not that a slightly different theology has been introduced, for example that submission follows from rather than precedes Lordly manifestation, but that the concept of self-surrender has fallen from the collect altogether.[57]

The Epiphany of the Lord (two Masses)

Vigil

CO II, 837a	2002: Vigil of the Epiphany
Corda nostra, quaesumus, Domine, venturae *festivitatis* splendor illustret, quo *et* mundi huius *tenebris carere* valeamus, et perveniamus ad patriam claritatis aeternae.	Corda nostra, quaesumus, Domine, tuae *maiestatis* splendor illustret, quo mundi huius *tenebras transire* valeamus, et perveniamus ad patriam claritatis aeternae.

Corpus Orationum 3003 IV, A and B	
Hostias tibi, Domine, pro nati Filii tui *apparitione* deferimus, suppliciter exorantes: ut, sicut ipse nostrorum auctor est munerum, ita sit ipse misericors et susceptor, Iesus Christus Dominus noster.	For the *manifestation/epiphany* of your new born Son, we bring offerings to you, humbly beseeching that, as he himself is the author of our gifts, so may he also be merciful and receive them, Jesus Christ our Lord.

In all the Tridentine missals the above prayer is the secret assigned to January 13.

On the relationship between *apparitio* and *epiphania* see also Thomas J. Talley, *The Origins of the Liturgical Year*, 145.

[55] "*qui hanc sollemnitatem electionis gentium primitiis consecrasti.*"

[56] 1 Tim. 2.4.

[57] Further, the word that is omitted here, *subditis* (or *subditus* in the nominative, masculine singular) which means "subject," was also omitted in the revised collect for the feast of the Holy Family. In the 1962 collect, the child Jesus is subject (*subditus*) to Mary and Joseph.

May the splendor of the *coming feast* shine on our hearts, we beseech you, O Lord, by which we may both have strength to hold ourselves aloof from the darkness of this world and arrive at the homeland of eternal light.	May the splendor of *your majesty* shine on our hearts, we beseech you, O Lord, by which we may have strength to *pass by* the darkness of this world and arrive at the homeland of eternal light.

Manuscript History

The source text, CO II, 837a, appears in codices dating from the eighth century through the sixteenth. It is always assigned to the vigil of the Epiphany or Theophany.[58] There is no warrant in the manuscript tradition for the changes made by the modern revisers. These are three: "your majesty" replaces "coming feast;" "et" is omitted changing the "both/and" construction of the original to a single "and"; "*tenebras transire*" replaces "*tenebris carere*" – the meaning of these Latin phrases is discussed below.

The Text

The omission of the mention of the coming feast is explained by the fact that the post-Vatican II revisers originally assigned this collect to Monday after the Epiphany. Only in the third typical edition is it assigned to the Mass of the Vigil of the Epiphany.

"*Careo*" has a range of meanings that include "to be free from," "to lack" or "to feel the want of" as well as "to abstain from." That is, the word refers both to the involuntary deprivation of poverty and to voluntary refusals to make use of something that is available. The latter is the intended meaning. The twofold petition asks that we may have the strength to hold ourselves apart from the "darkness" of this world and that we may arrive at the splendor of the heavenly homeland.

The word supplied by the revisers, *transire*, comes from *trans*, across, and *ire*, to go, pass, etc. It suggests movement. Here the intended meaning is that we may have the strength to pass over or pass by the darkness of this world, to leave it untouched.

The original prayer asks for strength of will to avoid dark things while the revision asks that we have the strength to pass them by without touching them. That is, the original prayer asks for a certain degree of Christian maturation, a strength of will, by which we will keep apart from dark things; the revised prayer is less explicit about the mechanics of leaving them untouched.

The both/and construction of the original text indicates that there are two requests. The two are logically interdependent. The simple "and" of the revised text does not change the meaning but is more suggestive of a

---

[58] Both names designate 6 January.

single, fluid movement from this world to the next which is reinforced by the substitution of *transire*.

Epiphany

No change was made to the collect of the Epiphany. The same prayer appears in both the pre- and post-Vatican II missals.

Pre- and Post-Vatican II Missals: Epiphany of the Lord[59]
Deus, qui hodierna die Unigenitum tuum gentibus stella duce revelasti: concede propitius; ut, qui iam te ex fide cognovimus, usque ad contemplandam speciem tuae celsitudinis perducamur.	O God, who on this day with a star as guide revealed your only-begotten Son to the Gentiles: mercifully grant that we who have already known you by faith, may be led to contemplating the vision/sight of your majesty.

Manuscript History
The prayer appears in over fifty extant codices from the eighth century forward. It is always used in connection with the Epiphany and, in all but three cases, serves as the collect for the feast. Bernard Capelle argues compellingly that the prayer was composed by Saint Gregory.[60]

The Text
The collects of feasts that celebrate particularly important mysteries of faith note the day. The collect for the night Mass of the Nativity, for instance, states that God has made "*hanc sacratissimam noctem*" [this most holy night] bright, and the collect of the Epiphany announces that "*hodierna die*," on this day, God revealed his Only-begotten Son to the Gentiles.

God is addressed simply as "Deus." The *qui* clause that follows states a fact: God revealed his Only-begotten Son to the Gentiles through the leading of a star. The *qui* clause provides the motive for the petition. The two clauses of the collect chart parallel movements on two different planes. The magi are led by a star, something they can see but also must believe has a significance that they cannot see, to the manger where they see a child whom they adore as God. We, who have already known God by faith, ask to be mercifully led to the contemplation of the sight or vision of God in heaven – that is, to the beatific vision.

The vocabulary echoes 2 Corinthians 5.7: *per fidem enim ambulamus et non per speciem* [we walk by faith and not by sight]. Paul opposes faith and

---

[59] CO II, 1673.
[60] B. Capelle, "La main de Saint Grégoire dans le sacramentaire grégorien," *Revue benedictine* 49 (1937) 13–28 at 14ff.

sight. The prayer presents a progression from one to the other. Those who know by faith (note: faith gives true knowledge) are led unto [*ad* is a going toward that arrives at] the contemplation of the vision of God in glory.[61]

This collect is like that of the 1962 collect of Christmas night in three ways. As we note above, both mark the day/night. Second, both have the word "*cognovimus.*" In the collect of Christmas night we are those who have known the mystery of God's light; in this, we are those who have known "you, by faith." Lastly both ask for heavenly life under a particular aspect. In the Nativity prayer, it is the full enjoyment of the Lord's gladness. Here it is contemplation of the vision of God.

The Baptism of the Lord

1962: Baptism of the Lord (13 January) and 1970/2002: Baptism of the Lord (alt. collect)[62]	1970/2002: Baptism of the Lord (collect)
Deus, cuius Unigenitus in substantia nostrae carnis apparuit: praesta, quaesumus; ut per eum, quem similem nobis foris agnovimus, intus reformari mereamur.	Omnipotens sempiterne Deus, qui Christum, in Iordane flumine baptizatum, Spiritu Sancto super eum descendente, dilectum Filium tuum sollemniter declarasti, concede filiis adoptionis tuae, ex aqua et Spiritu sancto renatis, ut in beneplacito tuo iugiter perseverent.
O God, whose only-begotten Son appeared in the substance of our flesh: grant, we beseech you, that through him, whom we have recognized to be like us outwardly, we may be deemed worthy to be inwardly restored/transformed.	Almighty everlasting God, who solemnly declared Christ, having been baptized in the river Jordan, as the Holy Spirit was descending upon him, to be your beloved Son; grant to the sons of your adoption who have been reborn through water and the Holy Spirit, that they may ever persevere in your good pleasure.

Manuscript History

The 1962 collect appears in numerous codices dated by scholars from the eighth/ninth century to the sixteenth when it was incorporated into the Tridentine missal. In all these it is assigned to the Octave Day of the

---

[61] B. Capelle, "La main de Saint Grégoire dans le sacramentaire gregorien," *Revue benedictine* 49 (1937) 15–19, calls attention to ways in which Saint Gregory adapted the language and thought of Paul expressed in this verse in his sermons.
[62] CO II, 1197.

Epiphany or Theophany.[63] In 12 codices, dating from the eighth to the eleventh and the thirteenth centuries, it is assigned to the Epiphany.[64]

The post-Vatican II collect is a new composition which draws almost exclusively from scripture, principally the accounts of the Lord's baptism.[65]

In a 1971 essay, Dumas mentions the 1962 collect in the context of explaining why the revisers included "entirely new compositions" in the new missal.

> ... It is also the case for orations that are not found in the former Missal, and that it was necessary to create in order to meet a new use when the above mentioned procedures proved insufficiently effective. See, for example, the three orations for the feast of the Baptism of the Lord ...[66]

Dumas's assertion of the absence of a suitable collect for the feast of the Lord's Baptism is particularly puzzling because that same year he also published a list of the sources for the proper Mass prayers. There he indicates that there are two collects assigned to the feast of the Lord's Baptism. He identifies the first, C1, as a new composition and the other, C2, as the collect assigned to 13 January in the 1962 missal.

The Text

1962 Collect // 1970/2002 alternate Collect

The prayer is addressed to God whose Only-begotten Son appeared "in the nature of our flesh" – that is, in our bodily human nature.

Substantia, literally "that which stands under," means "substance" as well as "essence," "being," and "nature." The assertion is not that the Son only seemed (appeared) to us to be enfleshed. Rather it is a statement that the Son assumed our fleshly nature and, thereby, became visible (appeared) to us.

Human beings have a composite nature, a nature comprised of a material (visible) body and a spiritual (invisible) soul. When the Only-begotten Son

---

[63] *CO* II, 1197 B.

[64] *CO* II, 1197 A.

[65] Cuthbert Johnson, "The Sources of the Roman Missal (1975)," *Notitiae* 32 (1996), p. 33 lists: Isa. 42.1–4, 6–7; Isa. 61.1–2; Mt. 3.16–17; Mk 1.9–11; Lk. 3.21–2; Jn 3.5; Rom. 18.15; Eph. 1.3, 5–6.

[66] "Les oraisons du nouveau Missel," *Questions Liturgiques* 25 (1971) 263–70 at 269: "C'est aussi le cas des oraisons inexistentes dans l'ancien Missel, et qu'il a fallu créer à l'usage du nouveau, lorsque les procédés ci-dessus mentionnés se révélaient insuffissiamment efficaces. Voir, par exemple les trois oraisons pour la fête du Baptême du Seigneur ..." The three orations are the collect, prayer over the offerings, and postcommunion prayer assigned to the feast in the Vatican II missals.

becomes human he, too, has a material body and a spiritual soul. The likeness between the Son and us does not extend only to what is apparent externally (*foris*), but also includes what is on the inside (*intus*). Put crudely, the Son is like us, inside and out, with respect to everything that is proper to human nature.

Sin, however universal in human experience, is not proper to human nature. Sin is the difference between the Son's human nature and our own. Our human nature has been defaced by sin, and our souls disfigured by it. His have not. Hence the petition that through the Son we may be deemed worthy to be restored within. The verb *formo* means to shape or fashion or form. *Reformo* is to reshape or remold or restore to what was before (the root words mean "to form back"). The prayer asks that we may be created anew in the Son, that through him our nature might become what it was before our first parents sinned.

Consideration of this prayer clarifies distinction between *cognovimus* and *agnovimus* mentioned above in the discussion of the collect of the night Mass of Christmas.[67] The perception of the Son's likeness to us comes from seeing what is visible. It is recognition. It is, we might say, skin deep (*foris*). Hence the use of "*agnovimus*" in this prayer. Knowledge of the "mystery of his light" must, of its very nature, be something more, and the word that conveys this is *cognovimus*.

1970/2002 Collect

The prayer addresses the Father as "almighty everlasting God." The statement of fact providing the motive for the petition which follows is "who solemnly declared Christ, having been baptized in the river Jordan, with the Holy Spirit descending upon him, to be your beloved Son." It is an unusually long *qui* clause (16 Latin words) which presents the events narrated in Matthew 2.16–17, Mark 1.10–11 and Luke 3.22 and uses the terms found in the Vulgate: baptized, Holy Spirit, descending, and beloved Son. For the third person Synoptic attestation of a "voice from heaven," the prayer substitutes the second person "*sollemniter declarasti*": you solemnly declared.

The collect petitions on behalf of "the sons of your adoption who have been reborn in water and the Holy Spirit." Again the language is from the Vulgate: "sons of adoption" echoes the "spirit of adoption as sons" of Romans 8.15[68] and "reborn from water and the Holy Spirit" is found in John 3.5, Jesus's words to Nicodemus.[69]

---

[67] See above on pp. 73–4 and nn. 34–5.

[68] "... accepistis Spiritum adoptionis filiorum." [... you have received the Spirit of adoption of sons].

[69] "... nisi quis renatus fuerit ex aqua et Spiritu non potest introire in regnum Dei" [... unless one is born of water and the Spirit, he cannot enter the kingdom of God."

The prayer's request is simply that these sons may ever persevere in God's good pleasure. *Beneplacitus* is not found in the Gospels but has the same root, *placeo*, as *conplacui* of Matthew 3.17 and Mark 1.11 and *conplacuit* of Luke 3.22: the voice from heaven says to/of the beloved Son, "with thee/ with whom I am *well pleased.*" *Beneplacitus* appears elsewhere in the New Testament and means "pleasing."[70]

Unlike so many Roman collects that ever so concisely name the heart of the mystery being contemplated, this new composition speaks of divine adoption without reference to its inner reality: the gift of grace, a share in divine life, a partaking of divine nature. Unlike human adoption, which is a matter of legal *fiat*, God makes us sons and daughters by making us partakers of his own divine nature. What Christ is by nature, the very Son of God, we become by grace – hence adopted.

The two prayers for the one feast are quite different. The chart below places them, element by element, side by side:

	1962, alt 1970/2002	1970
Address	O God	Almighty, everlasting God
Statement of fact	whose only-begotten Son appeared in the substance of our flesh	who solemnly declared Christ, having been baptized in the river Jordan, as the Holy Spirit was descending upon him, to be your beloved Son;
Words of petition	grant, we beseech you	grant
Those for whom the petition is made	we who recognize the Son to be like us outwardly	the sons of your adoption who have been reborn through water and the Holy Spirit
The petition	that, through him, we may be deemed worthy to be inwardly restored.	that they may always persevere in your good pleasure.

Above we note the scriptural references in the new prayer but not in the old. It would be a mistake, however, to conclude that the old prayer is informed by scripture to a lesser degree than the new one. Rather, the difference is

---

[70] 1 Cor. 10.5: "... with most of them, God was not pleased"; Eph. 5.10: "try to learn what is pleasing to the Lord."

in the way each draws upon scripture. The old text seems to come forth as prayer from a heart that has meditated deeply upon John's Prologue,[71] been struck by its truth, understood the Gospel's application to its own situation, and petitions from perceived need. The new text does not seem so much to reflect a heart that has made the meaning of the scriptures its own but from a mind that is anxious not to forget anything pertaining to the Lord's Baptism.

The petitions of the two collects are not commensurate. The old prayer asks, however succinctly, for the spiritual and moral renewal of the inner man. The new prayer asks to persevere/abide always in the Father's good pleasure. There are, to be sure, moral and spiritual dimensions to remaining in God's good graces, and these are enhanced by the use of the word *persevero* (persevere/abide) over, for example, *maneo* (remain/abide) because perseverance involves an active will. Nevertheless, the new collect, while clearly more focused on the event of the Lord's baptism and more explicit in its reference to our own (our adoption as sons), does not speak of the renewal or restoration of the inner man in Christ that is the concern of the older, less explicit prayer.

Conclusion

The changes made to the calendar of Christmastide are five: the feast of the Holy Family is celebrated on Sunday within the octave of the Nativity; 1 January is dedicated to Mary's Maternity; the Sunday celebration of the Most Holy Name of Jesus is suppressed and the day on which it was celebrated is now the second Sunday of the Nativity; the feast of the Baptism of the Lord is moved to the Sunday after the Epiphany (formerly the feast of the Holy Family); permission is given for the Epiphany to be celebrated on the second Sunday of the Nativity where 6 January is not a holy day of obligation.

The assignment of the Epiphany and the Baptism to Sundays is, perhaps, the calendar change with the most profound consequences for the faithful inasmuch as it places mysteries before them which they might not otherwise have the opportunity to celebrate – especially those who live in regions where the Epiphany is neither a civil holiday nor holy day of obligation.

The retention and reassignment of the feast of the Holy Family is noteworthy for two reasons. First, the feast was retained even though all but one of the calendar *coetus* members initially favored suppression. Second, as we shall discuss more fully in the next chapter, the calendar *coetus* had responsibility only for the calendar – the framework in which the Church celebrates the mysteries, so to speak, not the texts of particular

---

[71] The words *Unigenitus* and *carnis* ("Only-begotten Son" and "of flesh") suggest this.

celebrations. The responsibility of assigning lessons belonged to another *coetus*. In the case of the Holy Family, the suggestions of *Coetus* 1 with respect to the Gospel lesson prevailed – whether because they were actually accepted or for other reasons entirely. This will not always be the case.

The corpus of Christmastide Sunday and feast day collects of the new missal is very like the old corpus. Six collects are from the old missal. While three of these were edited, the adjustments were not extensive and, in one case they were reversed in a later edition of the missal. With respect to the five collects that are not found in the 1962 missal, only the prayers assigned to the feast of the Holy Family and the second Sunday of the Nativity are the only collects appointed to their respective days. And the latter is not celebrated where the Epiphany is celebrated on a Sunday. The collect assigned to the third Mass of Christmas is one of four appointed for the feast, and two of these are from the 1962 missal. The collect assigned to the Vigil of the Epiphany is one of two appointed for the feast; the other is from the 1962 missal. The new collect for the Baptism of the Lord is accompanied by an alternate collect taken from the old missal.

Comparative study of the two sets of Christmas collects and examination of each collect in the revised missal in relation to its source does not enable us to identify a central concern that guided the original post-Vatican II editors in their task, but we are able to make some cautious observations about their predilections:

1. There is an inclination to remove the titles of our Lord that appear in prayers. Examples are the collects of the Vigil of the Nativity and Mary, Holy Mother of God as well as the collects assigned to Advent Sunday I and II discussed in the previous chapter.

2. There is a tendency to tinker with the received text. In prayer after prayer the revisers make changes that have no warrant in the manuscript tradition. Often these do not discernibly improve the prayer. Two particularly striking examples are the collects of the night and dawn Masses of Christmas.

3. There is objection to the idea and/or vocabulary of submission or subjection. Examples are the new prayer assigned to the second Sunday of the Nativity, from which the word was edited, and the 1962 collect for the Holy Family which is not included in the new missal.

4. There is a tendency not to mention sin and/or the struggle against it. The only collect assigned to the Nativity of the Lord that mentions sin, actually a petition for liberation from it, is the one the revisers chose to replace with the ancient prayer that begs a share in the divine nature. A second example is the collect for the Epiphany vigil in which the revisers replaced *tenebris carere* with *tenebras transire* – instead of setting one's will against darkness, one glides past it.

5

Septuagesima

The short season of Septuagesima was suppressed in the post-Vatican II reform of the Church's calendar. This chapter, which examines both the reasons for the suppression and its effects, has three parts. The first briefly considers the origin, nature, and purpose of Septuagesima, for a proper appreciation of the suppression of a season in the Church's Sacred Year necessarily depends, in part at least, upon understanding why it was instituted in the first place. The second traces the decision to suppress Septuagesima through the records of *Coetus* 1. The third examines the collects of Septuagesima, the prayers that most particularly express the sentiments proper to the season.[1]

Duration, Origin, Nature, and Purpose of Septuagesima[2]

Septuagesima begins on the third Sunday before Ash Wednesday[3] and ends with first Vespers of the first Sunday of Lent.[4] The names of its three

---

[1] All are Sunday collects.

[2] The historical material is taken from Camille Callewaert, "L'oeuvre liturgique de s. Grégoire La Septuagésime et l'Alléluia" in *Sacris Erudiri*, Fragmenta Liturgica Collecta a Monachis Sancti Petri de Aldenbruggo in Steenbrugge ne Pereant (The Hague: Steenbrugis), 635–53. Henri LeClerq, "Septuagesime" in *DACL* vol. 15.1 (1950), cols. 1262–66 follows Callewaert.

[3] The ninth Sunday before the day of the Lord's resurrection.

[4] Ancient sacramentaries make a distinction not found in modern missals, namely that Wednesday of Quinquagesima marks the beginning of the fast and Sunday of Quadragesima the beginning of Lent. [Cf., for example, Leo Cunibert Mohlberg, *Liber Sacramentorum Romanae Aeclesiae ordinis anni circuli* (Rome: Herder, 1960) 19–20].

In the pre-Vatican II liturgical books, Ash Wednesday is designated *Feria Quarta Cinerum* [literally, Wednesday of Ashes] and the ferials following, Thursday after Ashes, Friday after Ashes, Saturday after Ashes until the First Sunday in Lent [*Dominica Prima in Quadragesima*].

Sundays are Septuagesima, Sexagesima, and Quinquagesima which mean 70, 60, and 50 respectively. The first Sunday of Lent is Quadragesima or 40. Ashes are distributed on Wednesday of Quinquagesima. Septuagesima Sunday, then, begins a not very literal countdown to the Pasch.[5]

From about the middle of the fifth century a period of pre-Lenten preparation began to be observed in the West. By the year 590 or 591, all three weeks of Septuagesima were an established part of the Roman church's annual preparation for the Pasch.[6] Camille Callewaert identifies five stages in the development of the season:

1. The station days of Quinquagesima, namely Wednesday and Friday of that week, were attached to the Lenten fast.

2. The intermediate days of Thursday and Saturday were added to bring the number of Lenten fast days to 40 – the length of Christ's own fast.

3. Penance or fasting was extended through the whole week of Quinquagesima.

4. Sexagesima was added in the sixth century.

5. The pre-Lenten period came to include the week of Septuagesima.[7]

The pre-Lenten observance arose through the initiatives of monks and the faithful. Indeed, initially it received mixed reactions from bishops.[8] The distinguishing characteristic of the season was penitence of devotion, not obligation.[9]

The post-Vatican II books use the same names for the ferials days from Ash Wednesday to the following Saturday. Sunday is designated: *Dominica I in Quadragesima*

Lent developed gradually in the West. In time it came to begin on the sixth Sunday before the Pasch. Since Sundays are never fasted, this arrangement provided only 36 fast days. Because the Lord himself fasted for 40 days, the beginning of the fast was eventually moved back to Wednesday of Quinquagesima. By the end of the seventh century a 40-day period of fasting was observed everywhere in the West.

[5] Septuagesima Sunday falls 64 days before Sunday of the Pasch; Sexagesima, 57 days; Quinquagesima the literal 50 days; Quadragesima 43 days. The fortieth day after the first Sunday of Lent is Holy Thursday which begins the Paschal Triduum. The origin of the nomenclature is unclear.

[6] Callewaert sees this verified in the text of a homily preached by Pope Saint Gregory I on Septuagesima Sunday at the station church of Saint Laurence Outside the Walls in 590 or 591. Cf. *Homiliae in evangelia* XIX.1 [*PL* 76, 1153C] and Camille Callewaert, "L'oeuvre liturgique de s. Grégoire La Septuagésime et l'Alléluia" 648 and 648, n. 46.

[7] Camille Callewaert, "L'oeuvre liturgique de s. Grégoire La Septuagésime et l'Alléluia" in *Sacris Erudiri*, Fragmenta Liturgica Collecta a Monachis Sancti Petri de Aldenbruggo in Steenbrugge ne Pereant (The Hague: Steenbrugis) 647.

[8] Camille Callewaert, "L'oeuvre liturgique de s. Grégoire La Septuagésime et l'Alléluia," 647–8.

[9] Camille Callewaert, "L'oeuvre liturgique de s. Grégoire La Septuagésime et l'Alléluia," 647–8.

The intuition of faith that gave rise to the season of Septuagesima, then, is a recognition of the goodness, or even the necessity, of preparing oneself mentally, physically, and spiritually for the ascesis of Lent. The same recognition expresses itself in the Eastern practice of observing the Sundays of Meat-fare and Cheese-fare on the second and first Sundays, respectively, that precede the last Sunday before Lent.[10] From Meat-fare Sunday the faithful lay aside all flesh foods until the Pasch. From Cheese-fare Sunday the faithful abstain from animal products such as eggs, milk, yogurt, butter, and cheese.

The Suppression of Septuagesima

The second schema of the Calendar *coetus* introduces discussion of Septuagesima in Question 15 under the heading *"De dominicis per annum."*[11]

Concerning the time of Septuagesima, these solutions are proposed:

a) *either* the names and formularies of the Sundays, Septuagesima, Quinquagesima, are preserved, but, the penitential character of this season is abolished;

b) *or* the season of Septuagesima is suppressed, and the formularies are used at another time;

c) *or* the season of Septuagesima is suppressed, but the formularies (with the names and penitential character removed: the *Gloria* and the *Alleluia* said, etc.) are used on the last three Sundays before Lent with, if necessary, other "post-Epiphany" formularies being omitted.[12]

Missing from the list of options are two possibilities. One is subsequently introduced by a *coetus* member; the other, which no one seems to have anticipated, is what actually came to pass. These are, respectively, that no

---

[10] If the Pasch is celebrated on the same day in both the East and the West, Meat-fare Sunday falls on Septuagesima and Cheese-fare on Sexagesima. That is, in both the East and the West, the period of pre-Lenten preparation begins on the same day.

[11] "Concerning the Sundays through the year." See Schema n. 61, *De Calendario*, 1 (12 February 1965), p. 2.

[12] Emphasis added. Schema n. 61, *De Calendario*, 1 (12 February 1965), pp. 2–3: "*Circa tempus Septuagesimae hac proponuntur solutiones: a) vel nomina et formularia dominicarum Sept., Quinq. serventur, tollitur tamen character paenitentialis huius temporis; b) vel tempus Septuagesimae supprimitur, formularia autem alio tempore adhibentur; c) vel tempus Septuagesimae supprimitur, formularia autem (ablatis nominibus et charactere paenitentiali: dicitur Gloria et Alleluia, etc.) adhibentur ultimis tribus dominicis ante Quadragesimam, omissis, si necesse est, aliis formulariis "'post Epiphaniam.'*"

change at all would be made and that the formularies of this season would
be removed altogether from the missal.

Question 15 distinguishes three aspects: (1) nomenclature, (2) formularies, and (3) penitential character.

"Nomenclature" refers to the names of these days: Septuagesima,
Sexagesima, and Quinquagesima. From the responses of the various *coetus*
members recorded in the second schema and reported below, it appears that
"the names" initially (March, 1965) were understood also to mean "the
season," so that a vote to retain or suppress the names was understood to
be a vote to retain or suppress the season.[13] A month later, in the schema of
April 1965, the two were distinguished for ecumenical reasons – the question
of retaining the names was left unsettled out of deference to the "separated
brethren" who continue to use them, while the determination to suppress those
things which marked Septuagesima as a distinct season was firm.[14] By the end
of the year the names were no longer a consideration as the seventh schema
of the calendar *coetus* speaks of "Sundays of time, once Septuagesima."[15]

"Formularies" refer to the texts of Mass and Office: scripture lessons,
chants, antiphons, prayers and so forth.

"Penitential character" refers to the two customs of using violet vestments
and omitting the *Gloria* and *Alleluia* throughout Septuagesima. That is, the
penitential character pertains to the liturgical environment or atmosphere.
It involves priest and sanctuary being clothed in violet and the omission of
the more exuberantly joyful prayers. It does not oblige the faithful to acts
of penance or add extra prayers of a penitential sort to the celebrations.

Rembert Van Doren's answer to the question about Septuagesisma
appears first. He added a solution d) according to which Septuagesima
would be retained as a period of austerity. He called Septuagesima "the
doorway of Lent" and voted that nothing be changed. In the event his
solution d) would not prevail, Van Doren preferred solution c): that the
name and penitential elements be removed but the formularies retained.[16]

---

[13] Schema n. 65, *De Calendario*, 2 (15 March 1965), p. 13.

[14] Schema n. 75, *De Calendario*, 4 (10 April 1965), p. 2. See footnote 25 below, last
paragraph.

[15] Schema n. 132, *De Calendario*, 7 (3 December 1965), p. 3: "... *pro dominicis temporis olim
Septuagesima.*"

[16] Schema n. 65, *De Calendario*, 2 (15 March 1965), p. 13: "*Posset ad hunc numerus addi
subdivisio d): Tempus Septuagesimae ut limen Quadragesimae, et ut transitus, cum nota
austeritatis, a tempore per annum (Epiphaniae) ad tempus poenitentiale, remaneat uti est.
Si haec solutio admitti non potest, accipendum est quod dicitur in c): formularia adhibentur
tribus dominicis ante Quadragesimam, ablatis nominibus et charactere poenitentiale.*" [A
subdivision d) might be added to this number: the Season of Septuagesima remains as the
entrance to Lent, and as a transition, with a note of austerity, from a time through the year
(of Epiphany) to a penitential season. If this solution cannot be permitted, what is stated in c)
ought to be approved: the formularies used on the three Sundays before Lent, with the names
and penitential character removed].

None of the other members voted for Van Doren's solution d). Aimé-Georges Martimort called for the suppression of Septuagesima. He did not comment on the formularies except to say that these were the responsibility of other *coetus*.[17] Pierre Jounel also voted for suppression of the season, but wanted its formularies used at another time.[18] Agostino Amore voted for suppression but divided the question of the formularies. He proposed that the breviary lessons be moved to Advent, and the Mass lessons retained in place.[19] Herman Schmidt preferred that everything but the penitential elements remain the same, but wanted the formularies retained even if the season were suppressed.[20] Ansgar Dirks voted that the season with its penitential elements be suppressed but the formularies retained.[21] Adrian Nocent said that Septuagesima should be abolished for pastoral reasons: so that the faithful may see the progress of the liturgical year clearly and not be confused by diverse "anticipations."[22] He does not mention the formularies, but summarizes: "The names and penitential character ought to be abolished: the *Gloria* and *Alleluia* said, the color green used, etc."[23]

In sum, counting also the second choice indicated by two of the members and omitting mention of the formularies, there was one vote for retaining everything, one for retaining everything but the penitential elements, and seven for suppressing the season.

---

[17] Schema n. 65, *De Calendario*, 2 (15 March 1965), p. 13: "*Supprimetur tempus Septuagesimae. De quaestione sub littera c) proposita, iudicium pertinet praecipue ad coetum de lectionibus in Missa et de cantibus Missae.*" [The season of Septuagesima will be suppressed. On the question proposed under letter c), the decision pertains chiefly to the *coetus* concerning the lessons at Mass and the chants at Mass].

[18] Schema n. 65, *De Calendario*, 2 (15 March 1965), p. 13: "*La proposition b) me plaît: Tempus Septuagesima supprimitur, formularia autem alio tempore adhibentur.*" [Proposition b) pleases me; the Season of Septuagesima is suppressed, but the formularies used at another time].

[19] Schema n. 65, *De Calendario*, 2 (15 March 1965), p. 13: "*a) Negative. b) Affirmative. c) distinguendum scilicet: 1) Quoad lectiones Breviarii poni possunt Tempore Adventus ... 2) Lectiones Missalis ibi manere possunt.*" [a) Negative; b) Affirmative; c) it is necessary to distinguish namely: 1) as far as possible the lessons of the Breviary be placed in the Season of Advent; 2) the Missal Lessons are able to remain there].

[20] Schema n. 65, *De Calendario*, 2 (15 March 1965), p. 13: "*Placet hoc ordine: a), c). Non placet b).*" [a) and c) are acceptable in that order; b) is not acceptable].

[21] Schema n. 65, *De Calendario*, 2 (15 March 1965), p. 13: "*Placet solutio c).*" [Solution c) is acceptable].

[22] Schema n. 65, *De Calendario*, 2 (15 March 1965), p. 13: "*Abolendum est tempus Septuagesimae. Non ad vanam archeologiam, sed ut fideles bene videant progressionem anni liturgici et non disturbantur per diversas "anticipationes." At tamen formularia retineantur.*" [The season of Septuagesima ought to be abolished. Not for empty archeologism, but that the faithful may see the progression of the liturgical year well and not be troubled by diverse "anticipations"].

[23] Schema n. 65, *De Calendario*, 2 (15 March 1965), p. 13: "*Abolenda sunt nomina et character paenitentiale: dicantur Gloria, Allelulia, adhibeatur color viridis, etc.*"

Turning to the matter of the formularies, options a) and c) both stipulated that the texts of the Mass and Office for the days of this season would be preserved. Four *coetus* members desired the Mass formularies to be retained (Schmidt, Van Doren, Amore, and Dirks); one wanted the formularies used at another time (Jounel); one did not mention the formularies at all (Nocent). Martimort dismissed the question of the formularies, stating that they were the responsibility of other *coetus*.

Less than a month later, the fourth schema of the *Coetus 1, De Calendario*, articulated the collective opinion as follows:

The time of Septuagesima presents a difficulty.

It would please all the consultors if the season of Septuagesima were suppressed with respect to both its name and penitential character (with only one member thinking otherwise).

The penitential character of the time of Septuagesima or pre-Lent (the suppression of the *Gloria* and *Alleluia,* the color violet) is difficult for the faithful to understand without many explanations. At present the exterior signs of a penitential season are used as in Lent, but are not retained for the sake of particular penance as in Lent. According to the mind of the *Constitution on the Sacred Liturgy*,[24] the arrangement of the liturgical year may become clearer through the suppression of the penitential character of this season.

As it pertains to the names Septuagesima, Sexagesima, and Quinquagesima: because these names are also used by some of our separated brethren, it is necessary to proceed cautiously in this matter and to promote conversations on this matter as on others.[25]

The text goes on to note that decisions regarding the formularies are the responsibility of other *coetus*.[26]

---

[24] No particular paragraph of *Sacrosanctum Concilium* is cited.

[25] Schema n. 75, *De Calendario*, 4 (10 April 1965), p. 2: "*Difficultatem praebet tempus Septuagesimae. Omnibus Consultoribus placeret si tempus Septuagesimae seu Prae Quadra. (uno tantem aliter sentiente).*

Character paenitentialis temporis Septuagesimae seu Prae-Quadragesimae (suppressio Gloria et Alleluia), color violaseus) difficile a fidelibus intelligitur, nisi cum multis explanationibus. Iam adhibentur signa exteriora temporis paenitentialis, sicut in Quadragesima, sed non tenentur ad paenitentiam particularem sicut in Quadragesima. Ad mentem Constitutionem "De S. Liturgia" ordinatio anni liturgici clarior fiat, suppresso charactere paenitentiali huius temporis.

Ad nomina Septuagesimae, Sexagesimae et Quinquagesimae quod attinet, cum haec nomina etiam a nonullis fratribus separatis adhibeantur, caute in hac re procedendum est, et colloquia de hac re, sicut de aliis, promovenda.

[26] Schema n. 75, *De Calendario*, 4 (10 April 1965), p. 2: *Ad formularia harum dominicarum quod attinet, haec questio pendet tum a coetu 11 (de lectionibus in Missa) tum a coetu 14 (de cantibus in Missa).*" [Concerning the formularies of these Sundays, this question rests partly with *Coetus* 11 (concerning the readings at Mass), partly with *Coetus* 14 (concerning the chants at Mass)].

It seems entirely possible that the majority of the *Coetus* 1 consultors did not realize what the suppression of Septuagesima would entail for the formularies inasmuch as Question 15 asks them to choose from among three possibilities and each possibility stipulates a specific disposition of the formularies. Four members stated that they thought the formularies should remain in place. It seems reasonable to read these votes, on the one hand, as favoring the suppression of (or, in the case of Van Doren, a perhaps reluctant willingness to accede to the suppression of) the penitential aspects of Septuagesima and, on the other, as favoring the preservation of the preparatory elements, for the formularies provide preparation.

Martimort's statement that the formularies were the responsibilities of other *coetus* is part of the official record, and his response appears in the schema in the order related above. That is, it seems that Jounel and Amore explicitly stated their preferences for the disposition of the formularies and Schmidt and Dirks selected options that stipulated particular dispositions of the formularies after Martimort stated, in effect, that *Coetus* 1 had no authority to determine the future use of the formularies. There is no indication that anyone heeded Martimort or asked why, if the members of the *Coetus* 1 had no say in the disposition of the formularies, the possibilities from which they had been asked to choose specified particular dispositions that each consultor, it seems reasonable to suppose, took into account when answering the question.

As it turned out, Martimort was right. The formularies did not fall within the mandate given to *Coetus* 1; the responsibility of deciding what texts would be used on specific days belonged to other groups. For their part, the various groups responsible for assigning formularies were obliged to make the assignments within the parameters of the new calendar that *Coetus* 1 configured. And the new calendar did not designate a pre-Lent period. That is, the calendar *coetus*, most of whose consultors said they wanted the Septuagesima formularies retained, failed to provide the necessary apparatus, so to speak, for the *coetus* responsible for formularies to retain them. There is no niche in the calendar in which to place preparatory texts so that they would be used every year immediately before Lent. This subject is revisited below.

The seventh schema of *Coetus* 1 bears the title "On the revision of the General Calendar." Its treatment of proper seasons[27] is divided into eight sections. The third of these, entitled "from the time after Epiphany until Lent," devotes a paragraph to Septuagesima. It reads:

> The time of Septuagesima, as a penitential season, is suppressed, with the question of using the present existing formularies more advantageously remaining untouched. – A desire was made manifest by several of the Fathers that, the penitential character of this season having been

---

[27] *Proprium de Tempore.*

suppressed, [its] character as preparatory for Lent be preserved in these three Sundays.[28]

Here it is certain *Consilium* members [the Fathers], the body largely consisting of bishops, not the members of *Coetus* 1, who want the three weeks immediately preceding Lent to prepare for it.

In his *The Reform of the Liturgy*, Annibale Bugnini writes: "Septuagesima loses its penitential character ... but by and large the present texts will continue in use"[29] and attaches the following footnote:

> There was disagreement on the suppression of the Septuagesima season. Some saw these weeks as a step toward Easter. On one occasion Pope Paul VI compared the complex [make] up, Septuagesima, Lent, Holy Week and Easter Triduum to the bells calling people to Sunday Mass. The ringing of them an hour, a half-hour, fifteen and five minutes before the time of Mass has a psychological effect and prepares the faithful materially and spiritually for the celebration of the liturgy. Then, however, the view prevailed that there should be a simplification: it was not possible to restore Lent to its full importance without sacrificing Septuagesima, which is an extension of Lent.[30]

Whereas Bugnini's focus in the body of his text is on the penitential character of Septuagesima, the focus of his footnote is on its preparatory character. On this account his final comment that it was not deemed possible to restore Lent to its full importance without sacrificing Septuagesima is unpersuasive. A period of preparation necessarily heightens, not diminishes, the importance of whatever event is being prepared for. In addition, preparation generally assures a fuller or better participation in the event itself. The present arrangement in which the faithful move from a *per annum* Tuesday to Ash Wednesday with no liturgical anticipation or preparation whatsoever is, to use Pope Paul's analogy, rather like ringing the church bells to signal Mass only at the moment the priest enters the sanctuary.

Bugnini errs when he writes "by and large the present texts will continue in use." They did not and, as we have stated, no niche in the calendar was provided for them to be used in the weeks immediately prior to Lent.[31]

---

[28] Schema n. 132, *De Calendario*, 7 (3 December 1965), p. 3: "*Tempus Septuagesimae, ut tempus penitentiale, supprimitur, intacta manente quaestione de formulariis nunc existantibus opportunius adhibendis. – A nonnullis Patribus manifestatum est desiderium ut, suppresso charactere paenitentiale huius temporis, servetur his tribus dominicis character praeparatorius ad Quadragesimam.*"

[29] Bugnini, *The Reform of the Liturgy*, 307.

[30] Bugnini, *The Reform of the Liturgy*, 307, n. 6.

[31] Even the Italian edition of Bugnini's book [*La riforma liturgica, 1948–1975* (Roma: CLV-Edizioni liturgiche, 1983] appeared after the promulgation of the new liturgical books. His statement seems to reflect an earlier expectation that Bugnini failed to correct when the Septuagesima formularies were not included in the revised missal.

Since the term formularies refers to all the proper texts used in the Mass and Offices of the season, a fairly significant number of texts are involved. In the missal, the Septuagesima formularies are the proper Mass prayers, antiphons, scripture lessons, and intervenient chants for the three Sundays.[32] The breviary formularies include all the lessons and responses for Matins, each day in the season having its own set, and the Septuagesima Mass collects which are also used at Office hours. None of this has been preserved intact so that any particular cluster, or even pair, of texts appears together in the revised missal or Office books.

Comparison of the pre- and post-Vatican II missals shows that only one of the nine proper Mass prayers of the three Septuagesima Sundays appears in the post-Vatican II missal. The postcommunion of Sexagesima serves as the postcommunion of Week I *per annum*.[33] None of the scripture lessons of 1962 Septuagesima Masses appears on any day that can fall during the three weeks immediately preceding Lent in any given year.

The collects, our interest, were the responsibility of *Coetus* 18*bis*. The first schema of *Coetus* 18*bis* that proposes a set of Mass orations for the entire liturgical year is dated 19 September 1966,[34] nine months after the decision to suppress Septuagesima had been made. The schema does not mention Septuagesima, but presents eight *post Epiphaniam* Sundays prior to the first Sunday of Lent.[35] None of the collects listed is from the season

---

[32] The Sunday Mass was repeated on the ferial days of the week following.

[33] It is impossible for the first week *per annum* to fall in the three weeks prior to Ash Wednesday, which means the prayer continues in use in another liturgical context.

There is a second prayer that continues in use to some extent, but this one in a different form as well as a different context. The first clause of the secret of Quinquagesima (also the 1962 secret of the third Sunday after the Epiphany) was pressed into service in what seems to be a newly composed secret for the Sunday II of Lent in the post-Vatican II missal. Compare:

1962: Secret, Sexagesima and Sunday III after the Epiphany	1970/2002: Secret, Sunday II in Lent
Haec hostia, Domine, quaesumus, emundet nostra delicta: *et ad sacrificium celebrandum, subditorum tibi* corpora, mentesque sanctificet.	Haec hostia, Domine, quaesumus, emundet nostra delicta, *et ad celebranda festa paschalia fidelium tuorum* corpora mentesque sanctificet.
May this host/victim/sacrifice/offering, we beseech you, O Lord, cleanse our offenses: and sanctify, *for the purpose of celebrating the sacrifice, the minds and bodies of those subject to you.*	May this host/victim/sacrifice/offering, we beseech you, O Lord, cleanse our offenses: and sanctify, *for the purpose of celebrating the paschal feast,* the minds and bodies of *[your] faithful.*

The revisers substitute *fidelium tuorum* for *subditorum tibi* and *festa paschalia* for *sacrificium*. The latter change moves the focus from the Mass being celebrated in the present to the future celebration of the Pasch. The former describes those who pray as "faithful," rather than as subject to the Lord.

This is the third instance in which we find that the revisers removed a form of the word [subject] from a prayer selected for use in the new missal. See pp. 79, 81, 83–5, 93, and p. 85, n. 57.

[34] Schema n. 186, *De Missali* 27 (September 19, 1966), pp. 17–20.

[35] Sometime later a decision was made to forsake the terms *"post Epiphaniam"* and *"post Pentecosten"* and use the *"per annum"* for both. The post-Vatican II reformers did not introduce the

of Septuagesima in the pre-Vatican missal and no reason why is given in the *Coetus* notes.

The Collects of Septuagesima

We proceed to a consideration of the three Septuagesima collects.[36]

Sunday in Septuagesima

Preces populi tui, quaesumus, Domine, clementer exaudi: ut qui juste pro peccatis nostris affligimur pro tui nominis gloria misericorditer liberemur.	The prayers of your people, we beseech you, O Lord, graciously hear, that we who are justly afflicted on account of our sins may for the sake of the glory of your name be mercifully freed.[37]

Manuscript History

The oration appears in codices dating from the eighth through the sixteenth century when it was incorporated without change into Tridentine missal for use on this Sunday. In early Mass books it serves as either the collect or *super populum* of Septuagesima.[38] In the 1962 missal the oration also serves as the collect following the fourth lesson of Ember Saturday in Lent and has everything but the last clause in common with the collect following the fourth lesson of Ember Saturday in Advent.[39]

---

term "*per annum*" into the liturgical books, but they did put it to an entirely new use. "*Per annum*" is found in pre-Vatican Office books, not missals, where it always designates prayers, antiphons or hymns that are used during more than one proper season. That is, prior to the post-Vatican II reforms, "*per annum*" was a collective term used to refer to more than one season, each of which had its own proper name. There were no weeks "*per annum*," but only "*per annum*" texts.

Further, all the proper names designating periods of time in the pre-Vatican II calendar identify the seasons of the Church year with the mysteries of salvation (or the feasts which celebrate the mysteries) either by looking forward to them, as in the case of Advent, Septuagesima, and Quadragesima (Lent), or recalling them, as in the seasons of the Nativity, after Epiphany, Paschaltide, and after Pentecost. The new *per annum* nomenclature abandons this custom.

[36] Again, each is prayed on the Sunday and on the ferial days of the week following.

[37] An effort has been made to follow the Latin word order in the English translation. Conventional English word order would dictate something along the line of: Graciously hear the prayers of your people, we beseech you, O Lord, that we who are justly afflicted for our sins may be mercifully freed for the sake of the glory of your name,

[38] CO VII, 4633A.

[39] "Preces populi tui, quaesumus, Domine, clementer exaudi: ut, qui iuste pro peccatis nostris affligimur, *pietatis tuae visitatione consolemur.* [The prayers of your people, we beseech you,

Text

Three aspects of the text are discussed below: (1) the rhetorical reversal of
the first line; (2) the word "*affligimur*," and (3) the *ut* clause.

The first word of the collect is the direct object of the imperative verb
which, however, appears at the end of the clause. As we saw in our consideration of the Advent collects,[40] this is not standard Latin word order but a
rhetorical device that puts special emphasis on both the verb and its object.
We blurt the word *prayers* first in our urgency that God *hear* them, and slip
in the adverb graciously/mercifully [*clementer*] just before the imperative
to soften what would otherwise be an impatient demand and to satisfy the
requirements of courtesy.

In her vocabulary notes on this prayer, Sister Mary Gonzaga Haessly
writes of the word *affligimur* [we are afflicted]:[41]

By whom or by what are we afflicted or distressed? 1) By God, with
punishment, in accordance with the measure of our sins; 2) by sin, with

---

O Lord, graciously hear, that we who are justly afflicted may be consoled by a visitation of
your mercy].

[40] See pp. 50–1 above.

[41] Use of the verb "*affligo*" (to afflict) in the the proper Mass prayers differs in the pre-
and post-Vatican II missals. The entry on page 21 of André Pflieger, *Liturgicae Orationis
Concordantia Verbalia* (Roma: Herder, 1964) presents three different ways in which the verb
is used in the pre-Vatican II missal: 1) in two Lenten collects the faithful describe themselves
as afflicting their flesh through abstinence (Monday after Sunday II and Saturday after Sunday
III); 2) collects assigned to Ember and Lenten days describe the faithful as being afflicted by
their sins (Or. 5 of Ember Saturday in Advent, Or. 4 of Ember Saturday in Lent), by the deserts
of their own actions (Sunday IV in Lent), and by their constant excesses (Wednesday in Holy
Week); 3) one votive postcommunion states that the Lord does not permit those who hope in
him to be afflicted beyond measure (*Missa pro gratiarum actione*).

Thaddäus Schnitker and Wolfgang Slaby, (eds), *Concordantia Verbalia Missalis Romani:
Partes Euchologicae*, (Münster: Aschendorff, 1983) 94, lists five prayers in which the verb
appears in the post-Vatican II missal but only two of these are proper Mass orations (the
others are two samples, *specimina*, of universal prayers, also called "General Intercessions" or
"Prayers of the Faithful," and one a blessing at the end of a Nuptial Mass). One of the two
proper Mass orations is the postcommunion to be used at Mass celebrated at the beginning of
the civil year. It asks that God's people not be afflicted by any dangers throughout the course of
that year. The other, a collect of a votive Mass for those who afflict us (*pro variis necessitatibus*
45), asks that we may extend sincere love to them.

The new missal has no proper Mass oration in which the faithful are described as "afflicted"
either by sin or by penance. Further, the verb does not appear in an oration of any Mass that
belongs to the annual cycle of feasts and seasons, but rather only in Masses for special needs. If
we extend our considerations to the noun *afflictio*, Schnitker and Slaby, 94, list six uses of the
word: three are in introit antiphons, one in a sample general intercession, and the remaining
two are collects of Masses for special needs: for those detained in prison (*Pro detentis in
carcere*) and in whatever need (*In quacumque necessitate*, collect B). The first of these asks that
God's imprisoned servants may be raised up (or supported, *subleventur*) through patience and
hope; the second that God might look mercifully upon our affliction. In context, the affliction
is the need that occasioned the use of this particular Mass.

the consequences of sin: remorse, distress, misery, etc.; our sins are our punishers ...[42]

The collect's *ut* clause consists of two parallel prepositional phrases which are divided by a verb and placed between two adverbs; there is a second verb at the end.[43] The parallelism is displayed in the following typographical arrangement:

ut qui	juste	pro peccatis nostris		affligimur
that we who	justly	for the sake of our sins		are afflicted
		pro tui nominis gloria	misericorditer	liberemur
		for the glory of your name	mercifully	may be freed

The verbs *affligimur* and *liberemur* are parallel in grammatical form and placement, but antithetical in meaning. The two prepositional phrases *pro peccatis nostris* and *pro tui nominis gloria* are also antithetically parallel: the first, our sins, lies in the past, belongs to us alone, and afflicts us in ways we cannot of ourselves escape; the second, the glory of God's name, lies in our future, is God's alone, and by appeal to it we beg from God a freedom only he can bestow.

The word *juste* is out of place both grammatically and structurally. Grammatically, because its position suggests it governs both *affligimur* and *liberemur* which cannot be the case: our affliction is just, but deliverance is not owed to us. Structurally, because *juste* like *misericorditer* is an adverb. If it had been placed immediately before its verb, *affligimur*, the two clauses would be perfectly parallel. The irregular placement of *juste* forms a chiasmus, **juste** *pro peccatis nostris* ... *pro tui nominis gloria* **misericorditer**, throwing "into relief the contrasted notions, 'justice' and 'mercy': 'we suffer *justly*; may we be *mercifully* delivered.'"[44]

Sunday in Sexagesima

Deus, qui conspicis, quia ex nulla nostra actione confidimus: concede propitius; ut, contra adversa omnia, Doctoris gentium protectione muniamur.	O God, who see that we trust in no deed of our own: mercifully grant that we may be defended against all hostile forces by the protection of the Doctor of the Gentiles.

---

[42] Haessly, *Rhetoric in the Sunday Collects of the Roman Missal*, 131–2.
[43] The discussion which follows both draws from and adapts the observations of Haessly, *Rhetoric in the Sunday Collects of the Roman Missal*, 42–3.
[44] Haessly, *Rhetoric in the Sunday Collects of the Roman Missal*, 42.

Manuscript Tradition

This oration appears in 45 codices dating from the eighth to the sixteenth centuries when it was incorporated into the Tridentine missals. Its only use is as the collect of Sexagesima.[45]

Text

Four aspects of the text are discussed below: (1) the reference to Saint Paul, (2) the *qui* clause, (3) the petition, (4) the thematic unity of the collect, the Station church, and the scripture lessons of the Mass.

First, the doctor of the Gentiles is Saint Paul[46] whom the Mass features prominently, perhaps because the Roman Station church of the day is the patriarchal basilica of Saint Paul Outside the Walls.[47] No other Sunday collect in the 1962 missal mentions a saint.

Second, the *qui* clause of the opening address obliquely praises God's omniscience in relation to our awareness of our own impotence. To paraphrase supplying a gloss that makes the implications explicit: "O God, you see all things and therefore see that we put no trust in any deed which we do of ourselves alone – that is, without the help of your grace." Trust in our own action here does not refer to the ability to act, *per se*, but the ability to do anything, unsupported by divine grace, that advances us to salvation or, conversely, the ability to stave off powers hostile to the health of our souls without heavenly protection.

Third, the petition: awareness of our own impotence prompts us to ask God in his mercy to afford us defense against all that is hostile through Saint Paul's protection. The statements of both the first and second clauses of the prayer are general and, therefore, all-embracing. As such they invite each member of the faithful to beg for what he understands himself to need and, at the same time, to have confidence because it simply is not possible for a single need to escape God's all-seeing eyes.

Fourth, the collect, Station, and the Mass lessons are thematically coordinated. The final verb of the collect echoes the name of the Station church, for the petition can also be translated "mercifully grant that we may be walled round against all hostile forces by the protection of the Doctor of the Gentiles." The *extra moenia* [outside the walls] of the basilica's name finds its antithetical counterpart in the *muniamur* [may we be walled round *or* may a wall be built around us] of the collect.[48]

---

[45] CO II, 1496.

[46] Cf. 1 Timothy 2.7: For this I was appointed a preacher and apostle (I am telling the truth, I am not lying), a teacher of the Gentiles in faith and truth.

[47] "*Statio ad S. Paulum*," otherwise called the "*Basilica Sancti Pauli extra moenia.*"

[48] The secret prayer of the same Mass continues the theme: *Oblatum tibi, Domine, sacrificium, vivificet nos semper et muniat.* [May the sacrifice which has been offered to you, O Lord, us give us life always and build a wall around us (*or* defend us as with a wall).]

But the deepest correspondence between the collect and Station is not the appropriation of the church's name in the petition of the prayer, but between the theology and spirituality of Saint Paul and that of the collect.

The Epistle lesson of the Mass, 2 Corinthians 11.19–12.9, presents Saint Paul to the faithful as a model, cause of hope, and heavenly patron and protector. The text is the saint's own description of the adversities he suffered which culminates in the confession that he was brought through them all by the grace of Christ. Indeed, just before closing Paul repeats the words that Christ spoke to him – words which explain that weakness is not an impediment to the Lord's power but the best ground, if not the necessary pre-condition, for its most perfect exercise: "*Sufficit tibi gratia mea: nam virtus in infirmitate perficitur.*"[49] This truth in turn offers hope to needy souls who recognize themselves in the poor or unpromising soil of the Gospel *pericope* of the same Mass: the parable of the sower of Luke 8.4–15. These connections are not belabored in the wording of the texts but become apparent, as might many others besides, though patient reading and consideration.

The method of the collect and its delicacy are noteworthy. The oration does not repeat the words of Saint Paul or paraphrase the scriptural text. Rather, the collect has put on the mind of Saint Paul, expressing with him the truth that the grace of Christ and its power are all that matters. Thus the collect imparts Paul's spiritual attitude to the faithful who sincerely pray "we trust in no deed of our own" and beg from God the protection that they therefore need.

Sunday in Quinquagesima

Preces nostras, quaesumus Domine, clementer exaudi: atque, a peccatorum vinculis absolutos, ab omni nos adversitate custodi.	Our prayers, we beseech you, O Lord, mercifully hear: and, when we have been freed from the fetters of our sins, protect us from every misfortune.

While the connection between the name of the Station church and the vocabulary of the orations is clear in the text, it must be stated that forms of the verb *munio* are commonly found in collects, secrets, and postcommunions, as well as in other Mass prayers whether of Sundays, ferials, feasts of saints or votive Masses. A search for the verb confined to Sunday Mass propers found *muniamur* in the 1962 collects for the second Sunday of Lent and Trinity Sunday and *muniat* in the 1962 secret for the Sunday within the octave of Epiphany as well as the fourth Sunday thereafter. While the first meanings of *munio* found in the Lewis and Short Latin-English Dictionary are "to build a wall around" and "to defend with a wall," the word also means to defend, protect, fortify, guard, shelter, strengthen, and support. It is, therefore, an obvious choice for use in petitions that seek God's protection. [Charlton T. Lewis, *A Latin Dictionary* (Oxford: Clarendon Press, 1879) s.v., p. 1176].

[49] 2 Corinthians 12.9: "My grace is sufficient for you; for my power is made perfect in weakness."

Manuscript Tradition

Like the two preceding, this oration appears in numerous codices dating from the eighth through the sixteenth century when it was incorporated into the Tridentine missal. In 38 of 41 pre-Trent missals, it serves as the collect of Quinquagesima.[50]

Text

Four aspects of the text are discussed below: (1) the rhetorical reversal of the initial clause, (2) the imperative verb of the second clause, (3) the word "*vincula*," (4) the word order of the final clause.

First, the initial clause of the collect employs the same rhetorical reversal as the collect for Septuagesima Sunday. The imperative verb is placed last and its direct object first, an arrangement that increases the emphasis on both words and conveys the haste and urgency of those who pray. Here, too, the demand expressed in the imperative is softened by an adverb: "mercifully" or "graciously."

Second, the second clause also contains an imperative verb. It is also placed last, but it is not softened by a deferential adverb. Thus the intensity of the petition, which begs God first to free us from the fetters of sin and then to protect us from every misfortune, rises as the prayer progresses.

Third, *vinculum* is anything by which something is bound: a tie, cord, rope, fetter, and so forth. The plural form, which we have here, refers especially to the fetters of prisoners. Thus the word conveys something more about the nature of sin and its hold on us. This, in connection with the absence of the possessive "our" modifying sins (which, however, is implied in the *nos* which follows), suggests that *vincula peccatorum* refers not only to our personal sins but to all the effects of original sin.[51] It is from the shackles of sin and concupiscence that the petition begs release and, after release, protection from any further danger or misfortune – by which we can understand both further entanglement in sin and adversity of other sorts. An explanation follows.

Lastly, Haessly tells us, the word order of the final clause is rhetorically significant. First, the *absolutos* is emphatic, both because it precedes *nos* and because it is separated from it. The effect is to include *absolutos* in *custodi*. "We ask God first to loosen the bonds of sin; it is only when we have been freed from sin that we may ask to be guarded against '*omni*

---

[50] CO VII, 4614. In addition to the collect of Quinquagesima, the oration appears as the collect of Saturday in Quinquagesima (or Saturday after Wednesday), the *super populum* of Sunday after the Octave of Pentecost, and a collect of "another daily Mass" [alia Missa cottidiana].

[51] Cf. Haessely, *Rhetoric in the Sunday Collects of the Roman Missal*, 44.

adversitate.'"[52] Second, the separation of *omni* from *adversitate* emphasizes *omni*: "... every kind of adversity and every kind of evil. But *omnis* ... often means (all) 'the rest', that is, everything beside sin."[53] This leads Haessly to offer two translations of the last line: "shield us from every kind of adversity" and "shield us from every other kind of adversity."[54]

As already noted, none of the collects of Septuagesima was included in the revised missal. Since the season itself was suppressed and, in the new arrangement of the calendar, the collects that are used on the last three Sundays before Ash Wednesday change from year to year according to the date of the Pasch, it is not possible to compare the Septuagesima collects to those which were chosen to replace them, for none were.

Conclusion

The three collects of Septuagesima share common themes: all express a consciousness of either sin and its effects (affliction, bondage) or our radical impotence ("no trust in our own deeds"), and all seek freedom from sin and/or protection from danger. As such they prepare the faithful to enter into the asceticisms of Lent conscious that the source of our afflictions is sin and that freedom from sin and protection from danger come only from the Lord. Awareness of these truths leads one not to trust in one's own deeds (including one's ascetical exercises) but in the grace of Christ.

In 2001 André Rose, a member of the *Consilium Coetus* 18*bis*, participated in a liturgical conference held at Fontgombault Abbey in France. In a paper entitled "The Problems of the Liturgical Reform" which he presented there and subsequently published, Rose says:

> Why do away with the pre-Lenten (Septuagesima) season? Because of this, the faithful find themselves, as it were, "parachuted" straight into Lent on Ash Wednesday with no preparation whatever. Yet we ought to be prepared for this. By all means, we could have made a new adaptation of this season, but why do away with it?[55]

The answer to Rose's question is sadly ironic. The records of *Coetus* 1 tell us that Septuagesima was suppressed for the sake of the faithful: "the penitential character of the time of Septuagesima or pre-Lent is difficult for

---

[52] Haessly, *Rhetoric in the Sunday Collects of the Roman Missal*, 45.
[53] Haessly, *Rhetoric in the Sunday Collects of the Roman Missal*, 46.
[54] Haessly, *Rhetoric in the Sunday Collects of the Roman Missal*, 46.
[55] Alcuin Reid, ed., *Looking Again at the Question of the Liturgy with Cardinal Ratzinger* (Farnborough: Saint Michael's Abbey Press, 2002) 91.

the faithful to understand without many explanations."[56] Further, Adrian Nocent said suppression of Septuagesima was necessary if the faithful were to see the progress of the liturgical year clearly and not be confused by diverse "anticipations."[57] But Callewaert's historical study shows us that the period of pre-Lenten penitence arose in the first place as an expression of the *devotion* of the faithful.[58]

This is key. Lent is a time of *obligatory* penance and fasting. Septuagesima, on the other hand, is a short season during which the devotion of the faithful impels them to prepare mentally, physically, and spiritually for Lent. Since the sixth century, the Church has encouraged and assisted the faithful in this preparation by appointing special Masses and Offices for this season and using a numeric nomenclature that marks off the time remaining until both Lent (in Latin, *Quadragesima* or 40) and the Pasch.

Most of the consultors assigned to the Calendar *coetus* seemed to have been of two minds about Septuagesima. Most voted to suppress the penitential elements, and most voted to preserve the formularies. While everything attached to the pre-Vatican observance of Septuagesima, the use of purple, the suppression of the *Alleluia* and *Gloria*, the names of the Sundays, and the formularies, are all integral parts of the pre-Lenten preparation that takes place during the season, there is a way in which the formularies are purely and only preparatory. The votes to retain the formularies, then, seem to have been votes to retain some kind of liturgical preparation for Lent. And, indeed, the *coetus* schemata witness to a continuing desire to preserve a period of pre-Lenten preparation.

The Calendar *coetus*, however, had no jurisdiction over formularies. When they failed to design a calendar in which Lent would be preceded every year by the same liturgical weeks, however these might be designated, they effectively closed the possibility of preparatory formularies being included in the new missal because they provided no place to put them.

This is unfortunate, for the absence of any liturgical preparation whatsoever for Lent ignores something about human nature that the liturgy had, heretofore, taken into account: the need to be ready. In consequence, even those who attend Mass and pray the Hours daily can find themselves, year after year, surprised by Lent.

---

[56] Schema n. 75, *De Calendario*, 3 (10 April 1965) p. 2.

[57] Schema n. 65, *De Calendario*, 2 (15 March 1965) p. 13.

[58] Camille Callewaert, "L'oeuvre liturgique de s. Grégoire La Septuagésime et l'Alléluia" in *Sacris Erudiri*, Fragmenta Liturgica Collecta a Monachis Sancti Petri de Aldenbruggo in Steenbrugge ne Pereant (The Hague: Steenbrugis) 647–8.

6

Lent

In the study of the Vatican II liturgical reform, the season of Lent presents a unique case for three reasons. First, it is the only proper season for which the Fathers of the Second Vatican Council may seem to have sanctioned a revision of the formularies.[1] Second, shortly after the close of the Council, Pope Paul VI relaxed the Lenten obligation when he modified the Church's laws governing fasting and abstinence – that is, as the revisers were working on the new corpus of Lenten liturgical texts, the disciplines the faithful were required to observe during Lent changed. Third, Lent is the only proper season that begins on a ferial day although, as we saw in the last chapter, this has not always been the case.[2]

This chapter has four parts. An introduction presents a brief history of Lent and the theological and spiritual principles upon which Lenten observance rests. The second discusses the specific nature of Lent and Lenten observance as these are presented in two documents: Vatican II's *Sacrosanctum Concilium* and Pope Paul VI's Apostolic Constitution *Paenitemini*. The third considers relevant schemata of Consilium *Coetus* 1 and *Coetus* 18*bis*. The fourth examines the Lenten Sunday collects of the pre- and post-Vatican II missals. Because it is the first day of Lent, we begin with a consideration of the collects assigned to Ash Wednesday in the two missals.

Introduction

Brief History of Lent

The season of Lent developed from an earlier pre-Paschal fast and reached its present duration of 40 days, exclusive of Sundays, in conscious imitation of the Lord's 40-day fast in the desert.[3]

---

[1] *Sacrosanctum Concilium* 109 directs that Lent's "two-fold character" be given greater prominence in the liturgy.

[2] See p. 95–6, n. 4.

[3] Thomas J. Talley, *The Origins of the Liturgical Year* (New York: Pueblo, 1986) 189–94.

This development took place in stages. From the fourth century until the first years of the seventh, Lent in the West was an uninterrupted period of 40 days of which only 36 were actually fasted.[4] While Sundays were not fasted, they were not without their ascetisms, for the obligation to conjugal continence, as well as to mortification of evil inclinations, generosity in pardoning injuries and reconciling enemies, works of piety and charity, and the more intense practice of humility, almsgiving, and fervent prayer bound the faithful on every day of Lent.[5]

The character of Lent changed over the course of centuries in response to changes in sacramental practice. In the fourth century, when there was a great number of adult converts to Christianity, Lent was an intense time of preparation for Baptism. Later, when infant Baptism became the normal way of initiating Christians, reconciliation of penitents became the principal focus of Lent. When sinners ceased to be reconciled publicly, Lent became a time of repentance, conversion, and penitence for all. But even when Lent was a time of preparation for Baptism and public penitence, the whole body of Christian faithful participated in Lenten observance because, as Thomas Talley puts it: "the redemption not of some but of all ... is at hand in the death and resurrection of the Lord."[6]

During the seventh century, the beginning of the fast was moved back to Wednesday in Quinquagesima in order that the number of days fasted would, like the Lord's own desert fast, be 40.[7] The practice of signing the

---

[4] John Cassian, *Conferences*, 21.25, and Saint Gregory, *Homil.*, xvi, *In Evang.* cited in F. Cabrol, "Caput Jejunii," *DACL* vol. 2.2 (Paris: Letouzey et Ané, 1913–53), col. 2134. Cassian, a fifth-century monk, and Pope Saint Gregory, who died in 605, gave spiritual meaning to the 36 fast days by calling them "a tithe of the year."

[5] Camille Callewaert, "La Durée et le Charactère du Carême Ancien," in *Sacris Erudiri*, Fragmenta Liturgica Collecta a Monachis Sancti Petri de Aldenbruggo in Steenbrugge ne Pereant (The Hague: Steenbrugis) 462–81, describes Lenten ascesis in various regions of the West during the fifth and sixth centuries on the basis of his examination of extant episcopal sermons of the period.

[6] Talley, *The Origins of the Liturgical Year*, 224. The information in this paragraph summarizes Talley's presentation, 222–25.

[7] When precisely it became widespread in the West to begin Lent, or more accurately to begin the fast, on Wednesday of Quinquagesima is a matter of some disagreement, but some time in the seventh century seems the most likely. Maximus of Turin reports the practice already in the fifth century – but this may be an isolated instance (Talley, *The Origins of the Liturgical Year*, 222). Amalarius, the ninth-century liturgical writer, claimed that beginning the fast on the Wednesday began in the seventh century and his view prevailed for about nine centuries (Talley, *The Origins of the Liturgical Year*, 222 and Cabrol, "Caput Jejunii," *DACL* vol. 2.2, col. 2134). Tommasi, writing in the early eighteenth century, argued that the practice dated from before Pope Gregory the Great on the basis of liturgical texts (Talley, *The Origins of the Liturgical Year*, 222), but see the excerpt of Gregory's Lenten sermon in Cabrol, "Caput Jejunii," col. 2134 and Cabrol on Tomassi in col. 2135. Others assign the practice to some time after Gregory (Cabrol, "Caput Jejunii," *DACL* vol. 2.2, col. 2134).

faithful with ashes, however, is not known before the eleventh century – and the name "Ash Wednesday" is later still.[8]

Theology and Spirituality of Lent

Integral to the traditional theology and spirituality of Lent, and of Christian ascesis more generally, is an understanding of the intimate relationship between body and soul in human beings who are composite creatures – who are incarnate spirits.

It is not simply that corporeal ascesis is one of the ways in which Christians have traditionally expressed their repentance and sought to atone for their own sins and those of others. It is also, and more importantly, that Christians recognize that freedom *for* God increases as one becomes more free *from* the demands of the body and the pull of worldly attractions.

The body is good, not evil. As a result of the Fall, the body is inclined to rebel against right reason and reason itself has been radically weakened in its natural powers. One of the fruits of physical ascesis undertaken with the proper dispositions is that, by God's grace, reason gains greater control over the body. Another, again by God's grace, is that in gaining greater mastery over physical urges we also grow in our ability to control interior inclinations to vice – to anger, pride, and so forth. Lastly physical asceticisms such as fasting cause us to experience our human weakness more intensely and this, by God's grace, makes us more open to God and more reliant upon his grace.

Catholic observance of Lent, then, is founded on the imitation of Christ's desert fast and thoroughly informed by an understanding of human nature that recognizes an intimate connection between body and soul.

The Nature of Lent and Lenten Observance

Sacrosanctum Concilium nn. 109–10

Paragraph n. 109 of the *Constitution on the Sacred Liturgy* states:

> The season of Lent has a twofold character: it disposes – especially through remembrance of, or preparation for, Baptism and through penance – the faithful who more diligently listen to the word of God and devote themselves to prayer to celebrate the Paschal Mystery. This

---

[8] Talley, *The Origins of the Liturgical Year*, 223–4.

two-fold character is to be placed in a clearer light in both the liturgy and in liturgical catechesis. Hence:

a) the baptismal elements proper to Lenten liturgy are to be used more abundantly; indeed, certain elements from an earlier tradition may be restored, as circumstances warrant.

b) the same may be said about the penitential elements. And with respect to catechesis, along with the social consequences of sin, the following are to be impressed upon the minds of the faithful: that the proper nature of penance is hatred of sin as it is an offense against God; that the Church's function in penitential acts is not to be neglected; and the necessity of prayer on behalf of sinners is to be urged.[9]

One of the elements of Lent's two-fold character is identified or defined as "remembrance of, or preparation for, Baptism." The "preparation for Baptism" aspect returns emphasis to what it was in antiquity before infant Baptism became the norm. But, while the new Rite of Christian Initiation of Adults gives renewed prominence to Lent as a time of intense preparation for Baptism, sacramental practice is not changed as a result of the Council. Infant Baptism remains the most usual way of making new Catholics.

In stating that the alternative, "remembrance of Baptism," belongs to the character of Lent, the Fathers of Vatican II seem to have charted a new direction in the theology and spirituality of the season for remembrance of Baptism is not mentioned in the standard histories of Lent.[10]

Sacrosanctum Concilium n. 109 envisions two types of revisions: those made to highlight Baptism and those made to highlight penance. The next paragraph, *Sacrosanctum Concilium* n. 110, describes the penance that befits this season:

Penance during the Lenten season ought to be not only interior and individual, but also exterior and social. Indeed, penitential practice should be fostered according to the possibilities as well as the conditions

---

[9] *Sacrosanctum Concilium* n. 109. Duplex indoles temporis quadragesimalis, quod praesertim per memoriam vel praeparationem Baptismi et per paenitentiam fideles, instantius verbum Dei audientes et orationi vacantes, componit ad celebrandum paschale mysterium, tam in liturgia quam in catechesi liturgica pleniore in luce ponatur. Proinde:

a) elementa baptismalia liturgiae quadragesimalis propria abundantius adhibeantur; quaedam vero ex anteriore traditione, pro opportunitate, restituantur;

b) idem dicatur de elementis paenitentialibus. Quoad catechesmi autem animis fidelium inculcetur, una cum consectariis socialibus peccati, illa propria paenitentiae natura quae peccatum, pro ut est offensa Dei, detestatur; nec praetermittantur partes Ecclesiae in actione paenitentiali atque oratio pro peccatoribus urgeatur.

[10] Cf. Camille Callewaert, "La Durée et le Charactère du Carême Ancien," 444–88; Talley, *The Origins of the Liturgical Year*, pp. 27–31, 163–230; E. Vacandard, "Carême," *DACL* vol. 2.2 (Paris: Letouzey et Ané, 1913–53), col. 2139–58.

of the faithful of our time and of the different regions, and as recommended by the authorities described in article 22.[11]

Nevertheless there will be a sacred Paschal fast, celebrated everywhere on Friday of the Passion and Death of the Lord and, according to suitableness, prolonged through Holy Saturday also, that in this way we may arrive at the joys of the Sunday of the resurrection with an uplifted and receptive spirit.[12]

By 4 December 1963, the date on which *Sacrosanctum Concilium* was promulgated, there was already an expectation that the strict Lenten fast then in force was to be relaxed, for the Council Fathers insist only on a Good Friday fast and, further, anticipate different modes of penance for particular regions.

In part the reason may be found in the preparatory documents, *Acta et Documenta Vaticano II Apparando*.[13] Prior to the Council, dioceses and religious communities around the world had been invited to comment on a number of topics.[14] Those which pertain to Lent include: a) the reform of the discipline of fasting and abstinence,[15] b) the reform of the law of fasting and abstinence,[16] c) the gravity of the obligation,[17] d) the Lenten fast[18] and e) the competence of the bishop to establish the law of abstinence.[19] Analysis of the responses lies outside the scope of this study, but the specifics of the Church's earlier discipline with respect to fasting and

---

[11] Art. 22 mentions first the authority of the Holy See and then that of legitimately established, competent, territorial bodies of Bishops.

[12] *Sacrosanctum Concilium* n. 110: Paenitentia temporis quadragesimalis non tantum sit interna et individualis, sed quoque externa et socialis. Praxis vero paenitentialis, iuxta nostrae aetatis et diversarum regionum possibilitates necnon fidelium condiciones, foveatur, et ab auctoritatibus, de quibus in art. 22, commendetur.

Sacrum tamen esto ieiunium paschale, feria VI in Passione et Morte Domini ubique celebrandum et, iuxta opportunitatem, etiam Sabbato sancto producendum, ut ita, elato et aperto animo, ad gaudia dominicae Resurrectionis perveniatur.

[13] *Acta et Documenta Concilio Oecumenico Vaticano II Apparando*, series 1, appendix volume II: (Typis Polyglottis Vaticanis, 1961), 218–36. A footnote to the Council discussion in which the bishops consider of *Sacrosanctum Concilium* n. 110 refers the reader to the preparatory documents. See *Acta Synodalia Sacrosancti Concilii Oecumenici Vatican* I, vol. 2.2 (Vatican: Typis Polyglottis, 1972) 272, n. 2.

[14] Footnotes identify not individual bishops or persons but the dioceses or religious congregations from which the responses came. Those from religious congregations came through the superiors general. For example *Acta et Documenta Concilio Oecumenico*, 220, n. 8 reads: "Sup. Gen. Congreg. Cister. Italiae, Sup. Gen. O.F.M., Sup. Gen. Inst. Cavanis."

[15] *Acta et Documenta Concilio*, 218–19, nn. 1–7.

[16] *Acta et Documenta Concilio*, 219–30, nn. 1–75. Many of these include suggestions about Lenten observance.

[17] *Acta et Documenta Concilio*, 230–2, nn. 1–12.

[18] *Acta et Documenta Concilio*, 232–4, nn. 1–16.

[19] *Acta et Documenta Concilio*, 234–6, nn. 1–97.

abstinence and the gist of the comments on the above-mentioned topics sent by dioceses and religious communities are relevant.

Prior to the Second Vatican Council, Catholics between the ages of 21 and 60 were required to fast on all the ferial days of Lent, the nine Ember Days that fell outside of Lent, and on the vigils of certain feasts. All Catholics who had attained the age of reason were required to abstain from meat on all the Fridays of the year and the vigils of certain feasts. Further, partial abstinence (that is, taking meat only at the principal meal) was to be observed on the Wednesdays and Saturdays of the four Ember weeks.[20] These obligations bound gravely.

Many responses recorded in the preparatory documents state that the law of fasting and abstinence should be changed so that either it binds lightly or is not law but counsel.[21] With respect to revising the laws pertaining to fasting and abstinence, most suggestions favored relaxing the discipline in some way.[22] While the bishops of Vatican II anticipate different penitential practices in different regions,[23] and this is suggested by some of the responses in the preparatory documents, a greater number of the respondents state that observance should be uniform throughout the whole Church.[24] Many give reasons why reform is desirable: several note that fasts are not being observed, others that the requirements were confusing to the faithful, and two dioceses said it was necessary that the Church's law of fasting be changed so that a greater part of the faithful would be able to observe it.[25] One suggestion reads: "That Lent no longer be called 'time of fasting'; that it be given another name, which better expresses the end of this season."[26]

The Apostolic Constitution Paenitemini[27]

Pope Paul VI modified the Church's laws of fasting and abstinence on 17 February 1966 with the promulgation of the Apostolic Constitution

---

[20] Ember Days were the Wednesday, Friday, and Saturdays of the first week of Lent, the week following Pentecost Sunday, the week following the Feast of the Holy Cross in September, and the week following 13 December. Traditionally Orders were conferred on the Saturdays of Ember weeks.

[21] *Acta et Documenta Concilio*, pp. 230–2, nn. 1–12.

[22] *Acta et Documenta Concilio*, pp. 219–30, nn. 1–75.

[23] See *Sacrosanctum Concilium* n. 110 above.

[24] *Acta et Documenta Concilio*, pp. 234–6, nn. 1–97.

[25] *Acta et Documenta Concilio*, p. 220, n. 5: Ieiunium in communi, ut dicit S. Thomas, cadit sub praecepto legis naturae et haec lex semper urget; legem autem ieiunii ecclesiasticam immutare opportet ut saltem hodie a maiore fidelium parte observari possit. [Fasting in common, as Saint Thomas says, falls under the precept of the natural law and this law always urges; however, it is necessary to change the ecclesiastical law of fasting so that today in any case it can be observed by the greater part of the faithful].

[26] *Acta et Documenta Concilio*, 233, n. 11: Quadragesima ne amplius vocetur "tempus ieiuniorum:" assumatur aliud nomen, melius exprimens huius temporis finem.

[27] *Acta Apostolicae Sedis* 58 (1966) pp. 177–98.

Paenitemini. The new law became effective on 23 February 1966 which, in that year, was Ash Wednesday.

Paenitemini, while asserting that Lent retains its penitential character,[28] reduces the universal days of obligatory fasting to two, Ash Wednesday and Good Friday, and the universal days of obligatory abstinence to Ash Wednesday and the Fridays of Lent.[29] *Paenitemini* also raised the age at which abstinence becomes obligatory to 14.[30] The "substantial observance" of the new regulations pertaining to fasting and abstinence "binds gravely."[31]

Paenitemi is not simply or primarily a document which relaxes the rules. It is a fervent and strongly worded exhortation to the faithful and to all men of good will, inspired by the Church's own self-examination during the Council, to do penance in response to divine law.[32] It spells out in detail what divine law requires and why penance is essential.

Affirming the constant tradition of the Church, the Holy Father teaches that abstinence from meat and fasts from food, accompanied by prayer and almsgiving, are the primary ways of obeying the divine command to do penance;[33] that our composite nature in which body and spirit are intimately connected requires bodily penance if we are to arrive at the freedom from attraction to things of this world, as well as the freedom from sin, vice, and concupiscence, to which Christians are called;[34] that baptism into Christ, which mystically incorporates a person into his death and resurrection, requires all Christians to offer themselves in sacrifice to God for their own sins and the sins of others – that is, the Christian has a duty to share in Christ's work of expiation.[35] And perhaps most relevant to this study, Pope Paul VI presents all this as part and parcel of the teaching of the Second Vatican Council.[36]

---

[28] *Acta Apostolicae Sedis* 58 (1966) p. 183, II.1.

[29] *Acta Apostolicae Sedis* 58 (1966) pp. 183–4, II.2 and 3.

[30] *Acta Apostolicae Sedis* 58 (1966) p. 184, IV.

[31] *Acta Apostolicae Sedis* 58 (1966) p. 183, II.2: "Eorum substantialis observantia graviter tenet."

[32] *Acta Apostolicae Sedis* 58 (1966), 177.

[33] *Acta Apostolicae Sedis* 58 (1966), 177: Imprimis id Ecclesia cupit significare tres esse modos praecipuos, antiquitus traditos, quibus divino paenitentiae praecepto satisfieri possit: scilicet precationem, ieiunium, opera caritatis, quamvis praesertim abstinentiam a carne et ieiunium tuita sit. [In the first place, the Church desires to signify three chief ways, in accordance with ancient tradition, by which the divine precept of penitence is able to be satisfied: namely prayer, fasting, works of charity, although she has upheld abstinence from meat and fasting especially].

[34] *Acta Apostolicae Sedis* 58 (1966) p. 181.

[35] *Acta Apostolicae Sedis* 58 (1966) p. 180.

[36] In his first sentence Pope Paul VI states that the impetus behind *Paenitemini* derives from the experience of the Church during the Second Vatican Council which had closed approximately two months before the Apostolic Constitution was published. The introduction declares that during the course of the Council, the Church: 1) "placed in a clearer light the

The Consilium *Coetus*

In this section we consider the two questions about Lent that *Coetus* 1 addressed and discuss again the third revision policy governing the work of *Coetus* 18*bis*.[37] Most of the *Coetus* 1 deliberations recounted below took place before the promulgation of *Paenitemini*. The policies that governed the revision work of *Coetus* 18*bis* were approved a little more than seven months after *Paenitemini* appeared.

Coetus 1

Questions 7 and 8 of the first schema of the Calendar *coetus* are about the beginning of Lent and the distribution of ashes. The responses are recorded in the second schema. Question 7 reads:

> Whether Ash Wednesday is to be retained as the beginning of Lent, or whether Ash Wednesday and the three following days are to be suppressed [and] the first Sunday of Lent (or Vespers I of that Sunday) restored as the beginning of Lent?[38]

Rembert Van Doren, whose response is first, does not answer the questions being asked but presents two of his own. The first is what does pastoral zeal require. The second is, given that fasting and abstinence are required on Ash Wednesday, whether pastors would be free to suppress the obligation were Lent not to begin on Ash Wednesday.[39]

Aimé-Georges Martimort votes no to the retention of Ash Wednesday and yes to suppression and transfer of the beginning of Lent to the Sunday but does not stipulate further. Pierre Jounel and Herman Schmidt agree, and further stipulate that Lent should begin after first Vespers of the first Sunday of Lent. Ansgar Dirks agrees in theory, but does not know whether it can

---

duty of sharing the work of Christ himself, and also his work of expiation, to the fulfilling of which all members are divinely called" (p. 177); 2) "became more and more conscious" that her members "stand constantly in need of conversion to God and renewal" (pp. 177–8); 3) "considered more attentively her duty" of exhorting men "to salutary abstinence, by which they may be fortified on all sides, lest sojourning to their heavenly homeland they allow themselves to be fettered by the use of the things of this world" (p. 178). Further, *Paenitemini* has 65 footnotes, 44 of which cite documents of Vatican II (pp. 185–98).

[37] See pp. 12–3, 17 above.

[38] Schema n. 61, *De Calendario*, 2 (12 February 1965) p. 2: Utrum feria IV Cinerum retinenda sit initium Quadragesimae, an suppressis feria IV Cinerum et tribus diebus sequentibus, initium Quadragesimae reponendum sit dominica I in Quadragesima (seu in Iis Vesperis huius dominicae)?

[39] Schema n. 65, *De Calendario*, 2 (15 March 1965) p. 6.

be done because the faithful are accustomed to beginning on the Wednesday before.[40]

Adrian Nocent responds at length:

That the beginning of Lent be restored to the first Sunday of Lent. Not for vain archeologism but for truth. For the beginning of Lent was brought forward to Ash Wednesday so that there might be forty days of fasting from food because fasting from food is not done on Sunday. But in his sermons Saint Leo declares there to be a fast also on Sundays from vices and sins and for cultivating charity towards one's neighbor. Not only the strict sense of fasting from food is seemly for the season of Lent. In our own day, because fasting is more rarely done through privation from food by the faithful or by clerics and religious, or even by monks, it is better, according to the truth, to begin the time of Lent on the first Sunday and to fast according to the true and more profound meaning of the time of Lent.[41]

Coetus 17, De ritibus peculiaribus in anno liturgico [on particular rites in the liturgical year] took part in this discussion inasmuch as the schema records the collective response of the members of Coetus 17 to the same questions. They unanimously favor transferring the start of Lent to Sunday.

Agostino Amore alone disagrees, voting yes for the retention of Ash Wednesday as the beginning of Lent. His reasons are pastoral: "the number of forty days for fasting recommends that the time of Lent begin on Ash Wednesday."[42] He cites Sacrosanctum Concilium paragraphs 4 and 23 in support. The latter reads:

There must be no innovations unless the good of the Church genuinely and certainly requires them; and care must be taken that any new forms adopted should in some way grow organically from forms already existing.[43]

---

[40] All responses Schema n. 65, De Calendario, 2 (15 March 1965) p. 6.

[41] Schema n. 65, De Calendario, 2 (15 March 1965) p. 6: Initium Quadragesimae dominice I in Quadragesima reponendum sit. Non ad vanum archeologiam sed ad veritatem. Etenim ieiunium protrehebatur ad feriam IV Cinerum ut sint dies quadraginta ieiunii ciborum, quia in dominica ieiunium ciborum non fit. Attamen S. Leo in sermonibus suis affirmat ieiunandum esse etiam diebus dominicis a vitiis et peccatis et colendo caritatem erga proximum. Sensus strictus ieiunii ciborum non convenit unice ad tempus Quadragesimae. In diebus nostris, quia rarius privatione cibi ieiunatur a fidelibus et etiam a clericis, religiosis, et etiam monachis, decundum veritatem meius est incipere tempus Quadragesimaea Dominica Ia et ieiunare secundum veram et profundoriem significatione temporis Quadragesimae.

[42] Schema n. 65, De Calendario, 2 (15 March 1965) p. 6: "Rationes pastorales: Numerus dierum pro jejunio suadent ut tempus Quadragesimale incipiat feria IV Cinerum."

[43] Sacrosanctum Concilium, 23.

Amore also mentions paragraph 4 which says: "Lastly, faithfully submitting to tradition, the sacred Council declares that holy Mother Church holds all legitimately recognized Rites to have equal right and dignity; she wishes them to be preserved for the future and fostered in

The second question concerning Lent, Question 8, follows:

> If affirmative with respect to the second part of Question 7, whether ashes are to be imposed after first Vespers of Sunday or on Sunday itself or on the Monday following the first Sunday of Lent?[44]

Amore simply refers the others to his answer to the preceding question. Saturday evening is acceptable to Van Doren, Dirks, the members of *Coetus* 17, Nocent and, seemingly Martimort,[45] but not to Jounel who understands Saturday evening to count as Sunday. All except Dirks deem Sunday unfitting because penance is not done on Sunday. Jounel states that the proper day for ashes is Monday. Dirks, *Coetus* 17 and Nocent find Monday an acceptable, but not the only acceptable, choice.[46]

Martimort favors Ash Wednesday for the imposition of ashes, even when Lent begins on the following Sunday, "because custom is stronger than law,"[47] but would allow imposition to be done also on the days following, up to and including Saturday. Schmidt would permit the imposition of ashes from Ash Wednesday up to the second Sunday of Lent, but with the Sunday excluded. Dirks is amenable to particular regions being left to their individual preferences. The only *Coetus* members who confined the blessing and distribution of ashes to a single specific day for the whole Church are Jounel, who deemed Monday the only fitting day, and Amore who voted that Ash Wednesday remain the beginning of Lent.

On 27 April, 1965 the Consilium members voted on the question as worded below:

> Is it pleasing that the time of Lent begin from the first Sunday, authority being left to episcopal conferences to appoint the day of ashes or imposition of ashes, either Monday after Sunday I, or the Wednesday preceding, as now, or another day or several days before Sunday I, so that the days from Ash Wednesday to the first Sunday of Lent may be a time of preparation for Lent.[48]

---

every way, and desires that, where there is need, they [the rites] be prudently and newly revised in the light of sound tradition and given new vigor for today's circumstances and needs."

[44] Schema n. 61, *De Calendario*, 2 (12 February 1965) p. 2: Si affirmative respondetur ad secundum partem Quaestionis 7: Utrum cineres imponendae sint sabbato post Ias Vesperas I dominicae, an ipsa die dominica, an feria II post dominicam Iam?

[45] See below. Martimort includes Saturday but does not specify "after first Vespers."

[46] Schema n. 65, *De Calendario*, 2 (15 March 1965) pp. 7–8.

[47] Schema n. 65, *De Calendario*, 2 (15 March 1965) p. 8: "quia consuetudo fortior est quam leges."

[48] Schema n. 93, *De Calendario*, 5 (10 May 1965) p. 3: Placetne ut tempus Quadragesima a dominica prima incipiat, relicta Conferentiis episcopalibus potestate diem cinerum vel impositionem cinerum indicere aut feria II post dominicam I, aut feria IV praecedenti, sicut nunc,

The members approved the measure with fourteen for, three opposed, and one abstention.[49] Subsequent Consilium reports affirm both parts of the decision: that Lent is to begin on Sunday and liberty is to be given to the episcopal conferences to fix the day or days on which ashes are blessed and distributed.[50]

Annibale Bugnini, discussing the general meeting that took place in April 1965, states that the Consilium members approved the recommendation that:

> [t]he season of Lent begins on the First Sunday of Lent. The imposition of ashes can be done, depending on the judgment of the episcopal conferences, from Ash Wednesday to the Monday after the first Sunday.[51]

In the accompanying footnote, Bugnini adds: "The Pope would eventually have the decisive word on the matter."[52] Ash Wednesday, as history is the witness, was retained as the beginning of Lent.

Coetus 18bis

As we state in Chapter 1, in the Fall of 1966 Placide Bruylants sought approval from the Consilium members for six principles to govern the revision of the orations. Before the members voted, Bruylants explained each request and provided illustrative examples.

Leading up to the question of whether the members wanted, in cases where there were discrepancies, the orations to be accommodated to the rules/customs (*instituta*) of Christian life,[53] Bruylants explained that the 1962 Lenten orations as a whole do not reflect the character of Lent described in *Sacrosanctum Concilium* n. 109 because references to Baptism are almost entirely absent and references to penitence are almost exclusively expressed in the language of fasting:

> For the memory of and preparation for baptism, which according to the Constitution on the Sacred Liturgy (n. 109, a) are the first character

---

aut alia die vel pluribus diebus ante dominicam I, ita ut dies a feria IV cinerum ad dominicam I Quadragesimae sint tempus praeparatorium ad Quadragesimam?

[49] Schema n. 93, *De Calendario*, 5 (10 May 1965) p. 3: "Placet, 11; Placet, servata IV cinerum: 3; Non placet: 3; Nullum (album): 1."

[50] Schema n. 104, *De Anno Liturgico*, 5 (10 May 1965) p. 3; Schema n. 188, *De Calendario*, 11 (22 September 1966) pp. 2–3 and Schema n. 188 addendum, *De Calendario*, 11 (22 September 1966) p. 3. The latter two, which are dated more than six months after the appearance of *Paenitemini*, reiterate that Lent begins on the Sunday, etc., and make no mention of the obligation to fast on Ash Wednesday.

[51] Annibale Bugnini, *The Reform of the Liturgy (1948–1975)* tr. Matthew J. O'Connell (Collegeville: The Liturgical Press, 1990) 307.

[52] Annibale Bugnini, *The Reform of the Liturgy (1948–1975)* 307, n. 7.

[53] Policy III, b.

[*prima indoles*] of this season, are almost entirely absent. With respect to the second character [*secundam indolem*], namely the penitential character, it is evident almost exclusively in the language of fasting and neither the spirit of penance in general nor preparation for the paschal mystery is sufficiently treated.[54]

And so he asks:

Does it please the Fathers ... that, in particular cases [such as those just described], orations may be accommodated to the custom/rules [*institutis*] of Christian life today.[55]

Sacrosanctum Concilium n. 109 describes Lent as having a "*duplex indoles*," a two-fold nature or character. Remembrance of, or preparation for Baptism, and penitence are, as it were, two aspects of a single nature. Bruylants speaks of a first character (*prima indoles*) – memory of, or preparation for, Baptism, and a second character (*secundam indolem*) – the penitenitial character (*characterem ... poenitentialem*). The distinction may be academic, for *Sacrosanctum Concilium* n. 109 itself speaks separately of the baptismal and penitential elements in paragraphs 109a and 109b respectively.

The Fathers of Vatican II called for a revision that brings a) the two-fold character of preparation for, or remembrance of, Baptism and penance into clearer light; b) that makes more abundant use of the baptismal elements proper to Lenten liturgy; and c) "the same ... about the penitential elements." Bruylants informs the members that the 1962 texts do not conform to the stipulations of *Sacrosanctum Concilium* n. 109 – as the Fathers of Vatican II themselves indicate when they call for a revision.

Between the promulgation of *Sacrosanctum Concilium* and Bruylants's meeting with the members, Paul VI's *Paenitemini* appeared and the Church's Lenten regulations were relaxed. It is significant that Bruylants says nothing about *Paenitemini* – that is, he says nothing about accommodating the Lenten orations to *Paenitemini* or to the regulations enacted therein. But the question he put to the members is whether the orations may be accommodated to the "*institutis*" of Christian life today.

---

[54] *De Missale* 27, Schema n. 186 (19 September, 1966) pp. 2–3: "Nam, memoria *et* praeparatio baptismi, quae secundum Constitutionem de sacra Liturgia (n. 109, a) *prima indoles* sunt huius temporis, fere omnino absunt. Quoad *secundam indolem*, characterem nempe poenitentialem, patet quod in orationibus fere unice de ieiunio loquitur et non sufficienter tractatur neque de spiritu poenitentiae in genere, neque de praeparatione mysterii paschalis."

[55] *De Missali* 27, Schemata n. 186 (September 19, 1966) p. 3: "Placetne Patribus ... ut, in casu, accomodentur orationes institutis vitae christianae hodiernae?" This is the third of the six principles.

The Lewis and Short *A Latin Dictionary* defines *institutum* as "purpose, intention, design; an arrangement, plan; mode of life, habits, practices, manners; a regulation, ordinance, institution; instruction; agreement, stipulation."[56] *Instituta* (pl.) is a very broad word which includes both practices or customs and rules or regulations. That is, although not what Bruylants specifically asked for or seemingly intended, the wording of the approved policy permits the revisers to accommodate the Lenten orations to the new Lenten regulations. These, however, stipulate only the indispensable minimum in observance, not the exterior and interior penance which divine precept and the Church enjoin. That is, applying the policy to bring the orations into conformity with a particular understanding of *Sacrosanctum Concilium* is appropriate in a way that accommodating the orations to the regulations enacted in *Paenitemini* is not.

Nevertheless, something of the sort seems to have happened, for Antoine Dumas, in his 1971 essay on the revision principles and their application, under the subheading "The truth of inspiration and of style," states "It suffices to assert that one no longer finds in the orations the mention of fasts that are no longer observed ..."[57]

The Collects

Quantitative Overview

The days of Lent, from Ash Wednesday to Wednesday of Holy Week, number forty-three: six Sundays and thirty-seven ferial days.[58]

The 1962 missal has six Sunday but 45 ferial collects. Nine ferial collects are assigned to the three Ember Days.[59] Wednesday after Sunday IV and Wednesday in Holy Week each have two collects. The other days have one. Since one prayer is assigned to two days,[60] there are forty-four different ferial collects in the pre-Vatican II missals.

The 1970 missal has forty-three Lenten collects, six assigned to Sundays and thirty-seven to ferial days. *Missale Romanum (2002)* adds one collect,

---

[56] Charlton T. Lewis, *A Latin Dictionary* (Oxford: Clarendon Press, 1879) s.v., p. 969.

[57] "Qu'il suffise d'assurer que l'on ne trouve plus, dans les oraisons, mention des jeûnes que ne sont plus observés ..." Antoine Dumas, "Les Oraisons du nouveau Missel Romain," *Liturgiques* 25 (1971): 263–70 at 264. Dumas makes the statement without reference to the Lenten orations.

[58] The overview does not consider the collects assigned to the Triduum.

[59] The arrangement is the same as Advent: two collects are assigned to Ember Wednesday, one to Ember Friday and six to Ember Saturday.

[60] The second collect assigned to Ember Wednesday is the collect for Thursday following Sunday I.

an alternate text that may be used on Friday of the fifth week of Lent.[61] Also, the third typical edition replaces the collect assigned to Saturday of the fifth week of Lent in the first two editions with a different prayer.

Disposition of the 1962 Lenten Collects

Of the six Lenten Sundays collects, only the one assigned to Palm Sunday is retained in the Vatican II missals. It was not revised. The other five 1962 Sunday collects do not appear anywhere in the Vatican II missals. Of the forty-four 1962 ferial collects, three are retained unchanged,[62] nine were edited for inclusion,[63] and thirty-two were omitted from the missal.[64]

Sources of the Vatican II Collects

A more complex picture emerges when we use the Vatican II missal as the point of reference. Of the six Vatican II Sunday collects only one is from the 1962 missal. It was not revised.[65] Three Sunday collects come from other Mass books or liturgical collections. Two of these three prayers were edited. The two remaining collects are new compositions. One takes something

---

[61] Thus the total number of Lenten ferial collects in the third typical edition is 38.

Friday in Passiontide was observed as the feast of the Seven Sorrows of the Blessed Virgin Mary from the fifteenth century in some local churches and by the Church universal from the eighteenth until the post-Vatican II reforms. The new prayer recovers that tradition: Deus, qui Ecclesiae tuae in hoc tempore tribuis benigne, beatam Mariam in passione Christi contemplanda devote imitari, da nobis, quaesumus, eiusdem Virginis intercessione, Unigenito Filio tuo firmius in dies adhaerere et ad plenitudinem gratiae eius demum pervenire. [O God, who in this season kindly give to your Church devoutly to imitate the blessed Mary as she contemplates the passion of Christ, grant us in these days through the intercession of the same Virgin, we beseech you, more firmly to cling to your Son and at last to attain the fulness of his grace]. Maurizio Barba, "Il Temporale, L'« Ordo Missae » e il Santorale del Nuovo « Missale Romanum, »" *Ephemerides Liturgicae* 116 (2002) 320–66 at 329 states that the prayer is a new composition.

[62] The collects assigned to Friday after the fourth Sunday of Lent and to Monday and Tuesday of Holy Week. The first was re-assigned to Monday of the fourth week of Lent, and the latter two retained in place.

[63] The 1962 collects for: Friday after Ash Wednesday; Monday, Tuesday, Wednesday (2nd collect), and Saturday (5th collect) after Sunday I; Friday after Sunday II; Wednesday after Sunday IV; Wednesday after Passion Sunday; Monday of Holy Week. All are assigned to the same days in the Vatican II missals except for the fifth collect of Ember Saturday which is assigned to Thursday after Ash Wednesday.

[64] Not included in the new missal are the 1962 collects assigned to Ash Wednesday and the following Thursday and Saturday; Ember Wednesday (the first collect), Ember Friday, and Ember Saturday (collects 1, 2, 3, 4 and 6); Monday through Thursday and Saturday after the Sunday II; all the ferial days after Sunday III; Monday, Tuesday, Thursday and Saturday after Sunday IV; every day but Wednesday after Sunday I of the Passion; and Wednesday of Holy Week The invocation, but not the petition, of the collect of Monday after Sunday III in Lent is used in the 1970 collect for Friday of the third week in Lent.

[65] The collect of Palm Sunday.

from a Mozarabic *inlatio*; the other combines part of an ancient prayer, words of a Sermon by Saint Leo the Great and newly composed phrases.[66] Only one of the five new Vatican II Lenten Sunday collects serves as Lenten Sunday collect in an earlier codex.[67]

Twenty-two of the 38 ferial collects are taken from the 1962 missal. As we indicate above, twelve of the twenty-two are collects of Lenten Masses, nine of which were edited for inclusion.[68] Four of the 22 appear in the 1962 missal as Lenten prayers, but are not Mass collects.[69] Only one of these was edited.[70] Six are imported from Sundays after the Epiphany or Pentecost; only one of these appears in edited form.[71] The last, the alternate collect assigned to Friday after the fifth Sunday of Lent in the third typical edition, is a new composition. There is no record of any of the post-Epiphany or post-Pentecost collects that the revisers selected ever being used in Lent prior to their appearance of the Vatican II missals.

Nine of the thirty-seven Lenten ferial collects are taken from other Mass books or liturgical collections.[72] Of these, all but one was edited.[73] The third typical edition of the *Missale Romanum* replaces the collect originally assigned to the Saturday of the fifth week of Lent with another ancient prayer which was not edited.

The corpus of Lenten collects in the Vatican II missal is, therefore, materially quite different from the corresponding corpus in the Tridentine missals. Indeed, only four collects appear in the very same form on the same day in the two missals. The new Lenten corpus is also materially very different from that of any other previous missal.

---

[66] The collect of second and fourth Sundays of Lent, respectively.

[67] The collect of the first Sunday of Lent.

[68] The collects of Thursday and Friday after Ash Wednesday; Monday, Tuesday, and Wednesday of the first week of Lent; Friday of the second week, Monday and Wednesday of the fourth week, Wednesday of the fifth week, and Monday, Tuesday and Wednesday of Holy Week. Only the collects of Monday of the fourth week and Tuesday and Wednesday of Holy Week were not edited.

[69] The collect of Ash Wednesday is the 1962 prayer after the imposition of ashes. The 1970/2002 collects of Thursday of the second week and Tuesday of the fifth week are blessings assigned to Wednesday after Sunday II of Lent and Tuesday after Passion Sunday in the 1962 missal. The 1970 collect assigned to Tuesday of the third week of Lent is the postcommunion prayer of Thursday after Sunday II in the earlier missal.

[70] The erstwhile postcommunion prayer that serves as the 1970 collect of Tuesday in the third week of Lent.

[71] The collect of Saturday after Ash Wednesday is that of the 3rd Sunday after the Epiphany. The collects of Thursday of the first week, Tuesday of the second week, Monday of the third week, Saturday of the fourth week, and Friday of the fifth week are the 1962 collects of 8th, 14th, 15th, 18th, and 23rd Sundays after Pentecost respectively. Only the collect for Thursday of the first week of Lent (the collect formerly assigned to the 8th Sunday after Pentecost) was edited.

[72] The collects of Friday and Saturday of the first week, Wednesday and Saturday of the second week, Thursday and Saturday of the third week, Thursday of the fourth week, and Thursday and Saturday of the fifth week.

[73] The collect assigned to Saturday of the second week of Lent was not edited.

Comparative Examination of the Collects of Ash Wednesday and the Sundays of Lent in the pre- and post-Vatican II missals

Ash Wednesday

1962 Ash Wednesday	1970/2002 Ash Wednesday
Praesta, Domine, fidelibus tuis: ut ieiuniorum veneranda solemnia, et congrua pietate suscipiant, et secura devotione percurrant.	Concede nobis, Domine, praesidia militiae christianae sanctis inchoare ieiuniis; ut contra spirituales nequitias pugnaturi, continentiae muniamur auxiliis.
Grant, O Lord, to your faithful: that they may both undertake the venerable solemn rites of fasting with fitting piety and persevere to the end in steadfast devotion.	Grant us, O Lord, to enter the defenses of Christian warfare with holy fasts; that we may be fortified by the aids of continence against the spiritual evils we are about to fight.

Manuscript History

The 1962 collect, with a *quaesumus* inserted before *Domine*, appears in *Gelasianum Vetus* as the collect for Ember Wednesday in September.[74] Both with and without *quaesumus*, it also appears in 18 codices dating from the eighth to the fifteenth century as the collect for Wednesday in Quinquagesima.[75] The post-Trent revisers adopted the text without modification and assigned it to the same day which they titled "*feria quarta cinerum*" [Wednesday of ashes].

The 1970 collect also appears in *Gelasianum Vetus* as an Ember Day collect, Wednesday in June,[76] but from the eleventh century it is used in connection with the blessing or imposition of ashes.[77] In the Tridentine missals it serves as the final prayer in the rite of blessing and imposition of ashes.

The Texts

1962 Collect

The 1962 collect describes Lent as *ieiuniorum veneranda solemnia. Solemnia* is a substantive meaning "religious or solemn rites," "ceremonies," "feasts," "festivals," or "sacred observances." *Suscipio* admits of a range of meanings from "receive" or "accept," which is the the most usual sense of the word in liturgical prayers, to "undertake," "enter upon" or "begin."

---

[74] *GeV* 1037.
[75] *CO* VI, 4416. During the seventh century the fast was moved back to Wednesday in Quinquagesima. The only codex that associates the prayer with "ashes" dates from the fourteenth century.
[76] *GeV* 631; it also appears in a Mass of the vigil of Pentecost, *GeV* 654.
[77] *CO* I, 673B.

In the collect *suscipiant* and *percurrant* are grammatically and logically parallel: "may they both begin ... and run through to the end ..."

The collect is straightforward and spare. It presents Lent as a venerable and sacred rite of fasting and asks that the faithful may receive or enter into this holy observance with fitting piety and complete the whole of it without the intensity of their devotion ever flagging.

1970/2002

The 1970/2002 collect describes Lent as *militiae christianae*, "Christian warfare," in which one fights against spiritual wickedness. *Praesidia* is a plural noun, literally meaning "that which presides over," but generally translated "defenses," "protections," "aids," or "helps." In military usage it also refers to places occupied by troops: "posts," "fortifications," "camps," or "stations." *Incoho* means "to lay the foundations" of something or "to begin."

The petition asks that our fasts be holy. If God grants that our fasts are holy, then, according to the logic of the prayer, continence will fortify, defend, and protect us in the fight against spiritual wickedness.

The 1962 collect, compelling in its petition that we begin Lent properly and persevere to the end without a diminishment in devotion, was perhaps replaced because of its description of Lent as a season of fasting. The 1970 collect instead describes Lent as a time of Christian warfare against spiritual evil which we ask to *begin* with a holy fast.

First Sunday of Lent

1962: Sunday I in Lent	1970/2002: Sunday I in Lent
Deus, qui Ecclesiam tuam annua quadragesimali observatione purificas; praesta familiae tuae: ut, quod a te obtinere abstinendo nititur, hoc bonis operibus exsequatur.	Concede nobis, omnipotens Deus, ut, per annua quadragesimalis exercitia sacramenti, et ad intellegendum Christi proficiamus arcanum, et effectus eius digna conversatione sectemur.
O God, who purify your Church through the yearly observance of the forty days; grant to your family that what it strives to obtain from you by abstaining, it may follow through upon by means of good works.	Grant to us, almighty God, that through the annual exercises of the Lenten mystery/sacrament, we may advance in understanding the hidden things of Christ and strive to carry them into effect by/in a worthy manner of life.[78]

[78] Or, alternatively: Grant to us, almighty God, that through the annual exercises of the forty day sacrament, we may make progress in understanding the mystery of Christ and seek to imitate the modes of its [the forty day mystery's] actions with fitting conduct.

Manuscript History

The 1962 collect was used widely and continually on the first Sunday of Lent from the eighth century until it was incorporated, without any change to the text, into the Tridentine missals.[79] It is not included in the post-Vatican II missal.

In his published list of sources, Dumas identifies this Vatican II collect as *Gelasianum Vetus* 104.[80] Four other manuscripts dating from the eighth, ninth and eleventh centuries also witness to the use of the 1970/2002 collect on the first Sunday of Lent.[81] It was adopted by post-Vatican revisers without any change to the text.

The Texts

1962

The 1962 collect describes Lent as an annual forty day observance in which God purifies his Church. Thus the nature (*observatio* = duty, service, precept, rule), duration (forty days) and purpose (purification of the Church) of Lent are succinctly set forth in the statement of fact or *qui* clause.[82] The petition identifies the Church as God's family, and then states its request in the most general terms: that whatever gifts and graces the family (or a member thereof) strives to obtain from God through abstinence, may be followed by good works. The generality accommodates every situation and makes it possible for every member of the Church, regardless of his or her spiritual circumstances, to pray the collect wholeheartedly.[83]

Sister Mary Gonzaga Haessly notes that the placement of *abstinendo* [by abstaining] before *nititur* [he, she, it strives], rather than in its usual place before *obtinere* [to obtain], puts greater emphasis on the word "abstain." *Nititur* is a "strong word stressing the need for vigorous effort." Together, in order, *obtinere abstinendo nititur* :

> brings out the paradox, so strange and yet so true: our loss, 'abstinere,' is our gain, 'obtinere.' This is in harmony with the whole teaching of the Gospel; hence abstinence is not a mechanical and fruitless piece of asceticism ..., but a means given by God for obtaining great spiritual graces.[84]

---

[79] CO II, 1554 lists 46 manuscripts.

[80] A. Dumas, "Les Sources du Nouveau Missel Romain," *Notitiae* 7 (1971) 39.

[81] Cf. CO I, 693.

[82] Haessly, *Rhetoric in the Sunday Collects of the Roman Missal*, 47.

[83] Haessly, *Rhetoric in the Sunday Collects of the Roman Missal*, 47 makes a similar observation: "Each individual has to direct his efforts to the needs of his own soul; hence, to cover all cases, the Church in praying, uses wide and general terms."

[84] All quotes: Haessly, *Rhetoric in the Sunday Collects of the Roman Missal*, 47–8.

Another aspect of the collect is the delicate balance of grace and human effort. It is God who purifies us, but we must both strive to obtain the graces we need from him by mortifying ourselves and follow through upon the graces we receive from him by doing good.

1970/2002

Exercitia is the plural form of a word which refers to "the performance of any activity involving effort, mental or physical, in order to attain proficiency in something or to maintain a proficiency already acquired by similar activity."[85]

Lent is called a "*quadragesimale sacramentum.*" From the age of the Fathers until the medieval period, before the word "sacrament" came to be associated almost exclusively with the seven, "sacrament" was used to refer to all the holy signs of which Christ was understood to be the author. The sign of the cross, the creeds, the Our Father, the rite of burial, the washing of feet and Lent itself are all sacraments in this broader sense.[86]

"*Sacramentum*" translates the Greek *mysterion* (mystery). But before it was pressed into Christian service, the Latin word referred to the oath formula or pledge of allegiance used by soldiers. Thus the word came to expresses both God's hidden workings (from the Greek) and human assent and moral duty to God (from the Latin).[87]

The 1970/2002 collect describes Lent as a sign of the reality of our salvation, an annual forty day period of grace that involves a human response requiring effort – the *exercitia*. It asks that we advance, or make progress, in understanding the *arcanum Christi*. What this means exactly is expressed in the last phrase of the prayer.

The key words are *effectus, conversatione,* and *sectemur. Sector* means "to follow," "strive after" or "eagerly pursue," but it can also mean "to imitate." *Conversatio* here means "conduct" or "manner of life." The *effectus* is not that of Christ simply, but of the *arcanum Christi* or the mystery of his forty day fast and struggle in the wilderness. *Effectus* is usually translated "effects" or "results" (the word here is an accusative plural), but may also mean "the carrying out (of purpose)" or "modes of action." The petition asks that we may make progress in understanding the mystery of Christ's forty day fast in the desert and imitate the modes of action exhibited, so to speak, in this mystery with fitting conduct.

---

[85] Roy J. Deferrari, *A Latin-English Dictionary of Saint Thomas Aquinas* (Boston: Saint Paul Editions, 1960) s.v., 371–72.

[86] Johann Auer, *A General Doctrine of the Sacraments* and *The Mystery of the Eucharist*, tr. Erasmo Leiva-Merikakis, tr. edited by Hugh M. Riley, *Dogmatic Theology* n. 6 (Washington, The Catholic University of American Press, 1985) 27 and 11.

[87] Johann Auer, *A General Doctrine of the Sacraments* and *The Mystery of the Eucharist*, 10–11.

This is the way that Camille Callewaert understands the collect which he says has a more "ancient outlook" than its 1962 counterpart, giving

> greater prominence to the divine Master who is proposed for our imitation and stresses the example so full of meaning (*arcanum*) which he has given to us by fasting during a mysterious period of forty days (*quadragesimalis sacramenti*).[88]

The collect expresses the same longing that pushed the beginning of the fast back to Wednesday of Quinquagesima: a conscious desire to imitate the Lord's own forty-day fast in the wilderness.

The Second Sunday of Lent

1962: Sunday II in Lent	1970/2002: Sunday II in Lent
Deus, qui conspicis omni nos virtute destitui: interius exteriusque custodi; ut ab omnibus adversitatibus muniamur in corpore et a pravis cogitationibus mundemur in mente.	Deus, qui nobis dilectum Filium tuum audire praecepisti, verbo tuo interius nos pascere digneris, ut, spiritali purificato intuitu, gloriae tuae laetemur aspectu.
O God, who see us to be destitute of every strength, watch over us within and without, that in body we may be protected from all adversity and in mind purified of perverse thoughts.	O God, who command us to listen to your beloved Son, deign to nourish us inwardly with your word, that with spiritual sight purified, we may rejoice in the vision of your glory.

Manuscript History

The 1962 prayer appears as the collect for Sunday II of Lent in numerous ancient codices dating from the eighth through the sixteenth centuries when it was assigned to the same day in the Tridentine missal.[89] It is not included in the Paul VI missals.

The 1970/2002 collect is a new composition. Antoine Dumas and Cuthbert Johnson both identify *Liber Mozarabicus Sacramentorum* 385

---

[88] *Sacris Erudiri*, 485–6: "… d'une allure plus ancienne, met davantage en relief le divin Maître, qui est proposé à notre imitation, et insiste sur l'exemple si plein de signification (*arcanum*) qu'il nous a donné en jeûnant durant une mystérieuse période de quarante jours (*quadragesimalis sacramenti*)."

Callewaert wrote 30 years before the appearance of the revised missal and was discussing *GeV* 104 in relation to the prayer for the first Sunday of Lent of his own day.

[89] CO II, 1494A lists 49 extant Mass books.

as the source of the new prayer.[90] The codex is a remote copy[91] of a manuscript that bears witness to the usages in Toledo, Spain in the second half of the eighth century.[92] *LMS 385* is the *inlatio*, a prayer like the Roman preface, of the Mass for Friday of the second week of Lent.

The Texts

1962:

The typographical presentation of the 1962 collect below displays the carefully crafted parallelism of the text:

Deus, qui conspicis	omni nos virtute	destitui:
O God, who see	us of every strength	to be destitute:
interius exteriusque	custodi;	
within and without	protect/guard [us],	

ut	ab omnibus adversitatibus	muniamur	in corpore
that	from all adversity	we may be protected	in body
et	a pravis cogitationibus	mundemur	in mente.
and	from perverse thoughts	we may be purified	in mind.

The *qui* clause provides the motive for the petition: God, who knows all things, sees that we are destitute of every strength. This is not a pious hyperbole but a theological fact, for Catholic faith understands that human beings of themselves are utterly incapable of any thought, word or deed which can advance them toward their eternal destiny without a prior and undeserved gift of divine grace that comes through the death and resurrection of Christ. The exact words of the *qui* clause are not found in scripture but flow from an internalization or appropriation of the words of Christ: "... for apart from me you can do nothing."[93]

"*Omni ... virtute destitui*" leads to the request: *interius exteriusque custodi*. "Within and without" or "inwardly and outwardly," like the expressions "A to Z" and "east to west," is a way of indicating everything. Imperative verbs usually appear first in their clauses. The placement of *custodi* at the end makes the imperative here even more intense.[94]

The compound *ut* clause, the parts of which are rigorously parallel to one another, is an expansion of "*interius exteriusque custodi*" and inversely

---

[90] Antoine Dumas, "Les Sources du Nouveau Missel Romain," *Notitiae* 7 (1971), 30; Cuthbert Johnson, "Sources of the Roman Missal (1975)," *Notitiae* 32 (1996), 43.

[91] Cyrille Vogel, *Medieval Liturgy*, 109 dates the manuscript as being from the tenth century; Eugenio Moeller and Joanne Maria Clément, *Corpus Orationum* report eleventh/twelfth century.

[92] Cyrille Vogel, *Medieval Liturgy*, 333. The modern critical edition is Marius Férotin, *Le Liber Mozarabicus Sacramentorum et Les Manuscrits Mozarabes* (Paris: Firmin-Didot, 1912). Hereafter *Liber Mozarabicus Sacramentorum =LMS*.

[93] John 15.5.

[94] Haessly, *Rhetoric in the Sunday Collects of the Roman Missal*, 49.

parallel to it: watch over us within and without ... in body (without) and in mind (within). The expansion makes the petition more specific: that in body we may be fortified, defended, protected from adversities of every sort, and that in mind we may be purified of all perversity of thought. Haessly writes:

> the two clauses ... are coordinate in expression, but in thought they are not on the same level; 'muniamur in corpore' serves as a background or foil for 'mundemur in mente'; 'as we are fortified in body, so may we be purified in soul'; 'may we be fortified in body, *so that* we may be purified in soul.' The fortifying of the body is a means for reaching the 'terminus ad quem' of the collect, namely, the purification of the soul.[95]

The 1962 collect for Sunday I states that God purifies his Church during Lent. The 1962 collect for Sunday II is a humble confession of utter powerlessness which begs God to purify us by attending to every external and internal need that purification requires. This does not preclude human effort, however. Indeed, the request that we may be fortified *in body* reminds us that we are striving "to obtain by abstaining."

1970/2002
LMS 385 is a long prayer:

> It is fitting and right, it is just and true and salutary, for us to give you thanks, almighty Father, and Jesus Christ your Son our Lord, in whom the faith of those who fast is nourished, hope is carried forward, and charity made strong. For he is the living and true bread, who is both the substance of eternity and the food of virtue. For he is your Word, through whom all things were made; who is not only the bread of human souls but also of their angels. By the nourishment of this bread Moses, your servant, fasted forty days and forty nights when receiving the law, and abstained from flesh foods so that he might have more room for your goodness; living and growing strong from your word, he drank in the sweetness of it in his spirit and received the light [of it] in his countenance. Whence he did not experience hunger, and was forgetful of earthly food: because he was glorifying that *appearance of your glory,* and, with the Holy Spirit overflowing, the discourse/word *nourished* [him] *inwardly*. Even now do not cease to give this bread to us, and exhort us to hunger for it unceasingly. By whose flesh, as we eat, we are made strong; and as we drink the blood, we are washed clean.[96]

---

[95] Haessly, *Rhetoric in the Sunday Collects of the Roman Missal*, 49–50.

[96] The italic type indicates the words which are found in the new collect of Sunday II of Lent.

Dignum et iustum est, equum et vere ac salutare est, nos tibi gratias agere, omnipotens Pater, et Ihesu Christo Filio tuo Domino nostro, in quo ieiunantium fides alitur, spes provehitur,

In *LMS* 385 Christ is the source of increase in the theological virtues. He is the living and true bread, the Word through whom all things were made, the bread of human souls. Christ is the one who nourished Moses, making his fast from food possible – a fast that made more room in him for God's goodness.

Moses is also said to have grown strong from God's word, to have drunk in its sweetness and received its light in his face. The word or discourse (*sermo,* not *verbum*) that nourished Moses interiorly seems not to be a reference to the Word and Second Person of the Trinity, but to Moses's conversations with God. As Moses glorified the appearance of God's glory, his hunger was taken away and he became forgetful of earthly food.

The petition of *LMS* 385 is that God may never cease to provide us with the Eucharist which both strengthens and cleanses.

LMS 385 draws on chapters 24 and 34 of Exodus – two accounts of Moses being on the mountain with God for 40 days and 40 nights. In the first, the glory of the Lord settles on the mountain as a cloud, and God calls Moses into it. In the second Moses receives the tablets of the law while fasting; when he comes down from the mountain his face shines from talking with God.

The correspondence between *LMS* 385 and the new collect is slight – the two phrases "*interius pascere*" and "*gloriae tuae ... aspectu*" comprise the whole of it. A stronger influence seems to have been the Gospel of the day which is always an account of the Transfiguration.

The collect's *qui* clause recalls the words spoken by the Father from the cloud: "This is my beloved Son; listen to him."[97] The petition which follows, "deign to nourish us inwardly with your word (*verbo*)," echoes *LMS* 385. In none of the typical editions is "word" (*verbo*) capitalized, however. That is, the prayer moves from the Son, whom we are to heed, to

---

charitas roboratur. Ipse est enim panis vivus et verus, qui est et substantia eternitatis et esca virtutis. Verbum enim tuum est, per quod facta sunt omnia: qui non solum humanarum mentium, sed ipsorum quoque panis est angelorum. Huius panis alimento Moyses famulus tuus quadriginta diebus ac noctibus legem suscipiens ieiunavit, et carnalibus cibis ut tue suavitatis capacior esset abstinuit: de verbo tuo vivens et valens, cuius et dulcedinem bibebat in spiritu et lucem accipiebat in vultu. Inde nec famem sensit, et terrenarum est oblitus escarum: quia et illum gloriae *tuae glorificabat adspectus*, et influente Spiritu Sancto sermo *pascebat interius*. Hunc etiam nobis panem ministrare non desinis, et ut indeficienter esuriamus hortaris. Cuius carne dum pascimur roboramur, et sanguinem dum potamus eluimur.

The postcommunion prayer for Sunday I of Lent in the 1970/2002 missal also uses phrases from the above prayer: Caelesti pane refecti, *quo fides alitur, spes provehitur, caritas roboratur,* quaesumus, Domine, ut ipsum, qui est *panis vivus et verus,* esurire discamus, et in omni verbo, quod procedit de ore tuo, vivere valeamus. [Having been refreshed by the heavenly bread through which *faith is nourished, hope is carried forward and charity made strong,* we beseech you, O Lord, that we may learn to hunger for him, who is *the living and true bread,* and may be able to live on every word that proceeds from your mouth].

[97] Mark 9.7. Cf. also Matthew 17.5: "This is my beloved Son with whom I am well-pleased; listen to him;" and Luke 9.35: "This is my Son, my Chosen; listen to him."

the word which is to nourish (the word of God, not the Word who is God). The anticipated effect of this nourishment is not strength, as in *LMS 385*, but the purification of spiritual sight so that, we come now to the collect's last phrase, we may rejoice in the vision of the Father's glory.

The imagery shifts twice: the command to listen or hear gives way to the word (something usually heard) that nourishes, and the nourishment (something that strengthens) purifies sight for the Beatific Vision. If one looks at only the images of the prayer, hearing is abandoned for sight. But if one starts from the scriptural passage to which the *qui* clause refers, the prayer moves from the apostles' vision of the transfigured Lord to our hope for the face-to-face vision of God in heaven.

Common to both collects is the necessity of inner purification – of mind in the 1962 collect, and of spiritual sight in that of 1970/2002. The 1962 collect presents purification as the result of God keeping watch over our every aspect, protecting us from the outside things that assail us and making our bodily ascetical efforts spiritually fortifying. The 1970/2002 collect presents purification as the result of God nourishing us interiorly with his word. The petition of the 1962 collect lacks the explicit request that we one day enjoy the Beatific Vision found in the 1970/2002 collect, while the 1970/2002 makes no mention of human weakness, of the difficulties that assail us, or of our bodily nature.

Third Sunday of Lent

1962: Sunday III in Lent	1970/2000: Sunday III in Lent
Quaesumus omnipotens Deus vota humilium respice atque ad defensionem nostram dexteram tuae maiestatis extende.	Deus, omnium misericordiarum *et* totius bonitatis auctor, qui peccatorum remedia in ieiuniis, orationibus et eleemosynis demonstrasti, hanc humilitatis nostrae confessionem propitius *intuere,* ut, qui inclinamur conscientia nostra, tua semper misericordia *sublevemur.*
We beseech you, almighty God, look upon the prayers of the lowly; and for our defense stretch out the right hand of your majesty.	O God, author of all mercies and the whole of goodness, who have shown [that] the remedies of sins [are] in fasting, prayer, and almsgiving, look graciously upon this confession of our humility, that we who are brought low by our conscience may always be raised up/ supported by your mercy.

Manuscript History

Use of the 1962 collect on this day has been continuous since the eighth century.[98] The exact prayer is not found in the revised missal, but the collect of Saturday after Ash Wednesday is similar.[99]

Dumas identifies the source of the 1970/2002 as *Gelasianum Vetus* 249.[100] The collect dates at least from the mid-eighth century but, prior to inclusion in the Vatican II missal, was always assigned to Saturday of the fourth week in Lent.[101] The ancient version of the prayer reads "omnium misericordiarum *ac* totius bonitatis auctor," and has "*respice*" and "*erigamur*" for "*intuere*" and "*sublevemur*," respectively. There is no precedent in the manuscript tradition for any of the changes made by the modern editors, but the substitutions are synonyms and do not significantly change the import of the prayer.

The Text
1962

The 1962 collect is both brief and intense. Beginning with *quaesumus*, it puts need before all nicety. God is addressed as "almighty." The difference between God and us is underscored: those who pray are lowly [*humilium*] and his right hand is one "of majesty." Like the collect of the preceding Sunday, this prayer is a cry for God's protection. The present collect is ever so much starker for, not even naming a specific need, it surrenders the details of our protection to divine wisdom and mercy.

1970/2002

God is addressed as the Father of all mercies and author of all goodness and further described as the one who has indicated that fasting, prayer, and almsgiving are remedies for sin. The second is an application of the first, underscoring that God extends his mercy to us in the two-fold fact that remedies for sin exist and he has told us what they are.

The collect asks God to look mercifully/graciously upon "this confession of our humility" that – an inversely parallel result clause follows:

---

[98] CO VII, 4915a lists 51 codices spanning the period from the eighth century to the Council of Trent.

[99] Compare: Omnipotens sempiterne Deus, infirmitatem nostram propitius respice, atque ad protegendum nos dexteram tuae maiestatis extende [Almighty, everlasting God, look mercifully upon our weakness, and stretch out the right hand/arm of your majesty to protect us.]

In the 1962 missal, the 1970/2002 collect of Saturday after Ash Wednesday served as the collect of the third Sunday after the Epiphany.

[100] A. Dumas, "Les Sources du Nouveau Missel Romain," *Notitiae* 7 (1971) 39.

[101] CO II, 1289. It is found in ten codices.

qui inclinamur	conscientia nostra,
we who are brought low	by our consciences

tua semper misericordia	sublevemur.
by your mercy always	may be lifted up

Our consciences and God's mercy are placed between two antithetical verbs. *Inclino* means to bend, bring low, diminish; and *sublevo* to raise up, lift up, support. The *sub* of *sublevo* carries with it the idea that the raising up takes place because of support from below – it means to lift up from beneath. We who are bent over or even flattened by the weight of guilt, a guilt which our consciences recognize, ask to be lifted to an upright position by the constant and underlying support of God's mercy.

Propitius, the adverb of the petition, can mean "mercifully" or "graciously." It is translated "graciously" above only because it is not *misericorditer*, an adverbial form of mercy having the same root as the other two mentions of mercy in the one prayer. God's mercy is the keystone of the collect and mentioned three times in all. The confession of our humility that we ask God to look upon or consider mercifully is not simply the collect that we are praying, but the way in which we have endeavored to fast, pray, and give alms – that is, the way in which we are giving ourselves to the divinely revealed remedies for sin.

This is the first Lenten Sunday collect in the new missal to mention our sinfulness or to speak of bodily asceticism – and it does both in a strong way.

The Fourth Sunday of Lent

The fourth Sunday of Lent is called *Laetare* Sunday from the Introit antiphon for the day:

Rejoice Jerusalem, and make assembly, all you who love her: rejoice with gladness you who were in sadness: that you may exult and be filled from the breasts of your consolation. I rejoiced in those who said to me we will go to the house of the Lord.[102]

---

[102] *Laetare* Jerusalem: et conventum facite, omnes qui diligitis eam: gaudete cum laetitia, qui in tristitia fuistis: ut exsultetis, et satiemini ab uberibus consolationis vestrae [Isaiah 66.10–11]. Laetatus sum in his, quae dicta sunt mihi in domum Domini ibimus [Psalm 121.1]. The antiphon is the same in both the pre- and post-Vatican II missals, but the Vatican II missal does not include the verse from Psalm 121.

1962: Sunday IV of Lent	1970/2002: Sunday IV of Lent
Concede, quaesumus, omnipotens Deus, ut qui ex merito nostrae actionis affligimur, tuae gratiae consolatione respiremus.	Deus, qui per Verbum tuum humani generis reconciliationem mirabiliter operaris, praesta, quaesumus, ut populus christianus prompta devotione et alacri fide ad ventura sollemnia valeat festinare.
Grant, we beseech thee, almighty God, that we who are justly afflicted on account of our actions, may find relief in the consolation of your grace.	O God, who wondrously work the reconciliation of the human race through your Word, grant, we beseech you, that the Christian people may be able to hasten to the coming solemnity with prompt devotion and ready faith.

Manuscript History

Use of the 1962 text on this day is continuous from the eighth century.[103]

The 1970/2002 collect is a new composition centonized from *GeV* 178, a Lenten ferial collect, and a Lenten sermon of Saint Leo the Great.[104]

Texts

1962 Collect

On this middle day of Lent when spirits may be flagging, the Church begs "almighty God" for the consolation of his grace. The affliction which we deservedly suffer is not simply the temporal punishments due to sin but, assumably, also the fasts and penances we have undertaken as part of Lenten observance. God's omnipotence (direct address) and our affliction (*qui* clause) are the two motives for the petition, for only God's grace, not affliction, however willingly undertaken, can revive. The parallelism of the result clause is presented below:

ut qui	ex merito *nostrae* actionis	affligimur,
that we who	from the merit of our action	are afflicted
	tuae gratiae consolatione	respiremus.
	by the consolation of your grace	may be revived

1970/2002 Collect

The 1970/2002 collect and its sources follow.

---

[103] CO I,760 cites 44 codices in which the prayer is the collect assigned to this same Sunday.
[104] Cf. Cuthbert Johnson, "The Sources of the Roman Missal (1975)" 32 (1996) 50 and A. Dumas, "Les Sources du Nouveau Missel Romain," *Notitiae* 7 (1971) 39. The revisers adapted Pope Saint Leo's *Sermo* 40, *De Quadragesima* II (*Patrologia Latina* 54, 151).

GeV 178: Wednesday of the second week of Lent, collect	Saint Leo the Great, Sermon on Lent 2	MR 1970/2004: Sunday IV in Lent
Deus qui per verbum tuum humani generis reconciliationem mirabiliter operaris, praesta, quaesumus, ut sancto ieiunio et tibi toto simus corde subiecti et in tua nobis efficiamur[105] praece concordes.	Quia ... dignumque est **ut populus Christianus** in quantacumque abstinentia constitutus, magis desideret se Dei verbo quam cibo satiare corporeo, **prompta devotione et alacri fide** suscipiamus solemne jejunium, ...	*Deus, qui per Verbum tuum humani generis reconciliationem mirabiliter operaris, praesta, quaesumus,* **ut populus christianus prompta devotione et alacri fide** ad ventura sollemnia valeat festinare.
O God, who do wondrously accomplish the reconciliation of the human race through your Word, grant, we beseech you, that in holy fasting we may be both subject to you with our whole heart and made to have one mind among ourselves in your peace.	Since ... and it is fitting that **the Christian people,** insofar as they are established in a greater abstinence, should have a greater desire to be filled with the word of God than with bodily food, let us undertake this solemn fast **with prompt devotion and ready faith,**...	*O God, who do wondrously accomplish the reconciliation of the human race through your Word, grant, we beseech you,* **that the Christian people** may be able to hasten to the coming solemnity **with prompt devotion and ready faith.**

Regular type in the left and middle columns indicates what the revisers left behind and, in the third column, what they introduced. The text adopted from the preface, *GeV* 178, is presented in italics and that from Saint Leo appears in bold type.

The editors adopted the opening clause from *Gelasianum Vetus* 178 without emendation, but took nothing from the result clause. The first part of the compound *ut* clause presents no grammatical difficulty, "that in holy fasting we may be subject to you with our whole heart," but the second part contains an obvious error: *praece*. *Praece* is unlikely to be an aberrant spelling of the ablative form of *prex*, the word for prayer or request, because "*tua praece*" appears in a context where the *tua* [your] refers to God. The same oration is found in other ancient

---

[105] *GeV* 178 has *efficiamus*. Text follows CO 1998.

sacramentaries,[106] some of which have *prece* (prayer) and others *pace* (peace).[107]

The translation given above assumes that *praece* is a mistranscription of *pace* rather than of *prece* because, quite aside from the difficulty already named, the petition "that through holy fasting ... we may come to have one mind among ourselves in your peace" seeks a practical effect of the reconciliation that the *qui* clause acknowledges God accomplishing through his Word. That is, God reconciles us to himself, which makes us *concordes* with him, establishing us in his peace, and we petition him to make us *concordes* with one another in the same peace. Thus the *pace* [peace] reading achieves a stronger parallelism of thought than any rendering using *prece* [prayer/request] is able to attain.[108] And, as we have seen, carefully balanced parallelism of grammar and/or ideas is characteristic of the ancient collects.

The revisers replaced the entire *ut* clause of the original prayer with: "that the Christian people may be able to hasten *to the coming solemnity* with prompt devotion and ready faith."[109] The source is a Lenten sermon

---

[106] CO III, 1998 lists 16 witnesses dating from the eighth to the twelfth centuries. The oration appears as a *super populum* in a Mass in time of fasting [*in Missa in tempore ieiunii*]; as, variously, *oratio ad vesperos, collecta,* and *oratio super populum* on Wednesday of the second week of Lent, and as the collect of Thursday of the fourth week of Lent.

[107] Uncharacteristically the CO entry, which has *pace*, does not report variants. But see Alban Dold and Leo Eizenhöfer, eds., *Das Prager Sakramentar [Cod. O. 83 (fol. 1–120) der Bibliothek des Metropolitankapitals]*, Texte und Arbeiten I, heft 38–42 (Beuron: Beuroner Kunstverlag, 1949), #56, 1: *prece*; Alban Dold and Klaus Gamber, (eds), *Das Sakramentar von Monza (Im Cod. F1/101 der Dortigen Kapitalsbibliothek)*, Texte und Arbeiten 3 (Beuron: Beuroner Kunstverlag, 1957), #170 which does not choose but reports on four other witnesses: *pace* (2), *prece* (1), *precede* (1); A. Dumas, ed., *Liber Sacramentorum Gellonensis*, Corpus Christianorum Series Latina 159A (Turnhout: Brepols, 1985), #368: *praece*; Odilo Heiming, ed., *Das Sacramentarium Triplex (die Handschrift C 43 der Zentralbibliothek Zürich)*, Corpus Ambrosiano Liturgicum 1, Liturgiewissenschaftliche Quellen und Forschungen, heft 49 (Münster: Aschendorffsche, 1968) #790: *pace*; Angelo Paredi and Giuseppe Fassi, eds., *Sacramentarium Bergomense Manoscritto del secolo IX della Biblioteca di S. Alessandro in Colonna in Bergamo*, Monumento Bergomensia 6 (Bergamo: Edizioni AMonumenta Bergomensia, 1962) #1448: *pace*; Patrick Saint-Roch, ed., *Liber Sacramentorum Engolismensis: Manuscrit B.N. Lat 816*, Corpus Christianorum Series Latina 159c (Turnhout: Brepols, 1987), #383: *prece*.

[108] Parallelism of one sort or another is, perhaps, the most common rhetorical device found in Roman orations. Therefore, everything else being equal, it seems safest to prefer the variant that brings the greatest parallelism to the text.

[109] The latter part of the discarded *ut* clause surfaces in the newly composed collect of Wednesday of the third week of Lent in the 1970/2002 missals. The entire prayer reads: Praesta, quaesumus, Domine, ut, per quadragesimalem observantiam eruditi et tuo verbo nutriti, *sancta continentia* tibi simus toto corde *devoti*, et in *oratione tua* semper efficiamur concordes. [Grant we beseech you, O Lord, that instructed through Lenten observance and nourished by your word, we may be devoted to you in holy continence and made to have one mind among ourselves in prayer to you.] This newly composed collect begins from the 1962 collect of Saturday following Sunday II of Lent.

in which Saint Leo the Great, after stating how fitting it is that "Christian people" fast, urges his congregation: "Let us undertake *this solemn fast* with prompt devotion and ready faith."[110]

The revisers combined two ancient texts centered on the Lenten fast to compose a Lenten collect that makes no mention of fasting. Also eliminated is mention of two blessings that fasting brings: from *GeV* 178, that through fasting we may become subject to God with our whole heart;[111] from Saint Leo, that fasting gives us a greater hunger for the word of God.

The literary quality of the new collect is inferior to that of the original. Above we saw that once the obvious error of the Gelasian text was corrected in accordance with the most compelling variant found in other ancient manuscripts, the collect's petition becomes conceptually parallel to the statement of fact of the *qui* clause. The *qui* clause of traditional Roman collects identifies the motive for the petition. The logic of *GeV* 178, the source text of the collect under consideration, is that since God wondrously works (present tense) the reconciliation of the human race through his Word, we are moved to ask him that we may be made subject to him with our whole heart through holy fasting (that is, reconciled to him) and be made to have one heart among ourselves in his peace (that is, be reconciled with one another).

The request that the Christian people be able, or be made worthy, to hasten with prompt devotion and ready faith to the coming solemnity is not an obvious or expected result of God wondrously reconciling the human race through his Word.

Of the many differences between the two collects, perhaps the most important is the way each petition portrays our condition. The 1962

---

[110] Cf. *Patrologia Latina* 54, 151b (*Sermo* LX, *De Quadragesima* II.4). The whole sentence follows with the relevant portion in italics: Quia ergo, dilectissimi, sicut Redemptoris nostri magisterio edocti sumus, non in solo pane vivit homo, sed in omni verbo Dei, dignumque est ut populus Christianus in quantacumque abstinentia constitutus, magis desideret se Dei verbo quam cibo satiare corporeo, *prompta devotione et alacri fide suscipiamus solemne jejunium*, non in sterili inedia, quam plerumque et imbecillitas corporis et avaritiae morbus indicit, sed in larga benevolentia celebrandum: ut scilicet simus de illis de quibus ipsa Veritas dicit: Beati qui esuriunt et sitiunt justitiam, quoniam ipsi saturabuntur. [Because, therefore, dearly beloved, as we have been instructed by the teaching of our Redeemer, "not by bread alone does man live, but by every word of God," (Mt. 4.4) it is fitting that the Christian people, insofar as they are established in a greater abstinence, should have a greater desire to be filled with the word of God than with bodily food, *let us undertake this solemn fast with prompt devotion and ready faith*, not in a useless hunger, that commonly both the feebleness of the body and the disorder of avarice betray, but celebrated with great generosity, so that indeed we may be among those concerning whom the Truth himself says: "Blessed are they who hunger and thirst for right-eousness, for they shall be satisfied." (Mt. 5.6)]

[111] The Latin word here is *subjectus*, the past passive participle of *subicio*. Like *subditus* (from *subdo*) it means to be subject to, or to submit to. This is the fourth time a word meaning "to be subject to" appears in a source prayer and the fourth time the revisers have not included it in the Vatican II collect. See above pp. 79, 81, 83–5, 93 and p. 85, n. 57 and p. 103, n. 33.

petition describes us as afflicted or self-afflicted and depleted human beings who need, or anyway long, to be revived *now* by the consolation of grace. The petition of the 1970/2002, with its request that we may hasten to a *future* feast with prompt devotion and ready faith, contains no suggestion that we are in the least worn down by the human condition or Lenten ascesis and in need of divine consolation.

Sunday I of the Passion // Fifth Sunday of Lent

1962: Sunday I of the Passion	1970/2002: Sunday V of Lent
Quaesumus omnipotens Deus familiam tuam propitius respice ut te largiente regatur in corpore et te servante custodiatur in mente.	Quaesumus, Domine Deus noster, ut in illa caritate, qua Filius tuus diligens mundum morti se tradidit, inveniamur ipsi, te opitulante, alacriter ambulantes .
We beseech you, almighty God, look mercifully upon your family: that, by your bounty, it may be guided aright in the things of the body, and, by your keeping, it may be guarded in mind/soul.[112]	We beseech you, O Lord our God, that through your aid, we may be found eagerly walking in that charity by which your Son, loving the world, delivered himself to death.

Manuscript History
From the eighth century the 1962 collect appears as the collect for this Sunday which, until the post-Vatican II reform, was called the first Sunday in Passiontide.[113] The collect is not included in the revised missal.

The 1970/2002 text is based upon *Liber Mozarabicus Sacramentorum* 706 which is the *oratio ad pacem* of the second Sunday after the octave of the Pasch.[114]

Texts
1962
The 1962 collect is a carefully balanced prayer which, like the two preceding 1962 collects (Sunday III and IV), puts need before nicety and finds its primary motive in the omnipotence of God:

---

[112] This translation follows that of Haessly, *Rhetoric in the Sunday Collects of the Roman Missal*, 53.

[113] *CO* VII, 4856 cites 48 witnesses. *De Cal.* 7, Schema n. 132 (3 December 1965) 3, #24 states: Passiontide, as it is now in force, is abolished, so that a series of six Sundays in Lent may be had of which the sixth is called "Passion or Palm" [Sunday]. The veiling of images in Passiontide, now in force, is suppressed.

[114] The *ad pacem* holds the same position in the Mozarabic liturgy as the Roman secret or prayer over the offerings.

Quaesumus omnipotens Deus
We beseech you almighty God

familiam tuam	propitius	respice
your family	mercifully	look down upon

	ut	te largiente	regatur	in corpore
	that	by your granting	it may be kept straight	in body

	et	te servante	custodiatur	in mente
	and	by your keeping	guarded	in mind

As in the 1962 collect for Sunday II of Lent, this prayer underscores the link between body and soul. God is the *paterfamilias* without whose lavish bounty the members of his household will not achieve the control over their bodies or lower appetites upon which the protection of their souls depends. *Rego*, the perfect passive participle of which is *rectus*, does not refer to asceticism but to the right or correct ordering of things. The sense is that excesses in matters of the body, whether they take the form of mortification or pampering, are not good for the soul. Nor is proper control over the body sufficient for the soul's protection which depends, in addition, on God's continual preservation.

The text is very carefully crafted. The two parts of the *ut* clause are grammatically parallel, word for word; each part contains exactly thirteen syllables.[115] The two final words, one in each part, are grammatically parallel and conceptually antithetical – body and soul. It is as though the author sought to achieve in the two parts of his subordinate clause the kind of perfect balance in the two parts of our composite nature that the prayer seeks for us from God.

1970/2002

The source prayer of the 1970/2002 collect is placed beside the new composition. The phrases common to both texts are in italics.

LMS 706	1970/2002 Collect: Sunday V
Christe Deus, qui inter inimicos suspendi passus est, crucis sustinendo iniuriam, dato nobis perfecte uite tolerantiam: ut *charitate illa* qua ipse *mundum diligens* pro eodem mortem subiisti *inueniamur ipsi te opitulante* perfecti. Sique [ad] passionis tuae exemplum inlata toleremus scandala, ut sanguine crucis tue omnia pacificante, capitis nostri mereamur effici membra.	Quaesumus, Domine Deus noster, ut in *illa caritate*, qua Filius tuus *diligens mundum* morti se tradidit, *inveniamur ipsi, te opitulante,* alacriter ambulantes.

---

[115] Haessly, *Rhetoric in the Sunday Collects of the Roman Missal*, 53–4 notes this.

O Christ God, who suffered suspended between enemies, by [your] bearing the injustice of the cross, the tolerance of the perfect life has been given to us: so that *we ourselves*, perfected *by your assistance [grace], may be found in that charity* with which you, yourself, *loving the world*, underwent death for the sake of the same. And as we suffer the scandals that have arisen according to the example of your passion so, by all making peace through the blood of your cross, may we be worthy to be made members of our head.	We beseech thee, O Lord our God, that *in that charity* by which your Son, *loving the world*, delivered himself to death *we ourselves may be found, through your assistance [grace]*, eagerly walking.

LMS 706 is prayed during Paschaltide. It is addressed to "Christ, O God." The substance is that Christ's suffering is the source of grace, perfection, peace, and, most importantly, the charity that makes us willing to suffer injustice as he did. And, the prayer implies, only by suffering in this way will we become worthy members of him.

The new collect addresses the Father, asking him that we may have the same charity with which Christ handed himself over to death. The emphasis is on charity, not on the process of being perfected, or on following Christ's example of suffering and becoming thereby worthy members of him as in the original. Indeed the somewhat jaunty phrase *"alacriter ambulantes,"* which is not found in the source prayer, strikes a discordant note when contrasted with the original's depiction of the suffering Christ suspended between enemies.

The pre- and post-Vatican II collects of this day have virtually nothing in common. The 1962 collect continues the themes first introduced on the second Sunday of Lent in that missal: our need for God's merciful protection of both body and soul and for a rightly ordered relationship between the two. The 1970/2002 collect, like the collect for the preceding Sunday in the same missal, stresses our dispositions and, possibly, movement: in the first, hurrying to the approaching solemnity with prompt devotion and ready faith; and here eagerly walking, or abiding (*ambulantes*), in the charity with which Christ delivered himself up to death.

Palm Sunday

1962 and 1970/2002: Palm Sunday	
Omnipotens sempiterne Deus, qui humano generi, ad imitandum humilitatis exemplum, salvatorem nostrum carnem sumere et crucem subire fecisti: concede propitius; ut et patientiae ipsius habere documenta et resurrectionis consortia mereamur.	Almighty everlasting God, who in order to give the human race an example of humility to imitate, has caused our Savior to take flesh and undergo the cross, mercifully grant that we may deserve to have both the lessons of his patience/ endurance/suffering and fellowship in his resurrection.[116]

Manuscript History
The same collect is used on Palm Sunday in the 1962 and 1970/2002 missals. Indeed the same collect has been in constant use on this day since the eighth century in either identical or variant form. In the variant, only the invocation is different having "*Deus*" for "*Omnipotens sempiterne Deus.*"[117]

Text
The collect for Palm Sunday is the first Lenten Sunday collect in the 1962 missal with a laudatory *qui* clause since Sunday II of Lent. Further, it is easily the longest of the Lenten Sunday collects in the 1962 missal – more than twice as long as the two shortest.[118] Except for Sunday I of Lent, all the Lenten Sunday collects in the 1970/2002 missal have *qui* clauses and the collect of Sunday III of Lent in the revised missal has the same number of words as the collect for Palm Sunday.[119] The dramatic contrast between the terse cries for divine assistance of the three preceding Sundays and the much longer collect of Palm Sunday of the 1962 missal has not been carried into that of 1970/2002.

The analysis of the collect that follows summarizes and synthesizes the commentary and notes on vocabulary and syntax presented by Sister Mary Gonzaga Haessly.[120]

---

[116] The translation is informed by, but is not an exact duplication of Haessly, *Rhetoric in the Sunday Collects of the Roman Missal*, 58.

[117] CO II, 1699 which lists 55 codices. For more on the variant, see CO II, 1699B.

[118] The word counts of the 1962 Sunday Lenten collects are: Sunday I, 22 words; Sunday II, 24 words; Sunday III, 14 words; Sunday IV, 15 words; Sunday I of the Passion, 19 words; Sunday II of the Passion or Palm Sunday, 31 words.

[119] The word counts of the 1970/2002 Sunday Lenten collects are: Sunday I and II, 22 words; Sunday III, 31 words; Sunday IV and V, 25 words; Palm Sunday, 31 words.

[120] Haessly, *Rhetoric in the Sunday Collects of the Roman Missal*, 55–7 and 137–8.

The *qui* clause is complex. Haessly calls it "unusually elaborate."[121] It contains a statement of purpose, *ad imitandum humilitatis exemplum* (for the purpose of an example of humility to be imitated), and two infinitive clauses governed by the one verb, *carnem sumere et crucem subire fecisti* (you caused to take flesh and to undergo the cross). God is addressed as omnipotent, and the divine deed which the *qui* clause names flows from his omnipotence. The subject of his activity is "our Savior" who has given us the first example of his humility in becoming human and the second in suffering the unspeakably ignominious death of crucifixion – something to which no Roman citizen would ever be subject. The *qui* clause is an impressive distillation, so to speak, of Philippians 2.5–9.

The prominent placement of *humano generi*, human race in the dative case, stresses

> two facts: 1) for the advantage of the human race the omnipotent God caused our Savior to become man; 2) man must cooperate with grace in order to share the fruits of redemption.[122]

The way in which we cooperate with grace, "our part in the drama of redemption," is to imitate the humility of Christ. *Imitandum* is emphatic, "amplifying and strengthening *exemplum*."[123] Haessly notes that this is the only collect in the Tridentine missal in which our Savior is presented as our model.[124]

The *qui* clause or statement of fact is the motive for the two-fold petition that God mercifully grant that we may deserve to have both the lessons of his patience/endurance/suffering (*patientia*) and fellowship in his resurrection. We shall focus on two aspects of the petition: the phrase "*patientiae habere ipsius documenta*" and the *et ... et* construction.

Of the first Haessly writes:

> *Documenta* is emphasized: 1) by position after the verb 'habere'; 2) by being separated from 'patientiae ipsis' ... ; 3) by position at the end of the colon. 'Patientiae ipsius documenta' is allied with 'humilitatis exemplum'. In the Statement of Fact the Church presents our Lord as our Model (exemplum); He is our Master because He imparts by His example the lesson of humility. In [the petition] we appear as pupils imploring God to enable us to 'hold' or 'possess' the 'lessons' or 'proofs' of His patience in such a manner that we may participate in His resurrection: 'resurrectionis habere consortia'. 'Documenta' is a kind of complement

[121] Haessly, *Rhetoric in the Sunday Collects of the Roman Missal*, 55.
[122] Haessly, *Rhetoric in the Sunday Collects of the Roman Missal*, 56.
[123] Haessly, *Rhetoric in the Sunday Collects of the Roman Missal*, 56.
[124] Haessly, *Rhetoric in the Sunday Collects of the Roman Missal*, 56.

or synonym of 'exemplum'. The phrases '[humilitatis exemplum]'[125] and 'patientiae ipsius documenta' recall the words of our Savior: "Discite a me, quia mitis sum, et humilis corde." [Learn from me, for I am meek, and humble in heart].[126]

There is nothing we can add to Haessly's analysis, and so proceed to the second consideration: the *et ... et* construction. Usually translated "both ... and," *et ... et* indicates a compound construction in which neither element is subordinated to the other – at least not grammatically.

Here, however, as we saw when considering the 1962 collect for Sunday II of Lent where a single *et* is used,[127] the ideas are grammatically parallel but not at all of the same order historically or spiritually.

> The 'documenta' were given to the world centuries ago, when our Lord suffered and died on the Cross; hence on this day we need not pray to *obtain* what we already possess. 'Et patientiae ipsius habere documenta' serves as a background or foil to the second clause 'et resurrectionis ipsius habere consortia mereamur'. We ask that 'we may deserve to have participation in His resurrection *even as* we possess the lessons of His patience', or that we may deserve *so* to possess the lessons of His patience *as* to have participation in His Resurrection.[128]

A share in the resurrection is the final end of having the lessons of Christ's *patientia*. On Sunday II of Lent the Church presents us with the Lord's transfiguration in which we see not only Christ in his risen state but the future to which we are called. "Today, full of solicitude that the lesson of Holy Week may not be too hard, she [again] reminds us of the triumph of the resurrection."[129]

Conclusion

This final section revisits the Consilium records, examines different ways the revisers appropriated ancient texts, compares the two sets of Lenten Sunday collects, and discusses the implementation of *Sacrosanctum Concilium* nn. 109–10.

---

[125] Haessly has "exemplum humilitatis" but it is "humilitatis exemplum" in the collect which means that the word order in the two parallel phrases is identical.
[126] Haessly, *Rhetoric in the Sunday Collects of the Roman Missal*, 57. The scriptural quotation is Matthew 11.29.
[127] See pp. 133–4.
[128] Haessly, *Rhetoric in the Sunday Collects of the Roman Missal*, 56–7.
[129] Haessly, *Rhetoric in the Sunday Collects of the Roman Missal*, 57.

Consilium Records

There are two matters mentioned in the Consilium records that deserve further consideration: (1) the proposals concerning the beginning of Lent and the distribution of ashes; (2) the statement about fasting from sin on Sunday.

Beginning of Lent and the Distribution of Ashes

The *periti* of *Coetus* 1 and the Consilium members approved a change in the duration of Lent that would have transferred the beginning of Lent to the sixth Sunday before the Pasch. Having decided this, they deliberated about the blessing and distribution of ashes and were unable to agree upon a single liturgical day on which ashes would be distributed everywhere in the Church as had heretofore been done on Ash Wednesday. Their quandary was occasioned by an anachronism that is not mentioned in the *coetus* records.

During the seventh century the beginning of the Lenten fast was moved back to Wednesday in Quinquagesima – that is, the revisers intended to restore the commencement and duration of Lent to what it had been before the year 700.[130] The use of ashes at the beginning of Lent, however, both for penitents and for the faithful, is later. The first reference in a "dateable liturgical book" to the practice of sprinkling ashes on penitents is 960 A.D.[131] The first reference to the practice of signing the faithful with ashes is from the beginning of the eleventh century.[132] It was not until 1091 that Pope Urban II, at a council in Benevento, "ordered the general imposition of ashes" on Wednesday of Quinquagesima.[133]

The Church which observed a Lent or pre-paschal fast that began on the sixth Sunday before the Pasch did not sign the faithful with blessed ashes.

The Sunday Fast

This earlier Lent is described as an *uninterrupted* 40-day observance. While Sundays were not fasted, they were not "days off" from Lent. As we note

---

[130] Some ancient liturgical books distinguish the beginning fast (Wednesday of Quinquagesima) and the beginning of Lent (Sunday of Quadragesima), but this distinction faded over time and does not pertain here for the issue at hand is the liturgical use of ashes.

[131] Talley, *The Origins of the Liturgical Year*, 223–4. The mention is found in C. Vogel and R. Elze, *Le Pontifical Romano-Germanique du dixième siècle*, II (Città del Vaticano, 1963) 21.

[132] Talley, *The Origins of the Liturgical Year*, 224. The witness is Aelfric, abbot of Eynsham in his *Lives of the Saints*. Talley cites H. Thurston, s.v. "Ash Wednesday," *The Catholic Encyclopedia* I (New York, 1913) 775.

[133] Talley, *The Origins of the Liturgical Year*, 224. Talley cites J. D. Mansi, *Sacrorum Conciliorum Nova et Amplissimi Collectio* (Florence 1759–87), 20.759.

above, Camille Callewaert's study of the Lenten sermons of the early period finds that the faithful remained obligated on Sunday to conjugal continence, generosity in pardoning injuries, works of piety and charity, the more intense practice of humility, almsgiving, and prayer, and, as always, the mortification of all evil inclinations.[134]

Adrian Nocent, arguing for a return to the Lent that commences on the sixth Sunday before the Pasch, says: "in his sermons Saint Leo declares there to be a fast also on Sundays from vices and sins and for cultivating charity towards one's neighbor."[135] One might assume that Nocent misspoke, or was recorded incorrectly, except that the same assertion appears in a second *coetus* report, where it is put forward to counter an anticipated objection:

> It can be objected that, if Lent begins from the first Sunday of Lent and Sundays are counted in the number forty, that there are no longer forty fast days (for Sundays are not fasted).
>
> To this difficulty it may be answered: 1) fasting (in the strict sense) is to be reduced to a few days almost everywhere in the world;[136] 2) and on Sundays fasting is to be from sins and vices and [for] the cultivation of charity toward neighbor. In this way a true and more perfect sense of fasting is able to be more easily inculcated.[137]

The problem, of course, is that "fasting from sin and vice" is not a penitential act, but something to which every human being is obliged by the natural law and to which every Christian is even more particularly obliged by Baptism.

Nocent claims the authority of Pope Saint Leo the Great but does not cite a specific text. While it is impossible to prove a negative, in this case that Saint Leo the Great did not say something, examination of Saint Leo's letters and sermons does not find an instance in which he speaks about fasting from sin and vice specifically on Sunday. Nor do word searches for different expressions for Sunday in various grammatical forms, or different

---

[134] Camille Callewaert, "La Durée et le Charactère du Carême Ancien," in *Sacris Erudiri: fragmenta liturgica collecta* (The Hague: Nijhoff, 1962) 462–81. See p. 114 above.

[135] Schema n. 65, *De Calendario*, 2 (15 March 1965) p. 6: S. Leo in sermonibus suis affirmat ieiunandum esse etiam diebus dominicis a vitiis et peccatis et colendo caritatem erga proximum.

[136] This seems to indicate that the members of the Calendar *coetus* were aware in advance what *Paenitemini* would require.

[137] *De Calendario* 4, Schema n. 75 (10 April 1965), p. 3: Obici potest quod iam non habentur 40 dies ieiunii, si Quadragesima incipit a dominica I Quadragesimae et dominicae numero quadragenario comprehenduntur (die dominica enim non ieiunatur). Ad hanc difficultatem respondetur: 1) ieiunium (sensu stricto) fere ubique terrarum ad paucos dies esse reductum; 2) etiam diebus dominicis ieiunandum esse a peccatis et vitiis et caritatem erga proximum colendam. Sic sensus verior vel perfectior ieiunii facilius inculcari potest.

forms of the nouns and verbs that mean fast and abstain, locate an instance where Saint Leo associates Sunday with a particular kind of fasting.

Nocent's appeal to Saint Leo may be based on Camille Callewaert, "La Durée et le Charactère du Carême Ancien." Discussing the observance of Lent in Rome, Callewaert says:

> Because, contrary to current opinion, the strict fast was neither the only practice of Lent nor one of the essential practices. Without doubt, Saint Leo insists in all his sermons on the necessity and advantages of bodily fasting. But he recommends no less other exercises of mortification and penitence suited to "purifying the soul and body," such as flight from sin and the more fervent practice of all good works and of all the Christian virtues.[138]

Flight from sin (*le fuite du pêché*),[139] however, is a different thing altogether from a fast from sin – for to fast, as an act of religion or asceticism, is to abstain voluntarily from something that is lawful. The sermon of Saint Leo to which Callewaert refers, On Lent IV, was delivered on the first Sunday of Lent. In context, Saint Leo's remarks refer to Lenten observance as a whole and do not pertain specifically to Sunday.

The Collects

The Lenten Sunday collects in each missal number six, but the respective sets of Lenten Sunday collects in the two missals have only the collect of Palm Sunday in common.

Selection

The set of Lenten Sunday collects in the Tridentine missals was already a set in the antecedent liturgical tradition and had been so for at least eight hundred years. The same six collects that were adopted in 1570 and used until 1969 had been assigned with the same wording to the same days from the eighth century to the sixteenth – this is attested by over forty extant

---

[138] *Sacris Erudiri: fragmenta liturgica collecta* (The Hague, Nijhoff, 1962) 480–1: Car contrairement à l'opinion courante, le jeûne strict n'était ni la seule pratique du carême ni un de ses pratiques essentielles. Sans doubte, saint Léon insiste dans toutes ses sermons sur la nécessité et les avantages du jeûne corporel. Mais si ne recommande pas moins les autres exercises de mortification et de pénitence aptes à "purifier les âmes et les corps" (Serm. IV, 1) ainsi que le fuite du pêché et la pratique plus fervente de toutes les bonnes oeuvres et de toutes les vertus chréttiennes." Cf. *PL* 54, 156 (*Sermo XLII, De Quadrigesima IV*)

[139] The Latin text of the traditional version of the Act of Contrition concludes: "Ideo firmiter propono, adiuvante gratia Tua, ... peccandique occasiones proximas *fugiturum*" [Therefore, I firmly resolve, with the help of thy grace ... *to flee* the near occasions of sin].

codices. The post-Trent reformers simply adopted, without any adaptation whatsoever, a corpus of long and widely prayed orations.

There is no single source of the set of Lenten Sunday collects in the Vatican II missals. The collects of Sundays I and III are, respectively, a Lenten Sunday and a Lenten Saturday collect from the mid-eighth century codex known as the *Gelasianum Vetus*. The collects of Sundays II and V are essentially new compositions loosely based, respectively, on a preface assigned to a Lenten Friday and an *oratio ad pacem* assigned to a Paschal Sunday in a tenth-century Mozarabic codex that reflects the liturgical practice of Toledo, Spain in the latter half of the eighth century. The collect of Sunday IV is a newly centonized composition which combines text from a collect assigned to a Lenten Wednesday in *Gelasianum Vetus* with phrases from a Lenten sermon of Pope Saint Leo the Great and words supplied by the revisers. The Palm Sunday collect is that of the *Missale Romanum (1962)* and the antecedent liturgical tradition; the same prayer has been used on this day from at least the eighth century.

There are no records which explain how or why the revisers selected, from all the documents in the Church's treasury, the texts that they did[140] – either those identified in the preceding paragraph or named elsewhere in this volume. We can only examine what the revisers did with the texts they selected.

Revision

The Palm Sunday collect was not revised, but the other five Sunday collects present examples of three different kinds of post-conciliar revision as well as one example of composition by centonization.

First, the revisers chose *Gelasianum Vetus* 104, a prayer that serves as the collect for the first Sunday of Lent in several ancient codices, and assigned it to the same day in the new missal without making any changes to the text. This is, perhaps, the most conservative sort of revision: replacing a particular prayer with the exact text of another prayer that was used on the same day and in the same setting in antiquity.

Second, the revisers chose *Gelasianum Vetus* 249 = CO II, 1289, which serves as a Lenten ferial collect in ten ancient codices, and assigned it to a Sunday, the third of Lent, where it also serves as a collect. They edited the prayer, but without changing its essential meaning: for three words they substituted synonyms not found in the manuscript tradition. This second example is of an instance in which the revisers retained the genre of the oration (Lenten collect) but changed both the setting (a ferial prayer is

---

[140] Cuthbert Johnson and Anthony Ward, "The Sources of the Roman Missal (1975)" *Notitiae* 22 (1986) 454.

assigned to a Sunday) and the text, but did not change the import of the prayer.

There are two examples of a third type of revision: the collects assigned to the second and fifth Sundays of Lent. Dumas identifies the source texts of these collects in the very same way that he identifies the sources in the two preceding examples, by codex and oration number. That is, he gives no indication that the texts of the prayers in the revised missal are not identical to, or substantially the same as, those in the ancient manuscripts.

The two source prayers are, respectively, *Liber Mozarabicus Sacramentorum* 385 (Sunday II) and *Liber Mozarabicus Sacramentorum* 706 (Sunday V). The first is a Lenten ferial prayer that corresponds to the Roman preface; the second is a Paschal Sunday oration preceding the kiss of peace for which there is no strict equivalent in the Roman liturgy. In the first case the revisers adopted a ferial prayer of a different genre from the same liturgical season (Lent), and in the second, they chose a Sunday oration of a different genre from a different liturgical season (Paschaltide).

When we compare *LMS* 385 with the collect of Sunday II, we find a difference of length: *LMS* 385 has 151 words and the 1970/2002 collect has 22. When we look to see if the new collect is a subset of the old, we find that the two prayers have only two disconnected phrases, five words, in common. Moreover the central ideas of the original, that God nourishes the one who fasts and fasting makes more room in a person for God and his goodness, are not found in the new collect.

Similarly *LMS* 706, which has 51 words, is considerably longer than the new collect of Sunday V, which has 22. Again, the new prayer is not a subset of the old. The two orations have only eight words in common and the eight come from three phrases in the original that are not continuous. And again the central idea of the ancient prayer, that Christ's suffering is the source of the charity that makes us willing to suffer injustice as he did and become thereby worthy members of him, does not appear in the new collect.

In these two instances, the revisers selected phrases that they inserted into new compositions essentially of their own making. The new compositions do not share the insights, longings, or other defining qualities of their respective sources.

Centonization

The 1970/2001 collect of Sunday IV is centonized from two pre-existing texts: a Lenten ferial collect found in *Gelasianum Vetus*, n. 178, and a Lenten sermon of Pope Saint Leo I, On Lent 2. As we note above, both sources speak of the blessings of fasting while the new collect makes no mention of fasting at all. Whereas Saint Leo enjoins his hearers "let us *undertake this solemn fast* with prompt devotion and ready faith," the collect asks that "the Christian people may be able to *hasten to the coming solemnity* with prompt devotion and ready faith."[141]

This matter, the way in which the revisers adopted, adapted or otherwise appropriated ancient texts, is revisited in the conclusion of the study.

The Two Sets of Lenten Sunday Collects

The 1962 Lenten Sunday collects praise God who purifies his Church through Lenten observances (Sunday I) and ask that: what we strive to obtain by abstinence, we may follow through upon with good works (Sunday I); God watch over us within and without so that we may be protected in body from adversity and purified in mind from perverse thoughts (Sunday II); God may look on the prayers of the lowly and extend his majestic right hand to defend us (Sunday III); we who are afflicted by our deeds may be refreshed by the consolation of his grace (Sunday IV); God, in his bounty, may guide us aright in body and, by his keeping, guard us in mind (Passion Sunday); that we may be worthy both of having the example of Christ's suffering and fellowship in his resurrection (Palm Sunday).

There is no explicit mention of fasting, almsgiving or prayer in these six prayers. But there is an abiding awareness of (1) God's omnipotence and mercy, and our frailty; (2) the season of ascesis; (3) the intimate connection between body and soul; (4) the relationship between grace and free will in which grace is always primary and free, graced, personal cooperation with grace always necessary. However succinctly, these prayers both presuppose and express theological anthropology and the ascetical theology of Catholic faith. Pope Paul VI presents the same doctrine in *Paenitemini*.

The 1970/2002 Lenten Sunday collects ask that: through the exertions of this 40-day sacrament we may grasp the mystery of Christ's fast and imitate it (Sunday I); God may nourish us with his word and make us, with purified sight, joyful in the vision of his glory (Sunday II); God may look upon our confession of humility and support us always by his mercy (Sunday III); we may hasten to the coming solemnity with prompt devotion and ready faith (Sunday IV); we may be found eagerly walking in that charity with which Christ handed himself over to death (Sunday V); we may be worthy both of having the example of Christ's suffering and fellowship in his resurrection (Palm Sunday).

The 1970 collect assigned to Sunday III makes explicit mention of the remedies for sin that God has revealed: fasting, almsgiving, and prayer. The most prominent themes of Tridentine prayers, the interdependence between body and soul and of the necessity of both divine grace and graced human effort, are not explicitly mentioned in the Lenten Sunday collects of

---

[141] Respectively, "prompta devotione et alacri fide *suscipiamus solemne jejunium*" and "populus christianus prompta devotione et alacri fide *ad ventura sollemnia valeat festinare*."

the new missals. More surprising is the absence of the baptismal elements called for in *Sacrosanctum Concilium* n. 109a and, apart from the collect of Sunday III and perhaps Sunday I, the penitential elements called for in *Sacrosanctum Concilium* n. 109b.

Sacrosanctum Concilium, Schema 186 and the Lenten Sunday Collects

Schema 186: Policy III and Sunday II of Lent

In the Fall of 1966, when Bruylants approached the Consilium members about accommodating orations to the *instituta* of Christian life today, he located the need to do so explicitly in the directives of *Sacrosanctum Concilium* n. 109. He told the members that elements that recall or prepare "for baptism ... are almost entirely absent" from the Lenten orations of the current missal, that the Lenten "penitential character ... is evident almost exclusively in the language of fasting," and that "neither the spirit of penance in general nor preparation for the paschal mystery is sufficiently treated."[142]

The schema in which Bruylants's presents the principles, as well as the reasons for them, also includes the Lenten Sunday collects that were drafted in conformity to both the stipulations of *Sacrosanctum Concilium* n. 109 and the revision principles being proposed.[143] Two of the collects, those assigned to Sunday I and Palm Sunday, appear in the Vatican II missals exactly as they appear in Schema 186. The other four were not included in the Vatican II missals and are discussed below.

The collect that Schema 186 proposes for Sunday II of Lent is *GeV* 178 as it appears above[144] with but one change: in holy continence [*sancta continentia*] replaces in holy fasting [*sancto ieiunio*] of *GeV* 178. This change is the sort that Bruylants seems to understand *Sacrosanctum Concilium* n. 109 to call for when he explains the reasons for the third revision policy to the Consilium members: there is a "penitential element,"[145] and it is not expressed in the language of fasting. In Schema 186 the *ut* clause of the collect [*GeV* 178] remains otherwise untouched and reads: "that in *holy continence* we may be both subject to you with our whole heart and made to have one mind among ourselves in your *prece*."[146] In the subsequent truncation and centonization of *GeV* 178 that produced the collect assigned

---

[142] *De Missali* 27 Schema n. 186 (September 19, 1966), pp. 2–3.

[143] *De Missali* 27 Schema n. 186 (September 19, 1966), pp. 20, 23, 26, 28, 31 and 34. The proposed ferial collects are presented on the intermediate pages.

[144] See p. 140 above.

[145] The 1962 collect for this day names none.

[146] See the discussion of *prece* above on pp. 140–1.

to Sunday IV of Lent in the Vatican II missals,[147] two things were lost to the prayer that were present when it was first proposed: the "penitential element" and a reference to the interdependence of corporeal restraint and spiritual progress.

Only *GeV* 178 of the Lenten Sunday collects proposed in Schema 186 was accommodated as the third revision provides. But five of the nine 1962 Lenten ferial collects that were retained in the 1970/2002 missal were also edited in the same way that *GeV* 178 was revised before it was included in Schema 186.[148]

Two of the remaining Lenten Sunday collects that appear in Schema 186 but not in the Vatican II missals were centonized compositions and are discussed below.

Schema *186: Policy VI and Sundays III and V*

The sixth policy provides for the composition of new orations chiefly by means of centonization.

The collect that Schema 186 proposes for Sunday III is centonized from four ancient prayers:

Ver 203 + Ver 552 + Ver 867 + Ver 995[149]	
Da, quaesumus, Domine, famulis tuis, quos ex aqua et Spiritu Sancto regenerare dignatus es, gratias tibi laudesque persolvere: et, ut plenitudinem adoptionis obtineant, ad tuorum observatiam mandatorum, tu omnium derige voluntates.	Grant, we beseech you, O Lord, to your servants, whom you deigned to regenerate through water and the Holy Spirit, to render praise and thanks to you, and that they may attain the fulness of adoption, direct the wills of all [of them] to the observance of your commandments.

We note both remembrance of, and gratitude for, the grace of Baptism in this proposed prayer, as well as awareness of graced, but freely willed, obedience to God.

---

[147] See p. 140.

[148] In the collect for: Friday after Ash Wednesday, the 1962 *ieiunia* becomes the 1970 *paenitentiae opera*; Monday after Sunday I, the 1962 *ieiunium* becomes the 1970 *opus quadragesimale*; Friday after Sunday II, the 1962 *ieiunio* becomes the 1970 *paenitentiae studio*; Wednesday after Sunday IV, the 1962 *ieiunio* becomes the 1970 *paenitentiae studio*; Wednesday after Passion Sunday (of Sunday V), the 1962 *ieiunio* becomes, with a grammatical shift, the 1970 *paenitentiam*.

[149] The revisers supplied "Da, quaesumus, Domine, famulis tuis." The sources are below, with italics indicating the text taken from each prayer.

Ver 203: Hanc igitur oblationem, quam tibi offerimus pro his, *quos ex acqua et spiritu sancto regenerare dignatus es*, tribuens eis remissionem omnium peccatorum, quaesumus, placatus accipias, eorumque nomina ascribi iubeas in libro uiuentium.

The collect which Schema 186 proposes for Sunday V of Lent is centonized from two ancient prayers:

GeV 254 + Ver 256[150]	
Concede, Domine, famulis tuis, ut sanctis edocti mysteriis, et fonte baptismatis, renovati, ad promissiones tuas te inspirante currant, te gubernante perveniant.	Grant, O Lord, to your servants that, having been instructed in the holy mysteries and renewed at the font of Baptism, they may hasten, by your inspiring, to your promises and, by your governing, attain [them].

Again, the collect proposed in Schema 186 recalls Baptism. It also recognizes the ongoing need for grace and begs for God's inspiration and governance.

Schema 186: Policy VI and Sunday IV of Lent

The collect that Schema 186 proposes for Sunday IV of Lent appears in the Vatican II missals in the ritual Mass for the second scrutiny. The revisers took it from the Gelasian Sacramentary and made no change to the text. It too includes the remembrance of Baptism called for in *Sacrosanctum Concilium* n. 109.

GeV 225	
Omnipotens sempiterne Deus, Ecclesiam tuam spiritali iucunditate multiplica, ut qui sunt generatione terreni, fiant regeneratione caelestis.	Almighty everlasting God, increase your Church in spiritual enjoyment, so that who are born of earth may be reborn of heaven.

Ver 552: Gratias tibi, domine, laudesque persoluimus, qui nos corporis et sanguinis dilectissimi filii tui domini nostro communione uegetasti; misericordiam tuam suppliciter exorantes, ut hoc tuum, domine, sacramentum non sit nobis reatus ad poenam, sed fiat intercessio salutaris ad ueniam.

Ver 867: Exaudi, domine, praeces nostras, ut in omni natione, quod uerbi tui promissum est euangelio, conpleatur; *et plenitudo adoptionis obtineat,* quod praedixit testificatio ueritatis.

Ver 995: Deus misericors, rex aeternae, da seruituti nostrae prosperum cursum; et ut tibi in populi tui deuotione placeamus, tu sancto praeside gregi; *et ad tuorum obseruantiam mandatorum tu omnium dirige uoluntates.*

[150] The revisers supplied "famulis tuis" for "electis nostris." The sources are below, with italics indicating the text taken from each prayer:

GeV 254: Concede, domine, electis nostris, *ut sanctis edocti mysteriis et renouentur fonte baptismatis* et inter ecclesiae tuae membra numerentur.

Ver 256: Quos tuos effices, domine, tua pietate circumtege, et fragilibus sanctorum omnium praetende subsidia; *ut ad promissiones tuas te inspirante currant, te gubernante perueniant.*

The point here is not to suggest that the collects originally proposed for the middle Sundays of Lent (Sundays II, III, IV, and V) are superior to, or more fitting than, the collects that were finally assigned. Rather, it is to note two things about the revision of the Lenten collects at the beginning stages of *Coetus* 18*bis*'s labors.

First, *Coetus* 18*bis* applied the second part of the third revision policy in the way Placide Bruylants described when he argued for its necessity. Broader and more general terms were substituted for the language of fasting.[151]

Second, the set of Lenten Sunday collects originally proposed in Schema 186 exhibits an effort to implement the directives of *Sacrosanctum Concilium* nn. 109–10 especially with respect to the inclusion of baptismal elements. A similar effort is not discernible in the Sunday collects that actually appeared in the Vatican II missals.

As we have noted elsewhere, there are no records that explain why the corpus of collects proposed in Schema 186 differs so greatly from the corpus found in the Vatican II missals.

---

[151] Cf. pp. 12–3, 17.

7

Paschaltide[1]

This chapter examines the post-Vatican II revision of the Paschaltide collects. It begins with a brief consideration of the revisions made to the Paschal calendar. The treatment of the collects is divided into two parts. The first discusses the disposition of the 1962 collects and the sources of the 1970/2002 collects. The second is a comparative examination of the two sets of texts.

The Calendar

The pre-Vatican Paschal season extends from *Dominica Resurrectionis* [Sunday of the Resurrection] to the octave day of the Pentecost or Trinity Sunday:

> *Dominica Resurrectionis* is followed by an octave which closes on *Dominica in Albis in Octava Paschae* [Sunday in White in the Paschal Octave].
> The four following Sundays are designated *Dominica Secunda, Tertia, Quarta,* and *Quinta post Pascha* [second, third, fourth, and fifth Sunday after the Pasch].
> Monday, Tuesday and Wednesday following the fifth Sunday after the Pasch, the three days before Ascension Thursday, are Rogation days. Wednesday is called the Vigil of the Ascension.
> Ascension Thursday.
> The Sunday following the Ascension is "Sunday after the Ascension."
> Pentecost has a vigil and an octave. The octave includes the summer Ember or fast days and closes on Trinity Sunday.

---

[1] *Missale Romanum (2002)* designates the season *"Tempus Paschale."* The new English translation of *The Roman Missal* published in 2011 has "Easter Time."

Coetus 1 considered three Paschaltide questions that pertain to our study: (1) whether to suppress the octave of Pentecost and close the Paschal season after Vespers (or Compline) of Pentecost Sunday;[2] (2) whether to name the Sundays of Paschaltide "of the Pasch" rather than "after the Pasch," making eight Sundays "of the Pasch" the last of which is Pentecost Sunday;[3] (3) whether to assign the Ascension to the Sunday before Pentecost (replacing the seventh Sunday of the Pasch) or to keep it on the Thursday but, in the latter case, according local authority faculties to transfer it to Sunday if needs warrant.[4]

All but Rembert Van Doren agreed to suppress the octave of Pentecost, thus giving Paschaltide a duration of fifty days exactly. Van Doren objected on the basis of antiquity – an octave of Pentecost had existed in Rome from the sixth century.[5]

All approved numbering the Sundays "of the Pasch." The consensus, however, was that these Sundays number seven and that Pentecost Sunday retain its proper title.[6]

The members were in agreement that the feast of the Ascension be celebrated on the fortieth day after the Pasch, and that faculties be given to local authority to transfer it to Sunday if needs warrant. If the Ascension were to be celebrated on a Sunday, however, Aimé-Georges Martimort preferred that it be celebrated on Pentecost Sunday, as a joint feast of Ascension and Pentecost, and not on Sunday VII of the Pasch. This, he said, was the practice in antiquity where the Ascension was not celebrated on Thursday.[7]

The post-Vatican Paschal season extends from *Dominica Paschae in Resurrectione Domini* [Sunday of the Pasch of the Resurrection of the Lord] to *Dominica Pentecostes* [Pentecost Sunday]:

Dominica Paschae in Resurrectione is celebrated with an octave that ends on Dominica II Paschae [Sunday II of the Pasch].

The Sundays are numbered "of the Pasch."

Thursday after Sunday VI of the Pasch is the Ascension of the Lord. There is a vigil but no octave.

The Sunday between the Ascension and Pentecost is Sunday VII of the Pasch.

Pentecost has a vigil but no octave.

---

[2] Schema, n. 65, *De Calendario*, 2 (15 March 1965) 3. The question is #3.

[3] Schema n. 65, *De Calendario*, 2 (15 March 1965) 4. The question is #4.

[4] Schema n. 65, *De Calendario*, 2 (15 March 1965) 5. The question is #6. The fifth question, also on p. 5, asks whether the Sundays of Paschaltide are to be observed as a feast of the first class, a designation that was abandoned in the new missal.

[5] Schema n. 65, *De Calendario*, 2 (15 March 1965) 3.

[6] Schema n. 65, *De Calendario*, 2 (15 March 1965) 3–4.

[7] Schema n. 65, *De Calendario*, 2 (15 March 1965) 5. The proposed joint feast would have its own proper formularies.

The consideration of the Sunday collects which follows does not include the collects assigned to the Paschal Vigil or Trinity Sunday.

The Collects

Quantitative Overview

Disposition of the 1962 Collects

Sundays and the Ascension

The table below indicates the disposition of each 1962 Sunday and Ascension collect. Differences among the various editions of the Vatican II missals are also noted.

Day	Missals	Disposition	Edited?
Sunday of Resurrection	**1970–2008**	**Retained/same day**	**yes**
Sunday *in Albis*	1970–2008	Retained/moved to ferial (Saturday after Sunday VII of the Pasch)	no
Sunday II after the Pasch	1970–5	Retained/moved to paschal ferial (Monday after Sunday IV) and *per annum* Sunday (14th)[8]	yes
	2002–8	Retained/moved to *per annum* Sunday (14th)	
Sunday III after the Pasch	1970–2008	Retained/moved to *per annum* Sunday (15th)	yes
Sunday IV after the Pasch	1970–5	Retained/moved to paschal ferial (Monday after Sunday V) and *per annum* Sunday (21st)	no
	2002–8	Retained/moved to *per annum* Sunday (21st)	
Sunday V after the Pasch	1970–2008	Retained/moved to *per annum* Sunday (10th)	yes[9]

---

[8] *Per annum*": means "through the year." The Sundays *per annum* of the Latin typical editions are called "Sundays in ordinary time" in the current English edition of the *Roman Missal*.

[9] The changes are to word order only.

Ascension of the Lord	1970–5	Omitted	
	2002–8	RESTORED/ALTERNATE PRAYER FOR SAME DAY	NO
Sunday after the Ascension	1970–2008	Retained/moved to *per annum* Sunday (29th)	no
Vigil of Pentecost	1970–2008	Retained/alternate prayer for same day	no
Pentecost	1970–2008	Retained/becomes the collect of votive Mass of the Holy Spirit	no

The bold typeface indicates the only collect that was retained on the same day. It was edited. All of the others, save one, were retained but moved to different days or celebrations. The small cap typeface shows that an originally omitted collect was restored in the third typical edition of the Vatican II missal.

Of the nine 1962 collects under consideration:

– Seven were transferred to ferial days and/or Sundays *per annum*.
– One was retained in place after editing.
– One was originally omitted but then restored as an alternate collect in the third typical edition of the Vatican II missal.
– None of the 1962 collects was retained in place without textual change in the first editions of the Vatican II missals.

Ferials

The 1962 missal has twenty ferial collects: six assigned to the Paschal octave, one to the rogation days, one to the vigil of Pentecost, and twelve to the Pentecost octave. Of the last twelve, two are assigned to Ember Wednesday, six to Ember Saturday (but two of these are not unique to the Pentecost Ember Days[10]) and one each to the remaining four days. The collect assigned to Thursday in the Pentecost octave is that of Pentecost Sunday. The number of unique Paschaltide ferial collects in the 1962 missal, then, is seventeen.

Of the seventeen, four were retained in the Vatican II missals, without editing, on the same days,[11] one was moved to a different day without any

---

[10] The two are the fifth and sixth collects assigned to Ember Saturday. The former serves as the fourth collect of Ember Saturday in September and the latter is the sixth collect of all four Ember Saturdays.

[11] The four are the collects assigned to Wednesday, Thursday, and Friday of the Paschal octave and to the Pentecost Vigil.

change to the text,[12] and two were moved to different days after undergoing textual changes.[13] The remaining ten do not appear in the Vatican II missals.[14]

Sources of the Paschal Collects of the Vatican II Missals

Sundays and Ascension Day

The following table indicates the source of each Paschal Sunday and Ascension collect in the Vatican II missals. Note is made of the differences among the various editions of the Vatican II missals.

Day	Missals	Source	Edited?
Sunday of the Resurrection	1970–2008	1962, same day	yes
Sunday II of the Pasch/Easter	1970–2008	early eighth-century codex	no
Sunday III of the Pasch/Easter	1970–2008	new composition; centonized from two texts	—
Sunday IV of the Pasch/Easter	1970–2008	ancient prayer	yes
Sunday V of the Pasch/Easter	1970–5	ancient prayer	yes
	2002–8	NEW COMPOSITION; CENTONIZED FROM TWO TEXTS	—
Sunday VI of the Pasch/Easter	1970–2008	new composition; centonized from 3 texts	—
VIGIL OF THE ASCENSION	2002–8 ONLY	ANCIENT PRAYER	YES
Ascension	1970–2008	new composition from Sermon of Saint Leo	—
	2002–8	1962 (ALTERNATE COLLECT)	NO
Sunday VII of the Pasch/Easter	1970–2008	ancient prayer	yes

---

[12] The second collect of Ember Wednesday in the Pentecost octave is assigned to Tuesday after Sunday VII of the Pasch.

[13] The collect assigned to Monday in the Paschal octave is assigned to Tuesday in the new missal; the one originally assigned to Tuesday is moved to Monday.

[14] The collects assigned to Saturday in the Paschal octave, the rogation days, and Monday and Tuesday in the Pentecost octave, as well as the first collect assigned to Ember Wednesday and all the collects assigned to Ember Saturday.

Vigil of	1970–2008	ancient prayer	yes
Pentecost		1962 alternate collect	no
Pentecost	1970–2008	ancient prayer	no

There are eleven Paschal Sunday and Ascension Day collects in the first two typical editions of the Vatican II missal. Two of these came from the 1962 missal. One was edited. Six came from ancient sacramentaries; four of these six were edited. Three collects are new compositions.

The third typical edition of the 2002 missal adds two more collects. As we note above, one collect was restored from the 1962 missal. The other, taken from an ancient sacramentary and edited, is the collect for the new Mass of the Vigil of the Ascension. In addition, the collect assigned to the fifth Sunday of the Pasch in the missals of 1970 and 1975 is replaced in the third typical edition by the collect assigned to Saturday after the fourth Sunday of the Pasch in the earlier Vatican II missals. This collect is a modern composition that was centonized from two ancient texts.

Ferial Collects

The 1970 and 1975 editions of the Vatican II missal have forty-four paschal ferial collects: forty-one are assigned to the ferial days of the seven weeks and three others provided for Thursday, Friday, and Saturday after the sixth Sunday of the Pasch for use in regions where the Ascension is celebrated on Sunday. Eleven collects are from the 1962 missal, seven without any change to the text and four after editing.[15] Twenty collects are from ancient liturgical codices, thirteen of which were edited for inclusion in the new missal.[16] The thirteen remaining collects are new compositions, each having been centonized from two or three ancient prayers.[17]

---

[15] The collects assigned to Monday through Friday of the Paschal octave came from Tuesday, Monday, and Wednesday to Friday, respectively, of the Paschal octave in the 1962 missal; that of Friday after Sunday II from Wednesday of Holy Week, Monday after Sunday II from Sunday III *post Pascha*; Monday after Sunday IV from Sunday II *post Pascha*; Monday after Sunday V from Sunday IV *post Pascha*; Tuesday and Saturday after Sunday VII, respectively are the second collect of Ember Wednesday in the Octave of Pentecost and Sunday *in albis*. The 1970 collects assigned to Monday and Tuesday in the Paschal octave and the Mondays following the third and fourth Sundays of the Pasch were edited.

[16] These are the collects assigned to: Monday, *Thursday, and Saturday after Sunday II of the Pasch; Tuesday, Friday, and Saturday after Sunday III; Tuesday, *Wednesday, Thursday, and Friday after Sunday IV; *Tuesday, *Wednesday, and Thursday after Sunday V; *Monday, Wednesday, *Thursday (when the Ascension is transferred to Sunday), *Friday (when the Ascension is transferred to Sunday), and Saturday (both collects) after Sunday VI; Friday after Sunday VII of the Pasch. The asterisk (*) designates ancient collects that were not edited.

[17] These are the collects assigned to: Saturday of the Paschal octave; Tuesday and Wednesday after Sunday II of the Pasch; Wednesday and Thursday after Sunday III; Saturday after Sunday

In spite of the fact that one of the revision principles agreed upon in 1966 is that the texts of orations are not to be repeated in the missal, seven of the ferial collects in the first two typical editions are assigned to more than one celebration, six to two and one to three.[18]

There are forty-five Paschal ferial collects in *Missale Romanum (2002)*. The third typical edition adds an alternate collect for Saturday following Sunday II of the Pasch, and includes eight new collects so that texts are no longer repeated.[19]

Seven of the forty-five Paschal ferial collects are from the 1962 missal, only two of which were edited.[20] Twenty-six are from ancient missals, eighteen of which were edited.[21] Eleven are new compositions centonized from ancient prayers.[22]

IV; Friday and Saturday after Sunday V; Tuesday and Friday after Sunday VI; Monday, Wednesday, and Thursday after Sunday VII.

[18] The collect of Monday after Sunday II of the Pasch is also assigned to the 19th Sunday *per annum*; that of Thursday after Sunday II of the Pasch also to Monday after Sunday VI; that of Friday after Sunday II of the Pasch also to Wednesday of Holy Week; that of Saturday after Sunday II to both Sunday V of the Pasch and the 23rd Sunday *per annum*; those of the Mondays after Sunday III, V and VI of the Pasch are also assigned respectively to the 15th, 21st and 19th Sundays *per annum*.

[19] The new texts are assigned to Monday, Thursday, Friday, and Saturday following Sunday II; Monday following Sunday III; Monday and Saturday following Sunday IV; Monday following Sunday V; Thursday following Sunday VI. The new collect assigned to Saturday following Sunday IV does not replace a duplication *per se*. Rather, in the third typical edition, the collect which was assigned to that Saturday in earlier editions of the Vatican II missals replaces the collect assigned to Sunday V in the first editions – a collect which was also assigned to two other days in the 1970/1975 missals.

[20] The seven are the collects assigned to Monday to Friday of the Paschal octave and to Tuesday and Saturday after Sunday VII. Only those of Monday and Tuesday of the Paschal Octave were edited.

[21] The 26 are the collects assigned to *Monday, Thursday, Friday, and Saturday following Sunday II (two collects are assigned to the Saturday); *Monday, Tuesday, Friday, and Saturday following Sunday III; Tuesday, *Wednesday, Thursday, Friday, and Saturday following Sunday IV; Monday, *Tuesday, *Wednesday, and Thursday following Sunday V; *Monday, Tuesday, Wednesday, and Saturday following Sunday VI; Friday following Sunday VII. Also taken from ancient codices are the collects assigned to *Thursday, *Friday, and Saturday following Sunday VI to be used in those regions where the Ascension is transferred to Sunday. The asterisk (*) indicates the eight ancient prayers that were not edited.

[22] These are the collects assigned to Saturday of the Paschal octave; Tuesday and Wednesday after Sunday II of the Pasch; Wednesday and Thursday after Sunday III; Monday after Sunday IV; Friday and Saturday after Sunday V; Friday after Sunday VI; Monday, Wednesday and Thursday after Sunday VII.

Examination of Texts

Sunday of the Resurrection

Dominica Resurrectionis (1962)	Dominica Paschae in Resurrectione Domini (1970/2008)
Deus, qui hodierna die per Unigenitum tuum, aeternitatis nobis aditum devicta morte reserasti: *vota nostra, quae praeveniendo aspiras, etiam adiuvando prosequere.*	Deus, qui hodierna die, per Unigenitum tuum, aeternitatis nobis aditum, devicta morte, reserasti, da nobis, quaesumus, ut, qui resurrectionis *dominicae* sollemnia colimus, *per innovationem tui Spiritus in lumine vitae resurgamus.*
O God, who on this day, death having been vanquished, unsealed the entrance to eternity through your only begotten Son: *attend also our prayers (or solemn promises), which by preceding [us] you inspire, with your assistance.*	O God, who this day, death having been vanquished, unsealed the entrance to eternity through your only-begotten Son: grant us, we beseech you, that we who celebrate the solemnity *of the Lord's* resurrection may, *through the renewal of your Spirit, rise in the light of life.*

Manuscript History

CO II, 1669A lists over 50 witnesses to the use of the 1962 prayer on *Dominica sancta Paschae* [holy Sunday of the Pasch] dating from the eighth to the sixteenth century.

There are ancient witnesses to a version of the prayer that has a different ending – the ending that Placide Bruylants cited in his discussion of revision policies with the Consilium members when he told the members that the 1962 collect was a corrupt text:

> Another change that all deplore occurred in the second part of the paschal collect which, without doubt, very much diminishes its theological import. The old Gelasian Sacramentary said it this way: *Deus, qui hodierna die per Unigenitum tuum aeternitatis nobis aditum devicta morte reserasti, da nobis, quaesumus, ut, qui resurrectionis sollemnia colimus, per innovationem tui spiritus a morte animae resurgamus.*[23]

---

[23] Schema n. 186, *De Missali* n. 27 (19 September 1966), p. 2: Alia mutatio, de qua omnes unanimiter dolent, in secunda parte collectae Paschatis, facta est, quo indubitanter momentum eius theologicum valde minuitur. In Gelasiano vetere sic sonabat: ... (as above, italics added). The prayer is *GeV* 463. The translation of the prayer appears below.

Seven extant eighth-century codices with the Gelasian version, or a variant of the same, exist, but this version of the prayer is not seen after the eleventh century.

Both forms of the prayer are used as the Paschal collect.

The Text
1962
In its mention of prevenient and concomitant grace, the collect makes use of Catholic theological concepts and vocabulary forged in the Pelagian and Semi-Pelagian controversies of the fifth and sixth centuries. Notwithstanding its technical character, the language of the prayer has considerable poetic force: God, acting first (*praeveniendo*), breathes into us (*aspiras*) our desires, prayers, solemn promises, vows, or longings (*vota nostra – vota* can mean any or all of these things). Having acknowledged that our longings, prayers, promises have been instilled in us by God, the collect then begs him to accompany, attend, escort (*prosequere*), one might say usher, them by his active assistance (*adjuvando*) toward their proper end: eternal life in heaven which, we know from the prayer's opening clause, has been opened to us by Christ's definitive victory over death (*devicta morte*).

The prayer progresses from God's action in unlocking the entrance way to eternity for us through his Son's victory over death to our request for the ongoing and accompanying assistance we need from him to make our way safely from temporal to eternal life. *Vota nostra*, the prayers and longings which God breathes into us and which we ask him to accompany and assist, is given special emphasis by being prominently placed at the start of the petition. Sister Mary Gonzaga Haessly identifies *vota* as the key word of the prayer.[24] If we assume, and we must, that the prayers and longings are those which celebration of the Lord's resurrection properly occasions, then the oration's petition, which seems at first glance to have been hijacked by the concerns of a doctrinal controversy, actually understands God to breathe the salvific event into the depths of our hearts and asks him to bring our hearts home to the eternity which he has opened for us.

1970/2002
Below, the Vatican II Paschal collect appears next to its source, the collect that Bruylants identified as the uncorrupt version.[25] Italic type indicates the differences between the two.

---

[24] Haessly, *Rhetoric in the Sunday Collects of the Roman Missal*, 59.
[25] The text Bruylants gave the Consilium members includes the words "*hodierna die*" [on today's day] which appear in the Tridentine, but not in the Gelasian, version of the prayer.

GeV 463: Dominicum Paschae	Dominica Paschae in Resurrectione Domini (Paul VI Missals, 1970–2008)
Deus, qui per Unigenitum tuum aeternitatis nobis aditum devicta morte reserasti, da nobis, quaesumus, ut, qui resurrectionis sollemnia colimus, per innovationem tui spiritus *a morte animae resurgamus.*	Deus, qui *hodierna die*, per Unigenitum tuum, aeternitatis nobis aditum, devicta morte, reserasti, da nobis, quaesumus, ut, qui resurrectionis *dominicae* sollemnia colimus, per innovationem tui Spiritus *in lumine vitae resurgamus.*
O God, who through your Only-begotten, unsealed for us the entrance to eternity by death having been conquered, grant, we beseech you, that we who celebrate the solemnity of [his] resurrection, may, through renewal of your Spirit, rise *from death of soul.*	O God, who this day, death having been vanquished, unsealed the entrance to eternity through your only-begotten Son: grant us, we beseech you, that we who celebrate the solemnity of the *Lord's* resurrection may, through the renewal of your Spirit, rise *in the light of life.*

GeV 463 begins with the same words as the 1962 prayer, except for the explicit reference to "this day," and introduces the theme of resurrection first negatively, but strikingly, with the words *devicta morte* [with death having been conquered], and then positively by naming the feast, *resurrectionis sollemnia colimus* [we celebrate the solemnity of the resurrection]. There follows the request that we may rise from death of soul (*a morte animae resurgamus*) through the renewal or the change (*per innovationem*) brought about by the Holy Spirit (*tui spiritus*). The movement here is from Christ's bodily resurrection from physical death, which signals his conquest over death and all that belongs to it, to our spiritual resurrection from spiritual death (*a morte anime resurgamus*) through the renewal of the Holy Spirit (*per innovationem tui spiritus*).

Antoine Dumas succeeded Placide Bruylants as *relator* of *Coetus* 18*bis*. In a 1971 article in which he identifies the principles used to revise the orations and explains how the principles were applied, he mentions the Paschal collect in a discussion about the ways in which revisers adapted ancient texts:

It happened sometimes that beautiful texts, retained after a rigorous selection process or even perfectly restored, and put in the place that suits them best, still do not give complete satisfaction. In this case a slight adaptation remained necessary. The most typical case is that of the collect of Sunday of the Pasch that, rescued from the Gregorian deformation in which it passed into the Missal of Pius V and made to conform to the best witness (*Gelasian* 463), ended with a regrettable collapse evoking death for the second time in a few words. We believed it good to put the ending in harmony with paschal joy by replacing *a morte animae* [from death of soul] with *in lumine vitae* [in the light of life].[26]

It is beyond our brief to determine whether the Tridentine form of the prayer is an example of corruption or of authentic development. Instead we consider the changes made to the ancient text.

There are three differences between *GeV* 463 and the Vatican II collect. The first is the presence of "*hodierna die*" which appears in a late eighth-century version of the Gelasian prayer.[27] In adopting this phrase, then, the revisers follow an ancient variant. The same is true for the second difference, the use of "*Dominica*" which is attested by every witness except *Gelasianum Vetus*.[28] The third difference, the use of "*in lumine vitae*" instead of "*a morte animae*," is without precedent in the manuscript tradition. It was introduced, as Dumas suggests, by the modern revisers and this, seemingly, without reference to an existing text. In any case, he cites none.

The movement in the revised prayer is from Christ's bodily resurrection from physical death, which signals his conquest over death and all that belongs to it, to our rising in the light of life (*in lumine vitae resurgamus*) through the renewal of the Holy Spirit.

The poetic parallelism of the Gelasian text is the literary expression of a theological truth: the bodily resurrection of Christ from physical death, by which death itself is conquered and the gates of eternal life are opened unto us, is the source of our spiritual resurrection from the death of sin. Therefore what Dumas describes as a "regrettable collapse evoking death for the second time in a few words" is something else entirely. It is an explicit acknowledgment that Christ's victory over physical death makes our escape from spiritual death possible. Since Christ was only capable of undergoing death because he assumed our mortal nature, it seems

---

[26] Emphasis added. Antoine Dumas,"Les oraisons du nouveau Missel," *Questions Liturgiques* 25 (1971) 263–70 at 268: Il est arrivé parfois que de beaux textes, retenus après une sélection sévère ou même parfaitement restaurés, et mis à la place qui leur convenait le mieux, ne donnent pas encore entière satisfaction. Dans ce cas, une légère adaptation demeurait nécessaire. Le cas plus typique est celui de la collecte du dimanche de Pâques qui, dégagée de sa déformation grégorienne passée dans le Missel de Pie V et rendue conforme au meilleur témoin (Gélasien 463), se terminait par une chute regrettable évoquant la mort pour la deuxième fois en quelques mots. On a cru bon de mettre la finale en harmonie avec la joie pascale en remplaçant *a morte animae* par *in lumine vitae*.

In this essay Dumas does not refer to the revision policies agreed upon in 1966 but instead identifies them as: truth, simplicity, and pastoral awareness. He also speaks of the revision as having three aspects: the selection, the revision, and the creation of texts.

[27] The *Sacramentaire de Gellone*, cf. CO III, 1992.

[28] Cf. CO III, 1992.

inadvisedly delicate for the revisers to avoid explicit mention of our vulner-
ability to death, either spiritual or physical, and the escape from it that God
in Christ has granted.

When Bruylants told the Consilium members that this collect had
suffered corruption, he did not suggest that there was anything unsatis-
factory about the version in *Gelasianum Vetus* which, in fact, he cited as
we quote above. Further, the first schema of Mass orations proposed for the
proper seasons presents the Gelasian version of the paschal collect without
the emendation Dumas says was necessary.[29] There is no extant Consilium
document that explains this change or verifies that the members explicitly
approved it.

The Octave of the Pasch // Sunday II of the Pasch

1962: Dominica in Albis: In Octava Paschae	1970–2008: Dominica II Paschae seu de divina Misericordia[30]
Praesta, quaesumus, omnipotens Deus: ut, qui paschalia festa peregimus, haec, te largiente, moribus et vita teneamus.	Deus misericordiae sempiternae, qui in ipso paschalis festi recursu fidem sacratae tibi plebis accendis, auge gratiam quam dedisti, ut digna omnes intellegentia comprehendant, quo lavacro abluti, quo Spiritu regenerati, quo sanguine sunt redempti.
Grant we beseech you, Almighty God, that we who have completed the paschal festivities may hold fast to them in character/morals and in life.	God of everlasting mercy who, in the annual return of the paschal feast, enkindle the faith of the people consecrated to you, increase the grace you have given, that all may grasp with worthy understanding by which bath they have been washed, by which Spirit they have been reborn, by which blood they have been redeemed.

Manuscript History

The 1962 collect appears in over 50 codices dating from the eighth century
to the sixteenth when it was incorporated into the Tridentine missal.[31] In

---

[29] Schema n. 186, *De Missali* n. 27 (19 September 1966), p. 36.

[30] Cf. CO II, 1268.

[31] CO VII, 4536.

all it is assigned to this day; in most it serves as the collect. There is only one variant: in some codices the words "*paschalia festa*" are transposed.

The post-Vatican II collect is not found in the Tridentine missals, but comes from the *Missale Gothicum*, a codex that dates from the beginning of the eighth century. There the prayer serves as the collect for Mass on Saturday in the Paschal octave. The collect does not appear in any other extant manuscript. The revisers did not edit the prayer, but the 2008 reprinting of the third typical edition capitalizes the S in spirit for the first time: "… by which Spirit they have been reborn …" The Octave day of the Pasch became Divine Mercy Sunday in 2000, at which time the invocation, "God of everlasting mercy," became especially apt.

The Texts
1962
This terse prayer begins with an imperative, *Praesta* [grant]. The urgency it expresses is softened by the *quaesumus* [we beseech you] that follows. God is addressed as "almighty." This attribute provides the motive for the request: that we who have completed observance of the Pasch may hold fast, interiorly and exteriorly (in character and in life), to the Paschal Mystery and, one understands, its fruits. To put it simply, we ask to become all that the event of the resurrection makes possible, all that the feast celebrates, and to act accordingly.

1970/2002–8
The opening clause of the Vatican II collect is unusually profuse for God is not only addressed as the "God of everlasting mercy," he is described as the one who, in the annual recurrence of the Pasch, enkindles the faith of the people consecrated to him. These statements of fact provide the motive for the request that follows: an increase of grace. The prayer goes on to name specific effects of the sought-for grace, effects which only God can cause: that all may grasp with proper understanding by which bath they have been washed, by which Spirit they have been reborn, by which blood they have been redeemed.

The key words of the *ut* clause are "*digna … intellegentia compre-hendant*." The verb means grasp, comprehend, to lay hold of something in its entirety. *Comprehendo* can mean to take hold of something physi-cally as in "seize," but here the clear meaning is to take into the mind, for "*digna … intelligentia*" means with fitting, proper, worthy, becoming … understanding. The objects of understanding are then listed: *which* bath, *which* Spirit, and *which* blood has, respectively, washed, regenerated and redeemed.

It is difficult to compare or contrast such very different texts, but, while the petition of the 1962 prayer begs that we hold to the paschal mysteries so firmly that we may be formed by them and live them, the 1970 prayer seeks a comprehensive and fitting intellectual grasp of these same mysteries which are named in images that recall Baptism, the death of Christ and the relationship between the two. There is a moral dimension to the Tridentine prayer that is only implied in the Vatican II prayer which instead emphasizes intellectual comprehension.

While this difference ought not be overlooked, it is also true that the two petitions, understood within the givens of Christian anthropology, include one another. One cannot live or become mysteries one has not properly grasped, for understanding orients the will and the will must be engaged, and one lives what one has been given the grace to understand truly and rightly if one's intellectual grasp directs one's will.

Sunday II after the Pasch // Sunday III of the Pasch

1962: Dominica II post Pascha	1970–2008: Dominica III Paschae
Deus, qui in Filii tui humilitate iacentem mundum erexisti: fidelibus tuis perpetuam concede laetitiam; ut, quos perpetuae mortis eripuisti casibus, gaudiis facias perfrui sempiternis.	Semper exsultet populus tuus, Deus, renovata animae iuventute, ut, qui nunc laetatur in adoptionis se gloriam restitutum, resurrectionis diem spe certae gratulationis exspectet.
O God, who, in the humility of your Son, have raised a fallen world: give unending gladness to your faithful that you may grant those, whom you have snatched from falls to unending death, to enjoy everlasting happiness.	May your people ever exult, O God, in renewed youth of soul, that they who, having been restored are now made glad in the glory of adoption, may await the day of resurrection in the hope of certain joy.

Manuscript History

The 1962 collect for Sunday II after the Pasch is found in over 50 ancient manuscripts dating from the eighth century to the sixteenth and, in over 40, is assigned to this same day.[32]

The Vatican II collect for the third Sunday of the Pasch is a centonized composition which combines the opening clause of a blessing used in Paschaltide from *Gelasianum Vetus* and the closing clause of a prayer for the faithful departed assigned to the eighth month (*October*) in the collection of liturgical texts known as the Leonine or Veronese Sacramentary.

The Text

1962

The collect's most striking aspect is the repetition of words and images.

---

[32] CO III, 1737.

First, there are the falls: *iacentem,* from *iaceo* which means to lie or be situated, to be thrown, to have fallen, to lie dead, to be cast down, to be prostrate, and *casibus,* is a plural form of *casus,* which is a falling down, a moral fall, a calamity, a euphemism for death. These words conveying disastrous descents stand in dramatic juxtaposition to both the voluntary descent of the Divine Son in his humility [*humilitate*] and the lifting that God accomplished through his Son's humility: *erexisti* [you have lifted or raised].

Second, there are words that have to do with joy: *laetitia* is unrestrained joyfulness, exultation, gladness, but a joy that shows itself externally; *perfruor* means to enjoy fully or thoroughly; *gaudium* is inward joy, gladness, delight – here in the plural: *gaudiis.*

Third, there are words that signify endlessness: *perpetuus:* continuous, uninterrupted, unending, perpetual, and *sempiternus:* everlasting. The word *perpetuus* appears twice. Once it modifies *laetitiam,* the joy we ask God to grant. Once it modifies death, from which God has snatched or delivered us (*eripuisti*). *Sempiternus* modifies the word for interior joys. The use of *eripuisti* [you have snatched or delivered] especially underscores God's victory over death for *eripio* also means to die suddenly or to be snatched away by death. God snatches from death using the very word that can refer to death unexpectedly snatching life away.

The *qui* clause or statement of fact describes the Father's redemption of all in terms reminiscent of Philippians 2.6–9, the hymn describing the Son's humility which is manifest first in his incarnation and then in his death. The hymn parallels the biblical account of the Fall, even as it tells the story of its reversal.[33] God's Son, not deeming equality with God something to be grasped, became human and obediently submitted to a death on a cross to save the human beings who ate forbidden fruit in order to grasp equality with God and through their disobedience became subject to death. Augustine tells us "Because, therefore, man fell through pride, he [God] applied humility in order to cure."[34] Or, in the image of the prayer, the Son's humility is the lever with which God lifts the fallen world.

The petition asks that God grant joy to his faithful who, in the next phrase, are described as those he has snatched from death. The resultant exultation is described with striking rhetorical redundancy: that they may completely enjoy everlasting joys.

---

[33] Genesis 3.1–7.

[34] *De Doctrina Christiana* 14.13 [PL 34, 23]: Quia ergo per superbiam homo lapsus est, humilitatem adhibuit ad sanandum. Similarly elsewhere, *De Catechizandis Rudibus* 4.8 [PL 40, 316] he writes: "The wretchedness of man's pride is great, but the mercy of God's humility is greater [Magna est enim miseria superbus homo, sed maior misericordia humilis Deus].

The collect's paschal character is evident in the voice it gives to the boundless joy that springs from escaping death.[35]

1970/2002
The new collect with its source texts are shown below:

GeV 515: Ad populum	Ver 1148: Mense Octobrio XXXIII. Super Defunctos	1970–2008: Dominica III Paschae
Populus tuus, quaesumus, Domine, *renouata semper exultet animae iuuentute, ut qui* ante peccatorum ueternoso in mortem uenerat senio, *nunc laetetur* in pristinam *se gloriam restitutum.*[36]	His, quaesumus, domine, sacrificiis, quibus purgationem et uiuentibus tribuis et defunctis, animam famuli tui benignus absolue; ut **resurrectionis diem spe certae gratulationis expectet.**	*Semper exsultet populus tuus,* Deus, *renovata animae iuventute, ut, qui nunc laetatur* in adoptionis *se gloriam restitutum,* **resurrectionis diem spe certae gratulationis exspectet.**
May your people ever exult, we beseech you O Lord, *in renewed youth of soul,* that they, who had previously come to death in the lethargic old age of sinners, *may now rejoice* to have been restored to their original *glory.*	Through these sacrifices, we beseech you, O Lord, by which you grant purification both to the living and the dead, kindly set the soul of your servant free, **that he may await the day of resurrection in the hope of certain joy.**	*May your people ever exult,* O God, *in renewed youth of soul,* that they who now rejoice to have been restored in the glory of adoption, **may await the day of resurrection in the hope of certain joy.**

The regular typeface indicates what is unique to each prayer. In the source prayers this is what the revisers left behind; in the new collect, it is what the revisers introduced or composed. Italic type indicates text taken from *Gelasianum Vetus* 515 (first column), and boldface type that taken from the *Veronense* 1148 (second column).

The Gelasian prayer is a blessing prayed over the people at the end of a Mass celebrated during Paschaltide. In other codices the same prayer serves

---

[35] The post-Vatican II revisers assigned this prayer to the 14th Sunday *per annum* after making one textual change: *perpetuam* [everlasting or unending] becomes *sanctam* [*holy*]. There is no warrant in the manuscript tradition for this change which destroys the parallelism of a carefully balanced composition: gift of unending joy // deliverance from unending death.
[36] Text corrected following *CO* VI, 4299.

as the blessing prayed on the Paschal *Annotina*, the first anniversary of Baptism of those who had been baptized at the Pasch the preceding year.[37] Death in the lethargic old age of sins or sinners (*peccatorum* is the genitive of both sin, *peccatum*, and sinner, *peccator*) recalls the spiritual state of the faithful before Baptism, and renewed youth of soul and restoration to original glory to their condition following Baptismal rebirth. Eden has been regained. Exultation and joy derive from one's having passed from the first state to the second.

The Veronese text is a prayer from a Mass for the faithful departed celebrated in the eighth month. It appears in no other codex.[38] Recognizing that God grants purification to both the living and the dead through the holy sacrifice of the Mass, the petition asks that the soul of the departed one might be set free to await the day on which the dead will be raised in hope of sure or determined (in the sense of resolved or settled) joy. The hope or expectation of joy can be *certain* in the case of the faithful departed precisely because his earthly sojourn has come to an end – that is, all his moral choices have been made.

Both texts present joy in relief to a former unhappy condition: in the first, the death of growing old in sin; in the second, the shackles forged by sins committed during life on earth. That is, both exhibit an acute awareness of something from which we need God's saving intervention, and, in consequence, the joy each prayer expresses is set against and heightened by what would have been had God not acted mercifully in response to human need.

The opening clause of the new composition takes, but rearranges, the opening clause of the blessing, omitting the deprecatory "we beseech you, O Lord" and supplying "O God" instead. Unusually, there is no statement of fact or the equivalent. The *ut* clause of the new prayer takes something from the closing clause of the blessing, but substitutes *"adoptionis"* for *"pristinam"* so that the people are *restitutum* (restored) in or by the "glory of adoption" rather than to "original glory." Since *restituo* means to restore something to a former condition and divine adoption is something completely new in Christ, something different from and greater than what was ours at the outset, the substitution is not a precise fit. Lastly, we note that the revisers took everything from this prayer but the mention of our plight in sin.

The prayer for the faithful departed was similarly looted. Neither the sacrifices that purify the living and the dead nor the request for the soul to be set free, statements which suggest the human being may be unclean and unfree, were brought to the new prayer. Only the request that particular persons, now those "restored in the glory of adoption," may await the day

---

[37] Cf. *CO* VI, 4299. The Pasch is a moveable feast; the *annotina* celebrates the first anniversary according to the actual date of Baptism.
[38] Cf. *CO* IV, 2919.

of resurrection in the hope of certain joy was incorporated into the new prayer. But here again there is a problem of theological imprecision. While "hope of *certain* joy" on the day of resurrection is possible for those who have died and who have reached Purgatory or Heaven, it is not for those who have not yet died. That is, while it is certain that God desires to bring all the baptized to heaven, their salvation cannot be sure or certain before they breathe their last breath because they remain free to turn away from God and his grace.

The internal logic of each prayer, with its missing premise, is given below:

> *GeV* 515: If God grants that his people exult always in renewed youth of soul, then those who had previously come to death in the lethargic old age of sinners will rejoice to have been restored to former glory.

> Missing premise: God's people are those who had previously come to death as sinners.

> *Ver* 1148: If God sets the soul of his servant free by means of the sacrifices through which he grants purification to the living and the dead, then his servant will await the day of resurrection in the hope of certain joy.

> Missing premise: the soul of God's servant stands in need of purification.

> *MR* 1970–2002: If God grants that his people exult always in renewed youth of soul, then they who now rejoice to have been restored in the glory of adoption will await the day of resurrection in the hope of certain joy.

> Missing premise: God's people are those who rejoice to have been restored through adoption.

"Restored in the glory of adoption" differs from what we are calling the missing premise of the other prayers because it does not explicitly mention the state of the faithful before God acted on their behalf. It names what they have been brought to, not taken away from. The constitutive elements of the old and new prayers are different not in the things they name, but in the *nature* of the things they name. The Vatican II collect also differs in this way from the 1962 prayer which is much more like *GeV* 515 and *Ver* 1148.

> *MR* 1962: If God, who raised the fallen world through the humility of his Son, gives unending gladness to his faithful ones, then those whom he has snatched from falls to unending death will enjoy everlasting happiness.

> Missing premise: the faithful are those who have been snatched from falls to unending death.

Sunday III after the Pasch // Sunday IV of the Pasch

1962: Dominica III post Pascha	1970–2008: Dominica IV Paschae
Deus, qui errantibus, ut in viam possint redire iustitiae, veritatis tuae lumen ostendis: da cunctis qui christiana professione censentur, et illa respuere, quae huic inimica sunt nomini; et ea quae sunt apta, sectari.	Omnipotens sempiterne Deus, deduc nos ad societatem caelestium gaudiorum, ut eo perveniat humilitas gregis, quo processit fortitudo pastoris.
O God, who show the light of your truth to those who stray that they may be able to return to the path of righteousness: grant to all who are known by profession of faith in Christ that they may both cast off those things which are inimical to his name and pursue those that are suited to it.	Almighty, everlasting God, lead us to the communion of heavenly joys, so that the humility of the flock may arrive there whence the strength of the shepherd has come forth/gone before.

Manuscript History

The 1962 collect, with the exact same wording, appears in over 40 codices dating from the eighth to the sixteenth century. In all these manuscripts, the collect is assigned to the third Sunday after the Pasch.[39]

The Vatican II collect appears in over 30 ancient codices dating from the eighth to the sixteenth century. It is always assigned to Paschal or Pentecost celebrations.[40] The revisers' emendations to the text, which are without precedent in the manuscript tradition, are discussed below.

The Texts
1962

Again the *qui* clause is a statement about God's redemptive work on behalf of mankind. Somewhat unusually, however, it is expanded by a purpose clause:[41] God shows the light of his truth to those who stray, wander, or err (all of mankind after the Fall) *so that* they are able to return to the way of

---

[39] Cf. CO II, 1582 B. In some codices the third Sunday after the Pasch is designated the second Sunday after the octave of the Pasch: same day, different nomenclature.

The post-Vatican II revisers assigned this prayer to the 15th Sunday *per annum* after omitting *justitiae*. This changes "way of righteousness" to "way" and leaves the path of return unspecified. The change follows two of the most ancient witnesses, *Gelasianum Vetus* and the *Prague Sacramentary*.

[40] CO VII, 3828. Dumas identifies *GeV* 524 as the source text.

[41] Ordinarily the purpose or *ut* clause extends the petition.

justice or righteousness.[42] There are two ways: the way of error shrouded in darkness and the way of justice or righteousness illumined by God's truth. Truth leads to moral righteousness – that is, God-given understanding makes it possible for the will to act justly.

The statement of fact is followed by a request for all who "*christiana professione censentur.*" The verb *censeo* shares its root with the noun *census* – the enrollment, counting, registering of citizens. Among the verb's meanings is "to be distinguished by a particular quality." The sense is "all who are enrolled by Christian profession" or "all who are distinguished, or identified, by profession of faith in Christ."

The petition presents two ways, moral opposites, in balanced antithetically parallel statements: that they may both reject (literally, spit out) those things which are inimical (or hostile) to this name and pursue those which are suited (or fitted) to it. The pronouns are all-inclusive: that Christians may reject every thought, word, deed, and inclination that is hostile to Christ and pursue every thought, word, deed, and inclination which befits one who follows him.

1970/2007

The fourth Sunday of the Pasch is known as Good Shepherd Sunday.[43] The revisers may have selected this particular collect for the day because of its use of pastoral language: *gregis* (of the flock), *pastoris* (of the shepherd), and perhaps the verb, *deduco* (lead). The source text and the Vatican II prayer are below:

CO VI, 3828	1970–2008: Dominica IV Paschae
Omnipotens sempiterne deus, deduc nos ad societatem caelestium gaudiorum, ut, *spiritu sancto renatos, regnum tuum facias introire atque* eo perueniat humilitas gregis quo *praecessit celsitudo* pastoris.	Omnipotens sempiterne Deus, deduc nos ad societatem caelestium gaudiorum, ut eo perveniat humilitas gregis, quo *processit* fortitudo pastoris.
Almighty, everlasting God, lead us to the communion of heavenly joys, so that *you may grant those who have been reborn in the Holy Spirit to enter your kingdom* and the lowliness of the flock may arrive there whence the *exaltedness* of the shepherd *has gone ahead.*	Almighty, everlasting God, lead us to the communion of heavenly joys, so that the humility/lowliness of the flock may arrive there whence the strength of the shepherd *has come forth/gone before or ahead.*

---

[42] The imagery is suggestive of different passages of John's Gospel, particularly the Prologue which speaks of the true light coming into the world and Jesus's statements that he is the "light of the world" and "the way, the truth and the life." Cf. John 1.4, 8.11, and 14.6.

[43] The Gospel lesson is always from John 10.

The opening clauses are identical in the two texts. There is no *qui* clause but the mode of address, "almighty, everlasting God," serves the same rhetorical function as a statement of fact. God's omnipotence prompts the request: that God will bring us into the company of those who are joyful in heaven. *Ut* [so that] follows, introducing the result clause. It is at this point that the two versions of the collect diverge.

In the original prayer the compound result clause mentions two hoped-for outcomes of the petition being favorably received and, in naming the first of these, also identifies the "us" of the petition. "Us" are those who have been reborn in the Holy Spirit – all the Baptized. The first hoped-for result is that God may grant those who have been reborn in the Spirit to enter his kingdom.

The second desired result is a descriptive interpretation of the first expressed with carefully crafted parallelism: that the lowliness (*humilitas*) of the flock may arrive there where the exaltedness (*celsitudo*) of the shepherd has gone ahead. There are four antithetically parallel couplets: *eo/quo* (to there/to or from where); *humilitas/celsitudo* (lowliness/highness); *gregis/pastoris* (of the flock/of the shepherd) and *perveniat/processit* (arrive/ gone ahead or before).

Humilitas and *celsitudo* are both examples of synecdoche – a literary or rhetorical device in which a part, here an attribute, is named for the whole. The prayer does not hope for the lowliness of the flock to reach heaven while the flock itself remains below, but rather names a characteristic of the flock, its lowliness, in asking that the whole flock might arrive where Christ has gone – for it is the shepherd who is understood to have arrived there, not merely his highness or exaltedness.

The revisers made three changes. They omitted the words "*spiritu sancto renatos regnum tuum tribuas introire atque*" [you may make those who have been reborn in the Holy Spirit to enter] and made two substitutions: *fortitudo* for *celsitudo* [strength for highness or exaltation] and *processit* for *praecessit* (translated below).

With the first change, the "us" of the prayer is no longer identified or described as those who have been reborn in the Holy Spirit. It is a significant loss because it is through rebirth in the Holy Spirit that we become members of the "flock."[44]

The most noticeable effect of the second change, exchanging *fortitudo* for *celsitudo*, is the disruption it causes in the balanced antithetical parallelism. In the new prayer, the *humility* of the flock is set off against the *strength* of the shepherd and strength is not an antonym of lowliness.

One effect of the third and last change, the substitution of *processit* for *praecessit*, is a confusion of sense. *Praecedo* means to have gone before or

---

[44] Cf. John 3.5: Jesus answered, "Truly, truly, I say to you, unless one is born of water and the Spirit, he cannot enter the kingdom of God."

ahead, to have preceded, to lead the way. *Procedo* can mean to go forth or to come forth. That is, the new final verb can express the hope that the flock will arrive at the place from which the shepherd's strength came or at the place to which the shepherd's strength has gone ahead. It seems likely that the latter is intended.[45] The point, however, is that the revisers exchanged an unambiguous verb for one that can mean opposite things.[46]

The moral content of the 1962 collect is strongly worded and uses general terms that include everything. The 1970/2002 is without explicit moral content, although mention of the flock's humility and the petition to reach heaven may bring moral matters to mind.

Sunday IV after the Pasch // Sunday V of the Pasch

1962: Dominica IV post Pascha	2002–8: Dominica V Paschae[47]
Deus, qui fidelium mentes unius efficis voluntatis: da populis tuis id amare quod praecipis, id desiderare quod promittis; ut inter mundanas varietates ibi nostra fixa sint corda, ubi vera sunt gaudia.	Omnipotens sempiterne Deus, semper in nobis paschale perfice sacramentum, ut, quos sacro baptismate dignatus es renovare, sub tuae protectionis auxilio multos fructus afferant, et ad aeternae vitae gaudia pervenire concedas.
O God, who make the minds of the faithful to be of one will: grant to your people to love what you command and desire what you promise; that amid the vicissitudes of this world our hearts may be fixed there where joys are true.	Almighty, everlasting God, perfect always the paschal mystery in us, that those, whom you deigned to make new in sacred baptism, may bear much fruit under the aid of your protection, and you may grant [them] to attain the joys of eternal life.

Manuscript History

The collect of the 1962 missal appears in over 40 codices dating from the eighth century to the sixteenth when it was incorporated into the Tridentine

---

[45] See the collect for the Ascension in the Vatican II missals which uses the word in this way: Fac nos, omnipotens Deus, sanctis exsultare gaudiis, et pia gratiarum actione laetari, quia Christi Filii tui ascensio est nostra provectio, et quo processit gloria capitis, eo spes vocatur et corporis. [Grant us, almighty God, to exult in holy joy, and to be glad in devout thanksgiving, because the ascension of Christ your Son is our advancement, and where the glory of the head has gone before, there the hope of the body is also called]. In this prayer, however, *provectio* [advancement or promotion] clarifies the meaning of *processit*.

[46] It may seem a silly distinction to bother making for, after all, the two describe the same place. The shepherd's strength comes from the heavenly realm to which the shepherd has now returned.

[47] In the first two typical editions (1970/1975) this collect is assigned to Saturday after Sunday VII Paschae.

missal. In most it is assigned to this day which, however, is sometimes designated Sunday III after the octave of the Pasch.[48]

The Vatican II collect is a new composition confected from two prayers, a preface and a *super oblata* [prayer over the offerings], assigned to two different Masses of the Paschal octave in the Bergomese sacramentary, a ninth-century Ambrosian text.[49]

The Texts
1962
The *qui* clause is a statement of fact that differs from others that we have examined. It does not name an attribute of God, like almighty and everlasting, or a saving deed like opening the gates of eternity or raising a fallen world. Rather, it names something intimate and interior that God accomplishes in his faithful. He makes their minds "of one will."

The nature of this singleness of will is clarified in the perfectly balanced infinitive phrases of the petition: to love what you command and to desire what you promise. The one will does not, in the first place, involve the faithful agreeing with one another. Rather, it causes each of them, in all the various aspects of his own particular life, to love (love is an act of the will) what God commands and to desire (an emotion that moves the will) all he promises. The "one will" is God's; the content of his will is revealed in what he commands and promises.

The practical effect of loving what God commands and desiring what he promises is stated in the result clause: constancy in the midst of change or even chaos. Or, in the words of the prayer, the effect is having a heart fixed

---

[48] CO II, 1632. In the Vatican II missals, the 1962 prayer was transferred without change to the twenty-first Sunday *per annum*.

[49] Bergomense 577, a Preface, Feria II in Albis. In Ecla Maior; Bergomense 571: Super Oblata, Fer. II in Alb. Mis. Pro Bapti. The modern critical edition is A. Paredi and G. Fassi, *Manoscritto Del Secolo IX Della Biblioteca Di S. Alessandro in Colonna in Bergamo* (Bergamo: Edizioni Monumenta Bergomensia, 1962). Hereafter, Bergomense = Berg.

In the 1970 and 1975 missals, this new composition was assigned to Saturday following the fourth Sunday of the Pasch. The collect appointed for the fourth Sunday in those editions was also assigned to Saturday following the second Sunday of the Pasch and the twenty-third Sunday *per annum*. In the third typical edition it is assigned only to the latter. The original prayer and its source are below:

CO 1310 A	1970/5: Sunday V of the Pasch
Deus, per quem nobis et redemptio venit et praestatur adoptio, *respice in opera misericoridae tuae*, ut in Christo renatis et aeterna tribuatur hereditas et vera libertas	Deus, per quem nobis et redemptio venit et praestatur adoptio, *filios dilectionis tuae benignus intende*, ut in Christo *credentibus* et vera tribuatur libertas et hereditas aeterna
O God, through whom both redemption comes and adoption is granted, *look upon the works of your mercy*, that upon *those who have been reborn* in Christ, both an eternal inheritance and true liberty may be bestowed.	God, through whom both redemption comes and adoption is granted to us, *look kindly on the sons of your love*, that upon *those who believe/trust* in Christ both true liberty and an eternal inheritance may be bestowed.

where joys are true even when one is dwelling amid the vicissitudes of this world.

2002/2008

The Vatican II collect assigned to this day and the prayers that were centonized to confect it appear below:

Berg 577: Preface, It. Mis. In Ecla Maior	*Berg 571*: Super Oblata, Fer. II in Alb. Mis. Pro Bapti.	2002–8: Dominica V Paschae[48]
Vere ... Christum Dominum nostrum, qui *semper in nobis paschale perficiat sacramentum*. Ut per initiata remedia continuis educare non desistat augmentis. Unde profusis gaudiis totus in orbe terrarum mundus exultat ...	Clementiam tuam supplices exoramus, **omnipotens Deus, ut** populum tuum, **quem sacro baptismate renovare dignatus es,** per haec paschalia munera, **ad aeternae vitae gaudia pervenire concedas.**	**Omnipotens** sempiterne **Deus,** *semper in nobis paschale perfice sacramentum,* ut, **quos sacro baptismate dignatus es renovare,** sub tuae protectionis auxilio multos fructus afferant, **et ad aeternae vitae gaudia pervenire concedas.**
Truly ... Christ our Lord, who *always perfects the paschal mystery in us.* So that through the remedies that have been begun he does not cease to nourish (foster, support) [them] with constant growth. Whence, with profuse joy the whole world through the globe of earth exults ...	Humbly we entreat your mercy, **almighty God, that you may grant** your people, **whom you have deigned to make new in sacred baptism, to attain the joys of eternal life** through these paschal gifts.	Almighty, everlasting God, *perfect always the paschal mystery in us,* that those, **whom you deigned to make new in sacred baptism,** may bear much fruit under the aid of your protection, and **you may grant** [them] **to attain the joys of eternal life.**

Again regular type in the two left columns indicates what the revisers left behind and, in the third column, what they introduced. The text adopted from the preface, *Berg 577*, is presented in italics and that from the *super oblata*, *Berg 571*, appears in bold type.

---

[50] 1970/1975 Saturday after Sunday VII Paschae.

The preface, *Berg 577*, is assigned to a Mass for Monday in the Paschal Octave. It praises Christ for always perfecting the Paschal Mystery in us – that is, bringing it to completion. Christ does not cease to bestow upon those in whom the remedies have been begun, the Baptized, graces in service of bringing his work to fulfillment. This perfecting is the cause of exultant joy throughout the whole world.

The *super oblata*, Berg 571, is from a different Mass for Monday of the Paschal octave, one to be offered for the newly Baptized. It is a deferential prayer which begins with the words: "Your mercy, humbly we pray, Almighty God." *Clementiam*, mercy, is the first word of the prayer. The request follows and is also presented with considerable deference: that you may grant your people, those whom you have deigned to make new in sacred Baptism, to attain the joys of eternal life through these paschal gifts. The "paschal gifts" are the sacrifice of the Mass and the Eucharistic elements that are about to be confected.

The revisers selected the address of *Berg 571*, delayed in the original, and added *sempiterne* to make the "almighty, everlasting God" with which the new prayer begins. From *Berg 577* they took the *qui* clause that describes the gracious action of Christ "who always perfects the paschal mystery (or sacrament) in us" and adapted it to make a petition expressed in the imperative: "perfect in us always the paschal mystery." Since the revisers did not adopt the "humbly we entreat your mercy" of *Berg 571* and did not supply a deprecatory phrase of their own devising, *perfice* appears bare of the polite softening which often accompanies imperatives.[51] The intensity of the imperative is diminished somewhat, however, by its delayed appearance.

The result clause follows. It is partly taken from *Berg 571* and partly composed by the revisers. The "us" of the opening clause comes to be identified in the new prayer as "those whom you have deigned to make new in sacred Baptism." The result clause understands God's perfecting the Paschal Mystery in the Baptized to have two effects: (1) that they, the Baptized, may bear much fruit under the help of his protection, and (2) that God may grant them to attain the joys of eternal life. The latter, "*ad aeternae vitae gaudia pervenire concedas*" is taken directly from *Berg 577*. The former, *sub tuae protectionis auxilio multos fructus afferant*, was supplied by the revisers and seems to be their own composition.[52] Uncharacteristically, the main verbs of the *ut* clause have different subjects and the effect is awkward – the compositional equivalent of two pieces of wood being put together without the preparatory sanding necessary to make the fit seamless. Moreover, the two thoughts could have been brought under the governance of a single verb with a change in but one syllable – for example, *ut sub*

---

[51] The 1962 prayer assigned to this day presents a bare imperative as well.

[52] The phrase is not found in the 1962 missal or in any of the ancient sacramentaries available through the web site at http://www.liturgia.it/

tuae protectionis auxilio multos fructus afferre, et ad aeternae vitae gaudia pervenire concedas: that you may grant [the Baptized] to bear much fruit under the help of your protection and to attain the joys of eternal life.

Sunday V after the Pasch // Sunday VI of the Pasch

1962: Dominica V post Pascha	1970–2008: Dominica VI Paschae
Deus, a quo bona cuncta procedunt, largire supplicibus tuis: ut cogitemus, te inspirante, quae recta sunt; et, te gubernante, eadem faciamus.	Fac nos, omnipotens Deus, hos laetitiae dies, quos in honorem Domini resurgentis exsequimur, affectu sedulo celebrare, ut quod recordatione percurrimus semper in opere teneamus.
O God from which all good things come, bestow upon those who humbly implore you that we may think, by your inspiration, those things which are right, and through your governance, do the same.	Almighty God, make us who are celebrating these days of joy in honor of the Lord's rising, to keep [them] with earnest love, that what we traverse through remembrance we may always uphold in action.

Manuscript History

The 1962 collect is found in more than 50 codices dating from the eighth through the sixteenth centuries. In most it serves as the collect for this day.[53]

The collect in the revised missal is a new composition centonized from three sources: 1) the preface of a Mass celebrated on the fast days following Pentecost (the June Ember Days), 2) a postcommunion prayer for the feast of Saint John the Evangelist in December, and 3) the collect of the Mass celebrated on the Paschal *Annotina*.[54] In other codices, the last prayer is assigned to Wednesday following the third Sunday after the Pasch, the midpoint of Paschaltide.[55]

The Text
1962

The *qui* clause identifies God as the source of *cuncta bona* [all goods].[56] The statement is general and all inclusive: good things, good thoughts, good

---

[53] CO II, 1085. In the Vatican II missals the collect is assigned to the tenth Sunday *per annum* with only a slight change in word order.

[54] Antoine Dumas names these specific prayers in "Les Sources du Missel Romain (II)," *Notitiae* 61 (February 1971) 75.

[55] CO II, 1308.

[56] It echoes James 1.17: omne datum optimum et omne donum perfectum desursum est descendens a Patre luminum. RSV: Every good endowment and every perfect gift is from above, coming down from the Father of lights ...

deeds, good lives, and so forth. The statement provides the motive for the petition that follows.

The request is on behalf of God's suppliants, those who humbly implore him [*supplicibus tuis*], further identified as the "we" of the prayer. The imperative verb, *largire*, the root of the English "largess," implies bountiful giving done with unstinting generosity. The two-fold gift that is sought is described in rhetorical chiasm:

ut	cogitemus,	te inspirante,	quae recta sunt;
that	we may think	by you inspiring	what is right

et,		te gubernante,	eadem	faciamus.
and		by you governing	the same	we may do

The verbs are stressed by being placed first and last, and the difference between thinking and doing underscored by the distance which separates them.[57] The means by which this thinking and doing are to be done are identified in the ablative present participles with their pronouns: "think by you inspiring // by you directing … do." *Inspiro* is to breathe into – we ask to think what God breathes into us. *Guberno* means, in the first place, to steer or pilot a ship; by extension it means direct, manage, govern, guide – we desire to act by God's steering, guiding, directing …

Just as the *cuncta bona* of the *qui* clause is general and all-embracing, so also are the direct objects of "think" and "do": We ask to think *quae recta sunt* – literally those things which are right, upright, correct, proper, appropriate, fitting, morally right, just, lawful, virtuous, noble. *Recta* means all these things. We ask to do *eadem* – the same, a pronoun that agrees with *recta*. The prayer asks that under God's direction we carry out in deed the just, noble, and good things he inspires us to think.

1970/2002

The centonized collect of Sunday VI of the Pasch in the Vatican II missals and its sources appear below.

Ver 229: Mense Maio XII in Jeiunio Mensis Quarti	Ver 1282: Mense Decembri XLI in Natale Sancti Iohannis Evang.	GeV 504: Orationes et Praeces de Pascha Annotina	Dominica VI Paschae

---

[57] Haessly, *Rhetoric in the Sunday Collects of the Roman Missal*, 69 writes: "… [O]ne of the important words, namely 'cogitemus', is placed at the beginning of the first colon, the other 'faciamus', at the end of the second; thus the *antithesis* between "thinking' and 'doing' is clearly brought out."

Vere dignum: post illos enim *laetitiae dies, quos in honorem Domini* a mortuis *resurgentis* et in caelos ascendentis exigimus, postque perceptum Sancti Spiritus donum necessariae nobis haec ieiunia sancta prouisa sunt, ut pura conuersatione uiuentibus quae diuinitus aeclesiae sunt collata permaneant.	Miserator et misericors domine, qui nos continuis caelestium martyrum non deseris sacramentis: praesta, quaesumus ut quae **sedulo celebramus affectu,** grato tibi percipiamus obsequio.	Deus, per cuius prouidentiam nec praeteritorum momenta deficiunt nec ulla superest expectacio futurorum, tribue permanentem peractae quae recolimus solemnitatis effectum, UT QUOD RECORDATIONE PERCURRIMUS, SEMPER IN OPERE TENEAMUS.	Fac nos, omnipotens Deus, hos *laetitiae dies, quos in honorem Domini resurgentis* exsequimur, **affectu sedulo celebrare,** UT QUOD RECORDATIONE PERCURRIMUS SEMPER IN OPERE TENEAMUS.
Truly is it fitting...: for after those *days of joy* which we spend *in honor of the Lord's rising* from the dead and ascending into heaven, and after the gift of the Holy Spirit has been received, necessarily these holy fasts have been provided for us who live, that they who have been brought into the church by divine providence may persevere in a pure way of life.	Compassionate and merciful God, who never forsake us in the ever present mysteries of the heavenly witnesses, grant, we beseech you, that what we **celebrate with earnest love** we may receive with a reverence that pleases you.	O God, through whose providence no moment of the past is wanting [and] no expectation for the future suffices, grant the abiding effect of the celebrated solemnity which we recall, THAT WHAT WE TRAVERSE THROUGH IN REMEMBRANCE WE MAY ALWAYS UPHOLD IN ACTION.	Almighty God, grant us who are fulfilling [carrying out] these *days of joy in honor of the Lord's rising,* to **celebrate** [them] with **earnest love,** THAT WHAT WE TRAVERSE THROUGH REMEMBRANCE WE MAY ALWAYS UPHOLD IN ACTION.

Regular type in the three left columns indicates what the revisers left behind and, in the fourth column, what they introduced. The text taken from *Ver* 229, a preface for the fast days following Pentecost, is presented in italics; that taken from *Ver* 1282, the postcommunion prayer for the feast of Saint John, is in bold typeface; and that from *GeV* 504, the prayer for the Paschal *Annotina*, is in small caps.

Ver 229 names three major events that the Church "honors" during Paschaltide, the season that has just come to a close: the Lord's rising from the dead, his Ascension and his bestowal of the Holy Spirit. The movement of the preface is from remembrance of the salvific events celebrated in Paschaltide, during which fasting is never done, to the necessity of fasting so that those who have been brought into the Church, that is redeemed and sanctified through the events just named, may persevere in purity of life. From this preface the revisers took the phrase "days of joy in honor of your Son's rising." That they deliberately omitted "from the dead" is apparent from the word order of the original text: *laetitiae dies, quos in honorem Domini a mortuis resurgentis* [of joy the days, which in honor of the Lord from the dead rising].

Ver 1282 is a somewhat difficult text. Most confounding is the presence of the word "*martyrum*"[of the martyrs/witnesses] in a prayer from the Mass in honor of Saint John the Evangelist – according to tradition, the one apostle who was not martyred. It seems best to understand "*caelestium martyrum*" as "of heavenly witnesses" in the manner of Hebrews 12.1.[58] If we do, the sense of the opening portion of the prayer is: "Compassionate and merciful God, who never forsake us (are always present to us) in the successive mysteries (successive celebrations of the feasts) of the heavenly witnesses, grant us we beseech you ..." Regardless of how the first part is understood, the prayer is clearly a sanctoral postcommunion.

The petition is expressed in a balanced parallel construction that pairs the celebration and reception of the Holy Eucharist.

ut	quae	sedulo		celebramus	affectu,
that	what	with earnest		we celebrate	love
		grato	tibi	percipiamus	obsequio
		with pleasing	to you	we may receive	reverence

The revisers took for adaptation only the first term of the bipartite parallel construction.

GeV 504 opens with a statement of fact about the embrace of God's Providence: through it he both supplies for deficiencies in our pasts and exceeds our hopes for the future. Its petition asks God to grant the "abiding

---

[58] Hebrews 12.1: Therefore, since we are surrounded by so great a cloud of witnesses, let us also lay aside every weight, and sin which clings so closely, and let us run with perseverance the race that is set before us. The Vulgate, however, has *testium* not *martyrum*.

effect of the celebrated, accomplished, finished [*peractae*] solemnity which we recall." The accusative participle modifying *effectum, permanentem*, comes from the verb *permaneo*: to stay to the end, hold out, last, continue, endure, remain; to persist, persevere; to abide in a rule of life; to live by.[59] The petition asks God to grant to those celebrating the enduring, constant, life-governing effect of the event they are recalling – Baptism at the Pasch for those celebrating the *Annotina* and Pasch itself otherwise. The result clause follows: "that what we traverse through in remembrance we may always uphold in action." To put it a tad differently, the prayer asks that those celebrating may not simply remember the event of their Baptism or the recently celebrated Pasch, but also live it always in their every act. The editors appropriated only the result clause, not the petition from which it flows.

The revisers created a new context for the words taken from the preface, *Ver* 229, by placing what they had selected between a new introduction, *Fac nos,* omnipotens Deus, hos ... [Make, cause or grant us, almighty God, these ...] and a verb *exsequimur* [we carry out, accomplish, fulfil]. To this start they appended the words taken from the postcommunion, *Ver* 1282, after changing the verb to an infinitive: *to celebrate* with earnest love. In the new setting, the direct object of celebrate becomes "days of joy," not one's own Baptism or the Pasch as in the original. The result clause, which was attached without any changes to the text, now also refers to the days of joy. The sense is that we not simply remember the days of joy we have been observing, but always hold fast to them in action. The result clause of the new collect is weaker than that of the source text because it is not bolstered by the "tribue permanentem ... effectum" [grant the enduring effect] of the older prayer.

We can now look at the new collect as an independent composition. The collect begins with an imperative verb – that is, with a certain intensity. There is no statement of fact about God, but he is addressed as "almighty" and this provides the motive for the petition. There is a statement of fact about "us," however – we are those who are following, pursuing, performing, one might say observing "these days of joy in honor of the rising of the Lord." The petition follows: to celebrate [these days] with earnest love (or earnest disposition, diligent affection). The petition is expanded by a result clause: that what we pass through in memory we may always uphold in action.

The centonized composition implies that if God grants us to celebrate the paschal days with earnest love or diligent devotion (however one chooses to translate the Latin), we will live what we have recalled. That is, the collect seems to assert that a particular disposition, although a gift from God, of itself obtains a good result. This is something different from

---

[59] Charlton T. Lewis, *A Latin Dictionary* (Oxford: Clarendon Press, 1879) s.v., p. 1347.

what is found in the source texts. The Veronese preface presents fasting as necessary for, but not productive of, perseverance in a pure way of life. The postcommunion for Saint John understands that it is God who grants us to receive the sacraments with a reverence that pleases him. The collect for the Paschal *Annotina* or midpoint asks God to grant the abiding effect that will enable us to hold fast in practice to what is liturgically recalled.

The theology of grace of the 1962 prayer for this day is the same as that found in the source texts of the newly confected Vatican II collect: namely, all good comes from God.

Ascension

The Vigil of the Ascension

The 2002 missal has a new Mass for the Vigil of the Ascension. There is no proper prayer for the vigil of the Ascension in either the 1962 missal or in the first and second typical editions of the Vatican II missal.

Manuscript History

The source of the new collect is an Ascension prayer that appears in 15 codices that date from the eighth to the eleventh centuries. It is not seen after the eleventh century until it is assigned to the Vigil of the Ascension in the third typical edition of the Vatican II missal. There are no warrants in the manuscript tradition for the changes made by the modern editors.

The Text

The new prayer and its source are below. The italics in the source prayer indicate what the revisers omitted, the boldface type what they changed. The italics in the new collect indicate what the revisers added or composed, the bold print how they changed what they changed.

CO II, 1337	2002–8 Vigil of the Ascension
Deus, **qui** *ad declaranda tuae miracula maiestatis post resurrectionem a mortuis* hodie in caelos apostolis adstantibus **ascendisti**, concede nobis *tuae pietatis auxilium*, ut secundum **tuam** promisionem et tu nobiscum semper in terris et nos **tecum** in caelo vivere mereamur.	Deus, **cuius Filius** hodie in caelos, Apostolis ad stantibus, **ascendit**, concede nobis, *quaesumus*, ut secundum **eius** promissionem et **ille** nobiscum semper in terris et nos **cum eo** in caelo vivere mereamur.

O God, **who** *to reveal the wonders of your majesty after rising from the dead,* today ascended to heaven as the apostles stood by, grant us **the help of your mercy,** that, in accordance with **your** promise, **you** may remain with us on earth and we may be deemed worthy to live with **you** in heaven.	O God, whose Son ascended to the heavens today as the Apostles stood by, grant us, *we beseech you,* in accordance with **his** promise, that **he** may always [be] with us on earth and we may be deemed worthy to live with **him** in heaven.

The source prayer addresses the Son. The new collect addresses the Father. This is in keeping with the decision of the Consilium members that, in general, orations were to address the Father.[60] "Whose Son" replaces the original description of Christ ascending to reveal or manifest the glory he possesses after his resurrection. "We beseech you," addressed to the Father, replaces the request for the help of "your mercy" addressed to Christ. The other changes simply transpose statements about Christ from the second person singular to the third.

The Son, not the Father, is the subject of the *qui* clause: he ascended while his apostles stood by. The petition begins with the imperative, *concede nobis* [grant to us], but the demand is immediately softened and deferred by the *quaesumus* [we beseech you] which the revisers supplied. *Ut* [that] follows, but the actual request is again deferred, this time by *secundum eius promissionem* [according to his promise]. We are only asking, we tell the Father, for what his Son promised. The request itself is twofold, a point that is underscored by the *et...et...* [both...and...] construction and a balanced parallel presentation:

et	ille	nobiscum	semper	in terris	
both	he	with us	always	on earth	

et	nos	cum eo	in caelo	vivere	mereamur
and	we	with him	in heaven	to live	may be worthy

The first request is that Christ always remain with us on earth. The second is that we may be worthy to live with him in heaven. From the theological perspective, the succession cannot be merely temporal; it is also causal. Because Christ remains with us on earth, we may one day be worthy to live with him in heaven.

Ascension Thursday
The collects assigned to Ascension Thursday in the pre- and post-Vatican II missals are:

---

[60] See pp. 13–4 above.

1962, 2002–8: In Ascensione Domini	1970–2008: In Ascensione Domini
Concede, quaesumus, omnipotens Deus: ut, qui hodierna die Unigenitum tuum Redemptorem nostrum ad caelos ascendisse credimus; ipsi quoque mente in caelestibus habitemus.	Fac nos, omnipotens Deus, sanctis exsultare gaudiis, et pia gratiarum actione laetari, quia Christi Filii tui ascensio est nostra provectio, et quo processit gloria capitis, eo spes vocatur et corporis.
Grant, we beseech you, almighty God: that we, who believe your only-begotten Son, our Redeemer, to have ascended to heaven this day, may ourselves dwell also in heavenly places in mind.	Grant us, almighty God, to exult in holy joy, and to be glad in devout thanksgiving, because the ascension of Christ your Son is our advancement, and where the glory of the head has gone before, there the hope of the body is also called.

Manuscript History
The 1962 Ascension day collect, which is the alternate collect of the feast in the third typical edition of the Vatican II missal, appears as the Ascension day collect in 50 liturgical manuscripts dating from the eighth to the sixteenth century as well as in all the Tridentine missals.[61] It was omitted from the first two editions of the new missal.

The 1970/75 collect is a new composition that draws upon an Ascension sermon of Pope Saint Leo the Great.[62]

The Text: 1962/2002
The collect opens with an imperative verb, followed by *quaesumus*, the address (almighty God) and a *qui* clause which is a statement of faith that affirms three truths: we believe 1) your only-begotten Son (relation to God), 2) our redeemer (relation to us), 3) ascended to heaven on this day (saving deed). The petition asks that we may remain, abide, dwell in heaven with Christ in mind, intention, purpose.

---

[61] CO I, 762.
[62] Antoine Dumas, "Les Sources du Missel Romain (II)," *Notitiae* 61 (February 1971) 75. See *Sermo LXX, De Ascensione Domini*, I.IV [PL 54, 292].

The Text: 1970/2002

Pope Saint Leo the Great: Sermon 73, 4	1970–2008: In Ascensione Domini
Quia igitur Christi ascensio, nostra prouectio est, et quo praecessit gloria capitis, eo spes uocatur et corporis, *dignis*, dilectissimi, *exultemus* gaudiis et pia gratiarum actione *laetemur*.	*Fac nos, omnipotens Deus, sanctis exsultare* gaudiis, et pia gratiarum actione *laetari*, quia Christi Filii tui ascensio est nostra provectio, et quo processit gloria capitis, eo spes vocatur et corporis.
Since therefore the ascension of Christ is our advancement, and where the glory of the head has gone before, there also the hope of the body is called, dearly beloved, let us exult with fitting joys and rejoice with devout thanksgiving.	Grant us, almighty God, to exult in holy joy, and to be glad in devout thanksgiving, because the ascension of Christ your Son is our advancement, and where the glory of the head has gone before, there the hope of the body is also called.

Pope Saint Leo's exhortation, to exult in fitting joy and to be glad in devout thanksgiving, becomes the petition of the new prayer after two changes. First, *dignis* [fitting, worthy, proper, becoming] modifying *gaudiis* [joys] was changed to *sanctis* [holy].[63] Second, the third person plural verbs, *exultemus* and *laetemur*, were recast as infinitives. In addition, the revisers supplied the opening imperative verb and salutation: *Fac nos, omnipotens Deus* [make, cause, grant us, almighty God]. In the confected collect, Leo's statement about the Ascension becomes a statement of fact that the revisers placed at the end of the new prayer, reversing Leo's order and that which is usual in prayers.

The statement of fact of this Ascension day prayer is very like the result clause of the collect appointed for Sunday IV of the Pasch in the Vatican II missals. In service of the same or similar ends, both present carefully balanced clauses that use synecdoche, antithetical pairs, and the word *processit*:

Sunday IV of the Pasch

ut	eo	perveniat	humilitas gregis,
that	there	may arrive	humility of the flock

	quo	processit	fortitudo pastoris
	where/whence	has gone before	the strength of the shepherd

Ascension

et	quo	processit	gloria capitis
and	where	has gone before	the glory of the head

---

[63] The revisers altered the 1962 collect of Sunday II *post Pascha*, now the 2002 collect of the 14th Sunday *per annum*, similarly: "*perpetuam ... laetitiam*" becomes "*sanctam ... laetitiam*."

eo	spes	vocatur	et	corporis
there	hope	is called	also	of the body

Individual elements of the two Ascension collects are presented side by side below.

Ascension day	1962, 2002	1970–2002
Mode of Address	Almighty God	Almighty God
Description of Christ	Your Only-Begotten Son, our redeemer	Your Son, our advancement (or progress, promotion); the head
Description of us	we who believe [your Son, our Redeemer] to have ascended to heaven today	the body
Petition	Grant that we too may abide with our minds in the heavenly places [where Christ has ascended].	Cause us to exult in holy joy and rejoice in devout thanksgiving.

Since either collect may be used at Mass on the Ascension, there is no change to remark upon.

Sunday after the Ascension // Sunday VII of the Pasch

Dominica post Ascensionem	Dominica VII Paschae
Omnipotens sempiterne Deus: fac nos tibi semper et devotam gerere voluntatem, et maiestati tuae sincero corde servire.	Supplicationibus nostris, Domine, adesto propitius, ut, sicut humani generis Salvatorem tecum in tua credimus maiestate, ita eum usque ad consummationem saeculi manere nobiscum, sicut ipse promisit, sentiamus.
Almighty, everlasting God: grant us always both to bear a will devoted to you and to serve your majesty with a sincere heart.	Be present, O Lord, to those who humbly implore you, that, as we believe the Savior of the human race to be with you in your majesty, so also may we experience him remaining with us unto the consummation of the world as he promised.

Manuscript History

The 1962 collect, without any variation in wording, serves as the collect for this day in over 40 codices that date from the eighth to the sixteenth century at which time it was incorporated into the Tridentine missal.[64]

The 1970/2002 collect appears in 30 liturgical collections that scholars date from the sixth/seventh century to the eleventh/twelfth with only one recorded variant and that appearing in only one codex.[65] The prayer is assigned to the Ascension or its vigil in numerous codices, but never to the Sunday following the feast. The modern editors revised the text. The changes they made do not follow the ancient variant and are without warrant in the manuscript tradition.

The Text

1962

The 1962 collect is simple, spare, and direct. It makes a two-fold request of God who is addressed/described as "Almighty, everlasting": that, at all times we have a will which is faithful to him and serve his majesty with a sincere heart – the *semper* [always], governs both infinitives: *gerere*, to bear, and *servire*, to serve. "Majesty" recognizes God's kingship and perhaps, in context, recalls the ascension of the Lord.

1970/2002

The 1970/2002 collect and its source are presented below. Differences in word order are indicated in italics, other differences in boldface type.

CO 153	Dominica VII Paschae
Adesto, domine, supplicationibus nostris, ut sicut humani generis salvatorem **consedere** tecum in tua maiestate **confidimus**, ita usque ad consummationem saeculi manere nobiscum **quemadmodum est pollicitus** sentiamus.	*Supplicationibus nostris, Domine, adesto* **propitius**, ut, sicut humani generis salvatorem tecum in tua **credimus** maiestate, ita **eum** usque ad consummationem saeculi manere nobiscum, **sicut ipse promisit,** sentiamus.
Be present, O Lord, to those who humbly implore you, that as **we trust** the Savior of the human race **to have taken his place** with you in majesty, so also may we perceive [him] to remain with us unto the consummation of the world, **as he promised.**	Graciously be present, O Lord, to those who humbly implore you, that as **we believe** the Savior of the human race **to be** with you in majesty, so also may we perceive [him] to remain with us, **as he promised,** unto the consummation of the world.

---

[64] CO VI, 3837 A. The prayer appears without textual change in the Vatican II missals as the collect of the 29th Sunday *per annum*.

[65] CO I,153. Dumas, "Les Sources du Missel Romain (II)," *Notitiae* 61 (February, 1971) p. 75, identifies *GeV* 580 as the source.

Since the editorial work of the modern redactors is mainly confined to substituting synonyms and reordering the text, the essential meaning of the prayer is not altered. But the revised prayer, while more deferential (propitius/graciously was added), is weaker in force and in poetry. In the original Christ is seated, or has taken his place, *consedere*, with the Father in majesty which is a stronger assertion that the implied "is" of the revision. Also the original alliteration *consedere/confidimus* was sacrificed in the editing of the same clause.

The new prayer combines elements found in the 2002 collect for the vigil of the Ascension and the 1962/2002 collect of the Ascension. Consider:

2002 Vigil of the Ascension	1962, 2002 Ascension	1970–2002 Sun VII Paschae
Deus, cuius Filius hodie in caelos, Apostolis adstantibus, adscendit, concede nobis, quaesumus, ut secundum eius promissionem **et ille nobiscum semper in terris** et nos cum eo in caelo vivere mereamur.	Concede, quaesumus, omnipotens Deus: ut, qui hodierna die Unigenitum tuum *Redemptorem nostrum ad caelos ascendisse credimus*; ipsi quoque mente in caelestibus habitemus.	Supplicationibus nostris, Domine, adesto propitius, ut, *sicut humani generis Salvatorem tecum in tua credimus maiestate,* ita **eum usque ad consummationem saeculi manere nobiscum,** sicut ipse promisit, sentiamus.
O God, whose Son ascended to the heavens today as the Apostles stood by, grant us, we beseech you, **in accordance with his promise,** that **he may always [be] with us on earth** and we may be deemed worthy to live with him in heaven.	Grant, we beseech you, almighty God, that, *we who believe your only-begotten Son, our Redeemer, to have ascended to heaven this day,* may ourselves dwell also in heavenly places in mind.	Graciously be present, O Lord, to those who humbly implore you that as *we believe the Savior of the human race to be with you in majesty,* so **also may we perceive [him] to remain with us, as he promised,** unto the consummation of the world.

In the Vatican II missals, the collect of the Mass for Sunday VII of the Pasch prolongs the feast of the Ascension by repeating sentiments expressed in the feast's own collects and by presenting a petition that recalls Christ's promise to remain with us until the end of time. The common themes are marked above in bold and italic typeface. The 1962 collect, equally conscious of the majesty of God, makes a different request: that we may be devoted to God and sincere in his service.

Pentecost

Vigil of Pentecost

The 1962 collect for this day is included without change in the Vatican II missals where it serves as the alternate collect for this day.

1962/1970–2008: Vigilia Pentecostes	1970–2008: Pentecostes: Ad Missam in Vigilis
Praesta, quaesumus, omnipotens Deus: ut claritatis tuae super nos splendor effulgeat; et lux tuae lucis corda eorum, qui per gratiam tuam renati sunt, Sancti Spiritus illustratione confirmet.	Omnipotens sempiterne Deus, qui paschale sacramentum quinquaginta dierum voluisti mysterio contineri, praesta, ut, gentium facta dispersione, divisiones linguarum ad unam confessionem tui nominis caelesti munere congregentur.
Grant, we beseech you, almighty God that the splendor of your glory may shine upon us, and, by the illumination of the Holy Spirit, the light of your light may strengthen the hearts of those who have been reborn through grace.	Almighty, everlasting God, who willed the paschal sacrament to be kept/ preserved in the mystery of fifty days, grant, dispersion of peoples having been effected, that by heavenly gift the division of tongues may be gathered together in a single confession of your name.

Manuscript History

The 1962 collect is found in over 50 codices dating from the sixth/seventh century until the sixteenth.[66] In most it serves as the collect for the Mass of the vigil of Pentecost. as it does in the 1962 missal.

The 1970/2002 prayer is found in over 30 codices dating from the sixth/ seventh century to the sixteenth in which it is used variously, but always in connection with the feast of Pentecost.[67] Eugenio Moeller and Joanne Maria Clément atypically do not list any textual variants but different forms of the prayer appear in the Veronese and Gelasian sacramentaries. Both have the same opening clause that Moeller and Clément present and that is found in the post-Vatican II missals. The respective petitions are worded differently, however, and are discussed below.

The Texts

1962 Collect and Alternate 1970/2002 Collect

Beginning with an imperative, *praesta* [grant], placed in the usual position and followed by *quaesumus* [we beseech you], this collect addresses

---

[66] CO VII, 4483.

[67] CO VI, 4015. Dumas, "Les Sources du Missel Romain (II)," *Notitiae* 61 (February 1971) p. 75, identifies the source as *GeV* 637.

"Almighty God." Light dominates as synonym after synonym appears in the *ut* clause: that the splendor (brightness, luster) of your brightness (glory, splendor) may shine forth (gleam, glitter) and the light of your light, by the illumination (brightness) of the Holy Spirit .... The actual request of the prayer is that God's light, by the illumination of the Holy Spirit, will strengthen the hearts of those who have been reborn through grace. In this way, the collect links the Paschal sacraments of Baptism and Confirmation.

1970/2002 Collect

Three different versions of the prayer are presented below. The Vatican II text is on the right. The differences are indicated in italics; the textual problem is in boldface type.

Ver 191	GeV 637	MR 1970–2002
praesta ut gentium facta dispersio *diuisione* linguarum ad unam confessionem tui nominis caelesti munere *congregetur*	praesta ut gencium facta dispersio *diuisiones* linguarum **ad unae confessione** tui nominis caeleste munere *congregentur.*	praesta ut, gentium facta dispersione, *divisiones* linguarum ad unam confessionem tui nominis caelesti munere *congregentur.*
grant that the dispersion of nations that occurred through the *division* of tongues may, by heavenly gift, be gathered together as one in confession of your name.	grant, dispersion of peoples having been effected, that by heavenly gift the *divisions* of tongues may be gathered together ... of your name.	grant, dispersion of peoples having occurred, that by heavenly gift the *divisions* of tongues may be gathered together in a single confession of your name.

The Veronese version of the prayer states that the dispersion of nations came about through the division of tongues and asks that the *dispersion* may be gathered (singular verb) by heavenly gift into a single confession of "your name." The Gelasian prayer has an obvious grammatical problem: *ad* governs the accusative but no accusative follows. Apart from this, the prayer asks that the *divisions* of tongues may be gathered (plural verb) by heavenly gift into [...] of your name. The post-Vatican II revisers chose the Gelasian version of the prayer but corrected the grammatical error. The result is a petition asking that, nations having been dispersed, the *divisions of tongues* may be gathered (plural verb) into a single confession of your name.

The collect addresses "almighty, everlasting God" and includes a statement of fact: the 50-day observance of the Paschal mystery is willed by God. It is God's will that the former be preserved, kept, held together, enclosed in the latter.

The petition alludes to the events recounted in Genesis 11, the confusion of tongues by God and consequent dispersion of nations, and Acts 2, the miracle following the descent of the Spirit upon the apostles whereby people "from every nation under heaven"[68] individually hear those who had received the Spirit speaking in his own [that is, the hearer's] language.[69] The actual request is that those of every language may be gathered into a single confession of "your name" – that is, united in profession of one faith.

Pentecost Sunday

1962 Pentecost	1970–2008 Pentecost
Deus, qui hodierna die corda fidelium Sancti Spiritus illustratione docuisti: da nobis, in eodem Spiritu recta sapere; et de eius semper consolatione gaudere.	Deus, qui sacramento festivitatis hodiernae universam Ecclesiam tuam in omni gente et natione sanctificas, in totam mundi latitudinem Spiritus Sancti dona defunde, et, quod inter ipsa evangelicae praedicationis exordia operata est divina dignatio, nunc quoque per credentium corda perfunde.
O God, who on this day, didst instruct the hearts of the faithful by the light of the Holy Spirit, grant us in the same Spirit to be truly wise and ever to rejoice in his consolation.[70]	O God, who in the mystery of today's feast, sanctify your whole Church amid every people and nation, pour down the gifts of the Holy Spirit upon the whole breadth of the world, and what divine condescension wrought amidst the very beginnings of Gospel proclamation now also pour into the hearts of believers.

Manuscript History
The 1962 text appears in 57 extant manuscripts dating from the eighth century to the sixteenth. In all it serves as a Pentecost Sunday prayer. In 52 it is the collect of the day as it is also in all the Tridentine missals. The only textual variant is the omission of "*semper*" in one codex.[71]

The collect of the revised missal appears in 30 extant codices dating from the eighth to the thirteenth century in connection with Pentecost, its vigil or

---

[68] Cf. Acts 2.5.
[69] Acts 2.5–12.
[70] Traditional English rendering.
[71] CO II, 1666. The Vatican II missals assign the prayer to the votive Mass of the Holy Spirit which purpose it also serves in the Tridentine missals.

its octave, but in none is it *the* collect of the feast.[72] It was included in the new missal without textual change.

The Text
1962
The 1962 collect of Pentecost Sunday opens in the same way as the 1962 collect of the Pasch: *Deus, qui hodierna die ...* [O God, who on this day ...]. *Hodierna die* also appears in the collect assigned to Ascension Thursday, but in none of the other collects of Paschaltide. That is, the solemnities celebrating the mysteries of the Lord's resurrection, ascension, and sending of his Spirit are denoted in the same way: "on this day." This phrase both elevates and connects these days.

The 1962 prayer continues the theme of light introduced in the Pentecost Vigil collect of the same missal by repeating one of its phrases. The petition of the vigil collect asks that the hearts of the baptized may be strengthened *Sancti Spiritus illustratione* [by the light of the Holy Spirit]. The *qui* clause of the Pentecost collect declares that the hearts of the faithful have been instructed *Sancti Spiritus illustratione* [by the light of the Holy Spirit]. With the word *docuisti* [taught/instructed] the theme of intellectual clarity, found in John's Gospel and implicit already in the light language of the vigil prayer, becomes explicit.[73] The faithful of this prayer are those who heard the apostolic preaching on the first Pentecost (*hodierna die*) and came to faith – the about 3,000 who were baptized that day.[74]

God's prior act of instructing the hearts of the faithful by the light of his Spirit on this day provides the motive for the petition, and "grant us" shifts the prayer from the past, the first Pentecost, to the present, this Pentecost Sunday. "Grant" governs two infinitive phrases, each making a request:

in eodem Spiritu	recta	sapere;
in the same Spirit	those things that are right	to understand

et	de eius	semper	consolatione	gaudere.
and	from his	always	consolation	to rejoice

We discussed *recta* above. It is a word with wide compass embracing all that is right, upright, correct, proper, appropriate, fitting, morally right, just, lawful, virtuous, and noble. The infinitive *sapere* means to taste or savor, but extends from discernment of palate to taking on the flavor, as in smacking of, and also to discernment of mind, as in know, understand, be

---

[72] CO III, 2057. Dumas, "Les Sources du Missel Romain (II)," *Notitiae* 61 (February 1971) p. 75, identifies *GeV* 638.

[73] Cf. John 14.26, the Spirit will teach (Vul. *docebit*) all things, and 16.13, the Spirit will teach (Vul. *docebit*) you all truth.

[74] Acts 2.42. This means the term "faithful" is used proleptically. See Haessly, *Rhetoric in the Sunday Collects of the Roman Missal*, p. 71.

prudent or wise. It shares its root with *sapientia*, wisdom. The first petition, then, asks that by the Spirit we may savor, smack of, know, understand, be prudent and wise about everything which is good, right, just, virtuous and noble. The second asks that we may ever (*semper*) rejoice in a consolation of which the Spirit is the source (*de*). The ever or always, which by its placement attaches to *gaudere* but not *sapere*, includes both the comfort of the Spirit in this world and everlasting happiness in the next.

1970/2002 Collect

This collect also begins "O God" followed by a statement of fact which continues a theme introduced in the collect of the vigil. Here it is the word "sacrament" or "mystery." The vigil collect speaks of the sacrament/mystery of both the Pasch and the 50 days, the Pentecost collect of the sacrament/mystery of "today's feast." God, in the mystery of today's feast, sanctifies his whole church in every people and nation. This statement of fact provides the motive for a two-fold request using two imperative verbs with the same root: *defunde* and *perfunde*. *Fundo* means to pour, *defundo* to pour down, *perfundo* to pour into or fill.

The first requested pouring, the pouring down, is for the gifts of the Holy Spirit to be poured upon the whole breadth [*in totam latitudinem*] of the world [*mundi*]. The second pouring is now also to pour into the hearts of believers what divine graciousness or condescension [*dignatio*] wrought [*operata est*: worked, caused, effected] at the very beginnings [*ipsa exordia*] of Gospel preaching.

The movement of the collect is from the statement that God sanctifies his *Church* amid every people and nation to a request that God pour the gifts of his Spirit on the whole *world* and fill the hearts of *believers* as he did, one interprets, on that first Pentecost Sunday (when the Gospel was first preached). The intended meaning or scope of the prayer is not clear but depends on whether the words "Church" (*ecclesiam*) in the *qui* clause and "believers" (*credentium*) in the second part of the petition are prolepsis[75] or not. The question arises principally from the first part of the petition, that God pour the gifts of the Holy Spirit on the breadth of the whole world, supported by the reference to the first Pentecost in the second part of the petition (*ipsa evangelicae praedicationis exordia*). For when the Gospel was first preached on Pentecost morning there were no believers in the multitude until those present heard the apostles speaking and God, in his graciousness, wrought in those hearts what he wrought.

That is, in one reading of the prayer, one that does not admit prolepsis, the movement is from the statement that God sanctifies his Church, which

---

[75] As are the "fidelium" of the 1962 Pentecost prayer – that is those who became faithful because they were taught by the light of the Holy Spirit, not those who were faithful when they were taught.

exists in every people and nation, to the request that those who already believe be infused with what divine graciousness wrought at the start of Christian preaching. In this case the petition for the gifts of the Spirit to be given to the whole world would be understood in the light of the statement of fact: gifts poured out upon the Church amid every people and nation, the believers of the second part of the petition. In the other reading, the one that understands Church and believers proleptically, the movement is from the statement that God sanctifies amid every people and nation, thus making his Church holy, to a petition that he pour the gifts of his Spirit upon the whole world and, working in human hearts as he did on the first Pentecost, effectively bring men and women to faith, to being believers (*corda credentium*).

The second reading places the Pentecost collect in narrative continuity with the collect of the vigil Mass, the petition of which is global in scope: "that the division of tongues may be gathered into a single confession of your name."

Conclusion

The nine Paschal *orationes* of Sundays and the Ascension of the 1962 missal are an ancient set. The same prayers, with the very same wording, are assigned to the very same days in more than 30 liturgical codices that date from the eighth through the sixteenth century. The compilers of the Tridentine missal simply continued a long and well-established tradition.

When the post-Vatican II revisers replaced the set, they departed from a tradition of usage that was at least twelve hundred years old. Examination of the collects assigned to these days in the new missals quickly finds that the post-conciliar reformers did not adopt a different, but equally ancient, set. Rather they confected a new one.

Below we consider each set, as a set, in turn.

The Corpus of 1962 Paschaltide Collects

The collects of Resurrection Sunday, Ascension Thursday, and Pentecost Sunday, the major feasts of Paschaltide, includes the phrase "*hodierna die*." The phrase gives these feasts prominence and brings them into particular association with one another.

The petitions for the Paschal Sundays and the Ascension ask (1) that God remain present assisting the desires and prayers he inspires in us (the Pasch); (2) that we may keep, possess, retain the paschal mystery in character and life (Octave Day/ Sunday *in Albis*); (3) that we, who have been saved from everlasting death, may enjoy everlasting happiness (Sunday II after the Pasch); (4) that Christians reject everything that opposes Christ and pursue all that is consistent with faith in him (Sunday III after the Pasch); (5) that we love what God commands and desire what he promises (Sunday IV after the Pasch); (6) that we think by God's inspiration all that is just, noble, and right, and under his direction do the same (Sunday V after the Pasch); (7) that our minds may abide in heaven with our ascended Lord (Ascension); (8) that our wills are ever faithful to the Lord and that we serve him always with a sincere heart (Sunday in Octave of Ascension); (9) that we may be prudent and wise about everything that is good, right, just, virtuous and noble, and enjoy always the consolation of the Holy Spirit (Pentecost).

Except for the collects of the Pasch and its Octave Day, no prayer explicitly mentions the Pasch or the resurrection. The collect of the Pasch begs God's constant assistance, that of the second Sunday after Easter for an unending joy which is all the more intense because it springs from awareness of our divinely executed escape from unending death. All the other collects speak of the way we are to live and comport ourselves in this life. These collects successively petition on behalf of the whole human person in its every aspect: character and life (*Sunday in Albis*); discerning choice that rejects all that is contrary to, and pursues all that is consistent with, Christ (third Sunday after Easter); love and desires (fourth Sunday after Easter); thoughts and actions (fifth Sunday after Easter); minds (sixth Sunday after Easter); wills (Sunday after the Ascension). In addition, the collect of Easter Sunday asks God to accompany with his grace the longings that he inspires, and that of Pentecost begs the gifts of practical wisdom and the constant consolation of the Holy Spirit.

All of these petitions are general, but concrete, and oriented to practical effect.

2002/2008

There is some development in the corpus of Paschaltide collects in the successive editions of the Vatican II missal. The summary below considers only the Paschal Sunday and Ascension collects of the third typical edition *Missale Romanum (2002)*.

The petitions of the revised set of collects seek: (1) that we may rise in the light of life through renewal in the Holy Spirit (Pasch); (2) that we may understand fittingly by which bath, Spirit, and blood we have been washed, reborn and redeemed (Sunday II of the Pasch); (3) that we may rejoice in renewed youth of soul so that we may await the day of resurrection with the hope of certain joy (Sunday III of the Pasch); (4) that we may be led to the communion of heavenly joys (Sunday IV of the Pasch); (5) that the paschal mystery may be perfected in us so that we may bear much fruit and attain the joy of eternal life (Sunday V of the Pasch); (6) that we may celebrate these days in honor of the risen Lord with earnest love and hold fast to them in action (Sunday VI of the Pasch); (7) that Christ will remain with us on earth and we may live with him in heaven (Vigil of Ascension); (8) that we may exult in holy joys and rejoice in devout thanksgiving (Ascension); (9) that our minds may abide in heaven with our ascended Lord (Ascension, alternate collect); (10) that we may experience Christ remaining with us (Sunday VII of the Pasch); (11) that the dispersion of tongues may be gathered into a single confession of faith (Vigil of Pentecost); (12) there may be a new outpouring of the Spirit through which God does now in the hearts of believers what he did when the Gospel was first preached (Pentecost).

Except for the collect assigned to Good Shepherd Sunday which uses pastoral images, the collects of the first six Sundays of the Pasch in the revised missal, that is those which occur before the Ascension, all contain an explicit reference to the Pasch or something intimately associated with it.[76] The remaining collects make specific mention of the Ascension or Pentecost.

A second difference is that two of the petitions in the revised set, the third and fifth, have *ut* or result clauses – particular gifts or graces are sought *so that* particular results will follow. For our purposes here, we ignore the implied causal connections and treat both the requests and their "results" as requests. In the following paragraphs we look at the *kinds* of things requested, and give particular attention to what we ask to be accomplished in or for us.

Four of the petitions of the revised missal explicitly ask that we may reach heaven.[77] A second request is attached to three of these petitions for heaven. These are that we may rejoice in renewed youth of soul (Sunday III), that we may bear much fruit (Sunday V), and that Christ may remain with us as he promised (Vigil of the Ascension). Of these requests for heaven only one includes mention of something going on in us or our doing something – namely, the prayer that asks God to perfect the paschal mystery in us that we may both bear much fruit and attain heaven (Sunday V).

Several of the petitions that speak of behaviors focus on dispositions or emotions or something akin, rather than deeds: for example, to rejoice in renewed youth of soul (Sunday III), to celebrate with diligent love (Sunday VI), to exult in holy joys and rejoice in devout thanksgiving (Ascension),

---

[76] Sunday I ... qui resurrectionis dominicae sollemnia colimus [... we who celebrate the solemnity of the Lord's resurrection]; Sunday II ... qui in ipso paschalis festi recursu [... who, in this annual return of the paschal feast]; Sunday III ... resurrectionis diem ... exspectet [... may await the day of resurrection]; Sunday IV: Good Shepherd Sunday; Sunday V ... semper in nobis paschale perfice sacramentum [... perfect always the paschale mystery in us]; Sunday VI ... quos in honorem Domini resurgentis exsequimur [which we celebrated in honor of the rising of the Lord].

[77] The older missal has one explicit and one implicit mention of eternal life (the collects of the second Sunday after the Pasch and Pentecost respectively).

to experience Christ with us (Sunday VII). It may be too harsh to call these "feel good petitions" but there is something of this about them. They are different from the pre-Vatican prayers assigned to these days not because they speak of love and joy, which appreciation of the Resurrection and Ascension must in fact evoke, but that they beg for us no further or more concrete response.

Three other petitions have a moral dimension. The collect of Sunday VI asks that we hold fast in action to what we celebrate in honor of the Lord's rising partially echoes the petition of the 1962 prayer for the Paschal octave. While general, it is concrete. The alternate collect of the Ascension, which asks that our minds may dwell in heaven with our ascended Lord, is a 1962 prayer that was inserted into the 2002 missal, not a newly selected or confected text. It exhibits the characteristics of the former missal. The collect of Sunday V requests that, under God's protection, we bear much fruit. Good fruit is meant, of course, and Jesus's teaching that only sound trees can bear good fruit is necessarily assumed. This prayer, then, is also a request that we become good.

Four petitions remain. The petition of the collect of Easter Sunday is that "through renewal of the Holy Spirit we may rise in the light of life." The phrase "rise in the light of life" has no technical or traditional meaning in biblical, liturgical, or theological usage. Attached to a collect prayed on the Pasch, it conveys a request that in some way we share in Christ's resurrection. But the language, while suggestive, is without concrete or explicit meaning. The petition was changed by the revisers from "... rise from death of soul." Aware of this, as no one at Mass on Easter Sunday is likely to be, we can surmise that "in the light of life" is meant to be a more positive way of putting "from death of soul." But the two expressions do not at all mean the same thing. Rather, clear language with specific meaning has been traded for pleasant, positive-sounding language of uncertain meaning.

The petition of Sunday II of the Pasch is for understanding – more accurately, to comprehend or grasp the named mysteries with fitting or worthy understanding. The formation of the intellect is essential if it is to direct the will properly, if the acts which follow are to be fully human, and if, to put it simply, the grace of redemption is to form our every aspect and faculty. That is, the petition of this prayer is good in itself. The difference between it and those of the 1962 missal, however, is that it goes no further than understanding the mysteries. It does not mention action (as does the 1962 prayer that we both think and *do*). Nor are there complementary prayers in the post-Vatican II Paschal set that address the needs of our will (like, for examples, the 1962 prayer that we bear always a will devoted to the Lord, or that we reject what is hostile to Christ's name and pursue what befits it).

The petition of the collect of the Pentecost Vigil is a prayer, not for the Christian community *per se* but for the conversion of the world: that by heavenly gift the division of tongues may be gathered together in a single confession of "your name." As we note above, it is not clear whether the Pentecost collect is principally a prayer for those who are already believers or those who have not yet become believers (in the latter case "believers" would be prolepsis). In either case, the essence of the petition is a new Pentecost in which God will do in hearts again what he did of old when the Spirit was first given and the Gospel first preached. The prayer asks that God's grace or working (*operatio*) may permeate the hearts of believers (*per corda* – throughout the hearts) but, unlike the 1962 Pentecost prayer which seeks wisdom concerning right things and the constant consolation of the Spirit, no specific gifts are sought.

It is hard, if not impossible, to compare and contrast two sets which do not have the same number of prayers (nine in the 1962 missal; twelve in the 2002 missal) and have only two prayers in common. After examining the petitions of each set, however, we can say that they do not have the same preoccupations and do not seek the same things from the Lord.

The 1962 corpus does not explicitly mention the feast or season in each prayer, which may be why the post-Vatican II revisers relegated six of them to *per annum* Sundays. As a set, however, the prayers beg that we, having been snatched by God from unending death, may be formed in our every aspect and faculty – prayers, character and life, choices, love and desires, thoughts and actions, minds and wills – and taught by the Holy Spirit so that we may be wise about all that is right and just and may rejoice always in his consolation. The graces which make this formation possible, we know from both our theology of redemption and the setting of these prayers, come only from the death and resurrection of the Lord.

All the prayers of the revised set, in contrast, remind us that we are celebrating the Pasch, the Ascension or Pentecost. They assert or beg for joy. The most frequently expressed desire is for the attainment of heaven. If there is a way in which these prayers embrace the totality of the human person that is at all like those of the 1962 missal it is not immediately apparent. They do not seem to be unified by a common vision or focus. This may be because the set was confected from different missals and certain prayers composed from multiple contributing texts. But, on the other hand, the fact that the revisers were not obliged to accept an existing corpus of Paschal orations and were free to assemble a new set and even to compose new prayers makes it all the more remarkable that the new corpus of Paschal Sunday and Ascension collects do not exhibit unity and depth.

While it is not possible to take the Paschal Mystery seriously, as these prayers certainly do, and be trite, it is also true that the revised set of Paschal Sunday and Ascension collects are relatively superficial – that is, in relation to the earlier set. The comparative superficiality is, perhaps, best appreciated when one looks at each set of petitions in the light of the New Testament understanding of the renewal and transformation of the human person that the grace of Christ is to effect in our mind, will, heart, spirit, thoughts, affections, and actions.

8

Summary and Conclusion

The first four sections of this last chapter discuss: 1) the uniqueness of the post-Vatican II reform of the Sacred Liturgy, 2) the way in which the revisers handled their sources, 3) centonization in the new missal, and 4) the character of the collect. These discussions are followed by a comparative evaluation of the two sets of collects and the conclusion.

The Uniqueness of the Post-Vatican II Reform

The *Missale Romanum (1570)*, the first typical edition of the Tridentine missal which is also called the Missal of Pius V, was commissioned by the bishops of the Council of Trent. The collects assigned to the Sunday and Holy Days of proper seasons in the first Tridentine missal are the same as those found in a great number of extant liturgical books the oldest of which go back to the eighth century. Those responsible for producing the Tridentine missal adopted *en bloc* a corpus of Mass collects that had been used for at least 800 years.

Surviving manuscripts indicate that Tridentine reformers made two textual changes to the corpus of Sunday and Holy Day collects assigned to proper seasons: they added *quaesumus* [we beseech you] to the collect of the fourth Sunday of Advent[1] and *Dominum nostrum Iesum Christum Filium tuum* [your Son, our Lord, Jesus Christ] to the collect of the Octave Day of the Nativity and Circumcision of the Lord (1 January).[2] Neither of these editorial additions changes the import of the prayer. The first increases deference, improves the cadence, and makes the opening clause of the collect identical to that of the first Sunday of Advent giving a greater unity to the collects of the season. The second, as we discuss above, names

---

[1] Cf. CO IV, 550.
[2] Cf. CO III, 2113 a, b, c.

the author of life and thereby makes explicit what the unrevised oration expresses implicitly.[3]

This same set of collects appears in the 1962 missal, the last typical edition of the Tridentine missal, except that new collects were added for the feasts of the Holy Name of Jesus (Sunday between January 2 and 5) and the Holy Family (Sunday within the Epiphany Octave) when they were placed on the universal calendar in 1721 and 1892 respectively. When the titles of the Octave Days of the Nativity and Epiphany were changed in the 1962 missal,[4] the collects of those days were not changed. They remained what they are in *Missale Romanum (1570)*.

As we have seen, the post-Vatican II revisers did not adopt an antecedent tradition of usage. They produced something unique. The four Sunday collects of Advent come from three different sources: two from a Romano-Frankish book (*Gelasianum Vetus*) and one each from the scroll of Ravenna (*Rotulus of Ravenna*) and the *Missale Romanum (1962)*.[5] The new set of six Lenten Sunday collects consists of one prayer from the *Missale Romanum*, two from the Romano-Frankish codex, and three new compositions. Two of the new compositions take something from a Mozarabic (Spanish) codex. The set of Pachaltide collects of *Missale Romanum* is likewise diverse. Three collects come from the 1962 missal, one in substantially revised form. Six come from ancient liturgical books, five from the Romano-Frankish codex and the sixth is unique to a Gallican codex (*Missale Gothicum*). Four are new compositions, three of which are centonized: one from two prayers in a Milanese or Ambrosian codex, one combining two prayers from the *Gelasianum Vetus*, and the third combining three prayers: two Roman prayers from the Veronese or *Leonine Sacramentary* and a prayer from the *Gelasianum Vetus*. The last new composition adapts a Sermon of Pope Saint Leo the Great.

The Handling of Sources

In the Fall of 1966, the Consilium members answered six questions and thereby laid out the course of action that the *periti* of *Coetus* 18*bis* were to follow in revising the orations. It was agreed that 1) texts be used only once; 2) corruptions be corrected; 3) references to events whose significance had been lost to the Church universal be removed and, where discrepancies existed, orations accommodated to the customs of present-day Christian

---

[3] See p. 82 above.

[4] January 1st ceased to be called the Circumcision and January 13 became the commemoration of the Lord's Baptism.

[5] The postcommunion prayer of the Annunciation in the 1962 missal is the collect of Advent Sunday IV in the Vatican II missals.

life; 4) proper literary genre be preserved or restored in, or inserted into, each prayer; 5) orations, in general, be addressed to the Father; 6) new texts, drafted chiefly by the method of centonization, be added.[6]

Initially there were lapses in the implementation of the first policy for texts are repeated in the first two typical editions of the Vatican II missals. This is corrected in the third typical edition, *Missale Romanum (2002)*, so there is no need to comment further. The sixth policy, which provides for the creation of new texts chiefly by means of centonization, is discussed in the next section. The matter of literary genre is touched upon both in this section and the next.

The second, third, and fifth policies name conditions that occasion the emendment of existing texts.

The fifth policy is implemented in only one collect among those considered in this study: the collect assigned to the Vigil of the Ascension. The source prayer is an ancient text addressed to Christ that is pressed into modern service for the first time in the *Missale Romanum (2002)*. As we saw above, every change the modern editors made to the source prayer (CO II, 1337) is explained by the decision to address the prayer to the Father.[7]

The third policy does not seem to have governed the revision of any collect in our study. With respect to the first situation named in the policy, the presence of references whose significance to the universal Church has been lost, none of the collects that we consider contain such a reference. With respect to the second, accommodating prayers to the customs of Christian life today, it is necessary to recall that Bruylants's explicit reason for asking the question was the discrepancy he saw between what the Fathers of Vatican II call for in *Sacrosanctum Concilium* n. 109 and the Lenten collects in the *Missale Romanum (1962)* – namely, that the latter contain no mention of Baptism and the references to penance in them are expressed exclusively in the language of fasting. The directives that the Council Fathers give in *Sacrosanctum Concilium* n. 109 are not carried into effect in the specific changes made to any collect that was adopted for Lenten Sunday use in the Vatican II missals.

The second policy calls for the correction of corrupt texts. Bruylants identified the 1962 collect assigned to Sunday of the Resurrection as a corrupt text and asked the Consilium members if they wanted the prayer restored according to the version found in *Gelasianum Vetus*. This was done. But later the collect was further revised, Dumas explains in his 1971 essay, because even after being perfectly restored it did not yet "give complete satisfaction."[8]

In the course of our examination we identify 12 other collects assigned to Sundays or holy days of proper seasons that were edited by the modern

---

[6] *De Missali* 27, Schema n. 186 (19 September 1966) pp. 1–4 and *addendum* p. 1.

[7] See above p. 190.

[8] Antoine Dumas,"Les oraisons du nouveau Missel," *Questions Liturgiques* 25 (1971): 263–70 at 268: "... ne donnent pas encore entière satisfaction."

revisers in ways that have no precedent in the manuscript tradition. These are the collects assigned to: Sundays I, II, and III of Advent; the Vigil, Night, and Dawn Masses of the Nativity of the Lord; Sunday I and II after the Nativity; the Vigil of the Epiphany; Sunday III of Lent; and Sundays IV and VII of the Pasch. Not included in the preceding list is the collect assigned to the Octave Day of the Nativity, the Solemnity of Mary Mother of God, which appeared in edited form in the first and second typical editions of the Vatican II missals but was restored to its 1962 form in *Missale Romanum (2002)*. In none of these cases had the source text suffered a corruption that the revisers corrected.

As the second adjustment to the collect of Easter Sunday and the twelve other examples illustrate, the revisers made changes to existing texts that were neither required nor justified by the agreed upon revision policies. The reasons for these changes are not recorded in the *Coetus* schemata.[9] An explanation may, however, be found in Antoine Dumas's 1968 reformulation of the revision policies and in his 1971 essay.[10]

The number of seemingly gratuitous changes made to these collects by the *periti* of *Coetus* 18*bis*, in contrast to the two very modest changes the post-Tridentine reformers made in the course of their labors, attests that the approach of the twentieth-century revisers to the received texts of our liturgical tradition was very different from that of their sixteenth-century counterparts.

The fourth revision policy stipulates that proper literary genre be preserved or restored in, or inserted into, each prayer. It is not clear how the revisers implemented this policy or even what it requires. In the first place the same texts are often used variously in antiquity, and it is difficult, if not impossible, to justify an assertion that one of the antique uses is not proper. Secondly, the revisers chose texts to use as collects in the Vatican II missals that had never served as collects before.

An example is the very first collect in the Vatican II missal. The revisers selected *GeV* 1139 as the new collect for the first Sunday of Advent. The same text is found in a variety of ancient codices where it is always either an Advent postcommunion prayer or an Advent blessing *super populum* [over the people]. There is no indication in the manuscript tradition that it had ever served as a Mass collect before its inclusion in the Vatican II missals. Both ancient uses enlarge the connotative significance of a prayer that speaks of Christ's coming because his sacramental coming, which is

---

[9] Many of these modern revisions are manifestly not improvements – for examples, the substitutions of *processit* for *praecessit* and *fortitudo* for *celsitudo* in the collect of Sunday IV of the Pasch which obscure the clarity and weaken the antithetical parallelism of the original text. See also the changes made to the collects assigned to the night and dawn Masses of Christmas.

[10] *De Missali* 56, Schema n. 319 (7 October 1968), p. 2 and Antoine Dumas, "Les oraisons du nouveau Missel," *Questions Liturgiques* 25 (1971) 263–70. See pp. 15–6 and p. 16, n. 44 for the 1968 rewording of the policies.

not explicitly named, is implicitly included whenever the prayer is prayed soon after Holy Communion. This is not to suggest that the prayer cannot be a proper collect, but to assert that its service as a postcommunion and blessing are also both wholly proper. And if so, we must acknowledge that the literary genre of particular liturgical prayers is a great deal more fluid than the fourth revision policy seems to suggest.

Centonization

Four of the collects in our study are newly centonized compositions, those assigned to: Sunday IV in Lent and Sundays III, V, and VI of the Pasch.

The creation of new liturgical prayers by means of centonization is an ancient practice. In Chapter 3 we discuss Pope Saint Gregory's use of the method to confect the collect assigned to the first Sunday of Advent in the Tridentine missals from two pre-Gelasian prayers that survive in the later codex known as the *Gelasianum Vetus*.[11] In this later volume, one of the source texts is an Advent prayer (*GeV* 1120) and the other is a prayer assigned to the month of December (*GeV* 1158). Both prayers ask for a heavenly coming – that is, they share a common theme. Pope Saint Gregory's new composition includes the entirety of the first clause of the first prayer and all but one word of the second clause of the second prayer – for the new composition substitutes *ut* for the original *et*. The Pontiff adds four words of his own. His work does not change the theme or the theology of the original prayers, but increases the intensity of the plea and, in so doing, puts greater emphasis on our reliance on, and need for, God.

The centonizing that produced the new collects in our study is somewhat different in character. The collect assigned to Sunday IV of Lent in the Vatican II missals is centonized from two texts that speak of fasting or, to be more precise, that name blessings that come from fasting. But the new prayer mentions neither fasting nor its benefits. The petition of the centonized collect asks that the Christian people may, with prompt devotion and ready faith, hasten to the coming solemnity. The notion of haste and the phrase "the coming solemnity" originate with the revisers for neither is found in either source. Rather the relevant source says "let us undertake this solemn fast with prompt devotion and ready faith."[12] In the process of centonization, then, the subject of both source texts is abandoned while certain expressions in each text are ordered to a purpose or sentiment that originates with the revisers. And whether by design or not, the new oration does not exhibit the customary parallelism between the statement of fact, which normally provides the motive for the petition, and the petition itself.

---

[11] See p. 33–5 above.
[12] *Patrologia Latina* 54, 151b (Leo, *Sermo* LX, *De Quadragesima* II.4).

The two source prayers of the newly centonized collect assigned to Sunday III of the Pasch do not share a common theme. The one, from Paschaltide, begs joy for those who have been restored to innocence after suffering the death of sin; the other, a prayer for the faithful departed, asks that the one who has died may be purified through the sacrifices offered on his behalf. Both source texts describe our state prior to God's saving acts. Indeed the joy expressed or hoped for in these prayers arises in no small part from a realization of what, except for God's mercy and goodness, would become of us. The new prayer adopts only phrases that describe what God has brought us to, not what he has saved us from. And, as we note in the discussion of these texts in Chapter 7, the newly confected prayer lacks the theological precision of its sources.[13]

The newly composed collect of Sunday VI of the Pasch is confected from three prayers. These do not share a common purpose or theme. From one composition the revisers took but three words. And as we indicate in Chapter 7, the theology of grace of the newly centonized collect differs from the one contained in all of the contributing texts.[14]

Questions pertaining to the policy which calls for the preservation of proper literary genre naturally surface as we examine the texts chosen for centonization. That a Lenten collect and a Lenten sermon were mined to confect the newly composed collect of Sunday III of Lent causes no surprise. The new paschal collects, however, were centonized from a variety of different types of prayers: the new collect of Sunday III is composed from a paschaltide blessing and an October prayer for the dead; that of Sunday V from a Paschal Octave preface and a Paschal Octave prayer over the offerings; that of Sunday VI from a fast day preface, a sanctoral oration from December, and paschal prayer. Again, it is not clear how the revision policy that requires preservation of the proper literary genre of prayers was observed in the practice of centonization or even what the policy requires.

Character of the Collect

The traditional Roman collects are highly sophisticated and stunningly concise literary compositions that overflow with surplus of meaning – connotation far outstripping denotation. In his classic essay "The Genius of the Roman Rite," Edmond Bishop says of them: "the ideas are as simple and elementary as the expression is pregnant and precise."[15]

The Tridentine missals use the term *oratio* for the prayers that we examine. The principal meanings of *oratio* have to do with speaking:

---

[13] See pp. 174–6 above.
[14] See pp. 188–9 above.
[15] *Liturgica Historica: Papers on the Liturgy and Religious Life of the Western Church* (Oxford: Clarendon Press, 1918) 3.

speech, set speech, formal discourse, speech delivered in public, mode of speaking. The word also means "prayer." Both meanings apply to the Mass *oratio*: the *oratio* is a prayer of a particular style that is publicly spoken. Joseph Jungmann describes it as "a prayer which has, to some extent, the character of public discourse."[16] The name *collecta*, assigned to these prayers in the Vatican II missals, originates in Gallican usage and suggests the gathering of petitions into this one prayer.[17]

The Roman *collect* or *oratio* is a prayer of petition expressed in a single, carefully crafted, concise, prose sentence having a somewhat elevated rhetorical style. The subject of the prayer is always plural[18] and the requests are always general (as befits a petition made on behalf of many). The single sentence of the prayer is comprised of short metrical units which flow rhythmically because each ends in a specific arrangement of stressed and unstressed syllables of Latin *cursus*. Also, collects are exceedingly brief. The shortest of the 1962 prayers in our study has 14 words (Sunday III of Lent), the longest 33 (Sunday III *post Pascha*); the shortest of the set in *Missale Romanum (2002)* has 20 words (Vigil of the Epiphany) and the longest 39 (Pentecost Sunday). The average length of the prayers in both sets is 25.9 words.[19]

Although scriptural allusions abound in the collects, the classic Roman orations generally do not quote or paraphrase scripture in either the *qui* clause or the petition itself. Rather, the typical Roman collect comes from scripture more in the manner of prayer that arises in the course of *lectio divina*, the monastic practice of reading and meditating – meditating in the ancient sense of ruminating and repeating – the sacred text until the heard and meditated Word of God pierces the heart and the heart naturally, as it were, responds in prayer.

Because, as Bishop says, "the ideas" of the collect "are as simple and elementary as the expression is pregnant and precise," their considerable riches and beauty continue to unfold as they are prayed not only year after year, but even hour after hour in the Offices of a single liturgical day. And as they are repeated again and again, the desires they express will hopefully take deeper and deeper root in those who pray them.

---

[16] Joseph Jungmann, *The Mass of the Roman Rite: its Origins and Development*, vol. 1, 360.

[17] Joseph Jungmann, *The Mass of the Roman Rite: its Origins and Development*, vol. 1, 361.

[18] Collective nouns such as family, flock, and people are "plural" in the sense intended here.

[19] The average for the Sunday and Holy Day collects of the 1962 missal carried to the third decimal point is 25.966; the average of the Sunday and Holy Day collects of the 2002 missal (which includes the alternate prayers) carried to the third decimal point is 25.971.

Comparative Evaluation

One of the objectives of this study is to discover whether the Sunday and Holy Day collects of proper seasons in the pre- and post-Vatican II missals assume the same posture before God, express the same convictions and sentiments about him, understand and describe the human situation in the same way, beseech God for the same or similar graces – and if they do not, to identify in what specific ways, and to what extent, they differ.

These are complex matters, and it is imperative that there be no misunderstanding. A comparative examination of the two missals with respect to only one type of prayer, the collect, is nothing more than a good start. And our examination of the collects is limited to those assigned to the Sundays and holy days of proper seasons. A summary of our findings in this first and very limited inquiry follows.

Advent

The 1962 collects focus those who pray them on the present as they seek immediate protection from danger and transforming interior effects.[20] The 1970/2002 collects orient those who pray them to the future. Three ask that we may enter heaven,[21] the fourth that we may arrive at and celebrate the joys of the coming feast.[22]

The 1962 collects call upon God to act or move: that he rouse his power and come, rouse our hearts, listen to our prayer and illumine our mind with the grace of visitation, rouse his power and come and help.[23] Our action, in the one 1962 collect in which it is mentioned, follows a delicate description of the interplay between divine gift and human response. We ask that God rouse our hearts to prepare the ways for his Son so, ultimately, we may serve him with pure minds. Between God's rousing and our service, however, the Son comes to those who have, by God's granting, prepared his way and, having come, purifies their minds.

The 1970/2002 collects, except for that of Sunday IV, present the human person as acting and in motion. They ask God to give a particular will to

---

[20] Sunday I: Protection and freedom from the threatening danger of sin; Sunday II: a heart that is roused to prepare for Christ and a mind purified for service to serve God; Sunday III: illumination of mind through the grace of divine visitation; Sunday IV: mercy to speed what sins impede.

[21] The petition is worded differently in each case. The collect of Sunday I asks that we may possess the heavenly kingdom; that of Sunday II, that we may be co-heirs with the Son; that of Sunday IV: that we may be brought to the glory of his resurrection.

[22] The prayer describes us as "people faithfully awaiting the feast of the Lord's nativity," and asks that we may be able to arrive at and celebrate the joys of such a great salvation with solemn prayers and ready rejoicing.

[23] The 1962 collects assigned to Sundays I, II, III, and IV respectively.

the faithful as they hasten, to grant that they are not impeded by earthly deeds as they hasten, to make them to arrive at the feast of the Nativity and the joys of salvation.[24] These are requests that we act or achieve or, in the one case, that we not be prevented from attaining.

The human situation is depicted differently in the two sets. In the 1962 prayers, human beings are threatened and impeded by sin, and their minds stand in need of purification and illumination. This bad news, so to speak, is off-set by the good news: the Lord comes in power to rouse, illumine, succor, protect, deliver, purify, and speed. In the 1970/2002 Advent Sunday collects, there is scant awareness of danger[25] and no mention of sin, recalcitrance, or human weakness.

Christmas

The differences between the two sets of Christmas collects are very difficult to name and then assess – especially the differences which are likely to have a formative effect on the faithful. One reason is that the pre- and post-Vatican II missals have a relatively large number of common collects. Another is that a number of the textual changes which the revisers made to the texts of the 1962 missal do not significantly alter the import of the prayers.

The most important differences between the two sets are two. The new missals give a prominence to the mystery of the Lord's Baptism that is lacking in the old. Similarly, the decision to transfer the feast of the Epiphany to Sunday in those regions where it is not a holy day of obligation insures that all the faithful consider and celebrate this mystery of the Lord's life. In the latter case, the change is a matter of giving the feast greater exposure or, more accurately, of exposing more of the faithful to the feast. In the former case, the 1962 collect is retained as an alternate. That is, the new collect assigned to the Lord's Baptism does not replace the old. The two collects are very different, however, and bring those who pray them into different aspects of the Paschal Mystery.

The 1962 collect is taken up with the mystery of the Incarnation and the hope it offers us. The divine Son took our flesh. He became exactly what we are, except that his nature is not marred by sin. The prayer asks nothing less for us than utter likeness to Christ through re-creation in grace. The prayer does not mention Baptism, either Christ's or our own.

The focus of the 1970/2002 collect is divine sonship: the real Sonship of Christ which the Father declares and our own adopted sonship. There are two explicit references to Baptism. The first is to the Lord's, the occasion of the Father's declaration. The second is to our own, for it is in the sacrament

---

[24] The 1970/2002 collects assigned to Sundays I, II, III, and IV respectively.

[25] There is only one request: that no earthly deed impede us as we hasten (Sunday II).

that God adopts us. The petition asks that we persevere in God's good pleasure – that is, be like the Son with whom the Father has declared he is well-pleased.

Each corpus of Christmas Sunday and Holy Day collects has a cumulative import and effect to which each prayer contributes. Thus it cannot be said that the new prayer for the Baptism substitutes consideration of Baptism and sonship for meditation on the mystery of the Incarnation, for the latter is beautifully and effectively presented in the new collect assigned to the day Mass of Christmas. It does, however, introduce something which is not found among the Christmas Sunday and Holy Day collects of the Tridentine missals: consideration of our adopted sonship.

Two other differences between the two sets of Christmas Sunday and Holy Day collects seem not to be significant in themselves, but will prove so if it they are discovered to be instances in a pattern of revision decisions. The first difference is that there is no mention of sin in the Vatican II set. The one prayer which mentions sin in the 1962 corpus, the collect of the Day Mass of Christmas, was omitted from the revised missals. Second, there is no mention of submission in Vatican II missals. Submission is only mentioned once in the texts of the 1962 missal that we consider here. The collect of the feast of the Holy Family describes Jesus as being subject to his human parents. What catches attention, however, is that the same root word also appears in the source prayer of the new collect assigned to the second Sunday of the Nativity, but the modern revisers edited it changing "the people subject to you" to "all people."[26]

Septuagesima

The Septuagesima collects of the 1962 missals prepare the faithful to enter into the asceticisms of Lent mindful of vital spiritual truths, the most important of which is the primacy of grace. It is the Lord who frees us from sin and its effects, who protects us from danger, who makes our ascetical exercises fruitful. The person who understands these things does not put his trust in himself, in his own deeds, or even in his Lenten efforts, but in the grace of Christ.

The suppression of Septuagesima means that the faithful who worship by means of the revised missal receive no liturgical preparation for Lent. There is no liturgical notice that Lent is drawing near, and there is no exposure to lessons and prayers that foster spiritual attitudes and importune graces especially conducive to fruitful Lenten observance.

---

[26] *Subditis tibi populis* becomes *cunctis populis*.

Lent

Comparison of the Collects

The collect assigned to the first Sunday of Lent in the 1970/2002 missals is infinitely suggestive. Lent is an imitation of Christ's time in the desert. His 40-day fast is a mystery, something full of meaning. The petition that we grasp this meaning and live all that it signifies is bottomless.

The collect of Sunday I in the 1962 missal is also bottomless, but more specific. Lent is a period in which God purifies his Church. God's family (= Church) participates willingly (strives) in this purification by abstaining but, recognizing that purification is insufficient because it is essentially negative, asks God that we may follow upon the purification gained by abstinence with good works. Both the primacy of God's action and the necessity of graced, free, human response are deftly presented.

The Palm Sunday collect is the same in both missals. Those assigned to the intervening Sundays,[27] however, are different. The following chart presents four aspects of each of these intervening collects: 1) the address and description of God; 2) the description of us; 3) the petition; 4) the result which follows if the petition is granted. In only two of the Lenten Sunday prayers in each missal does a named result accompany the petition.

	Su	1962	2002
1. God	II	God, who see us to be destitute of every strength	God, who command us to listen to your beloved Son
	III	almighty God	God, author of all mercies and the whole of goodness, who have shown that the remedies of sins are in fasting, prayer, and almsgiving
	IV	almighty God	God, who wondrously work the reconciliation of the human race through your Word
	Pass./V	almighty God	O Lord, our God

---

[27] Sunday I to IV of Lent and Passion Sunday I in the 1962 missal, and Sunday I to V of Lent in the 1970/2002 missals.

2. Us	II	destitute of every strength	those whom God commands to listen to his Son
	III	lowly	those who confess humility
	IV	justly afflicted on account of our actions	Christian people
	Pass./V	your family	we
3. Pet.	II	watch over us within and without	deign to nourish us inwardly with your word
	III	look upon the prayers of the lowly and stretch out the right hand of your majesty for our defense.	look graciously upon this confession of our humility
	IV	grant that we may find relief in the consolation of your grace	that the Christian people may be able to hasten to the coming solemnity with prompt devotion and ready faith
	Pass./V	look mercifully upon your family	that through your aid, we may be found eagerly walking in that charity by which your Son, loving the world, delivered himself to death
4. Result	II	that in body we may be protected from all adversity and in mind purified of perverse thoughts	that with spiritual sight purified, we may rejoice in the vision of your glory.
	III		that we who are brought low by our conscience may always be raised up by your mercy

	Pass./V	that, by your bounty, your family may be guided aright in the things of the body, and, by your keeping, it may be guarded in mind/soul.	

The 1962 collect of Sunday II calls upon God as one who sees that we are completely powerless; the remaining three address him simply as "omnipotens Deus," all-powerful God. Taken together these addresses express and inspire both humility and confidence.

The 1970/2002 collects describe God variously and there is nothing to distinguish them from the opening clause descriptions with which we have become familiar. God bids us heed his Son, is the author of all mercy and goodness who has revealed the remedies of sin, and the one who reconciles the human race in his Son. The first is particular to the Gospel of the day to which it is assigned (an account of the Transfiguration), the second to Lent as a penitential season, the third to the Christian Pasch.

The descriptions of us – the ones on behalf of whom the collects are prayed – in the 1962 missal are: destitute of all strength, lowly, justly afflicted on account of their deeds, and God's family.[28] In the 1970/2002 missal we are those whom God bids to heed his Son, who confess their humility, the Christian people, and "we."[29] There are no parallels in the post-Vatican II missals for the Tridentine confessions that we are destitute of strength and justly afflicted because of our deeds. These are statements about the spiritual condition and/or inner life of the ones praying. The 1970/2002 confession that God has commanded us to listen to his Son and the descriptive "Christian people" are of a different order entirely, for they say nothing of the inner state of the ones praying.

The first two petitions of the 1970/2002 missal, while not the same as any in the 1962 set, are like them. The "look graciously upon this confession of our humility" of the 1970/2002 collect assigned to Sunday III echoes the "look on the prayers of the lowly" of the 1962 collect assigned to the same day. And "deign to nourish us inwardly with your word" (1970/2002, Sunday II) though different, is the same sort of request as "grant that we may be revived by the consolation of your grace" (1962, Sunday IV).

The other two 1970/2002 petitions, that we hasten to the coming solemnity with prompt devotion and ready faith and be found eagerly walking in that charity by which the Son delivered himself to death are unlike anything in the 1962 Lenten Sunday collects. They strike a new

---

[28] Sunday II–IV of Lent and Passion Sunday, respectively.
[29] Sunday II–V of Lent, respectively.

note. The same note is heard in one of the Advent Sunday collects of the revised missal, and we return to this subject below. In contrast to the movement suggested in these two 1970/2002 prayers, the 1962 collects beg God's action and say nothing of our own: watch over us within and without, stretch out your hand to defend us, console us with your grace, look mercifully.[30]

We come now to the last aspect: the expected result. Only two petitions in each set are attended by a result clause. In the logic of the 1962 collect for Sunday II, if God watches over us within and without, we will be protected in body from all adversity and purified in mind of perverse thoughts; in that of the collect assigned to Passion Sunday, if God looks mercifully upon his family, it will be, by his bounty, guided aright in the things of the body, and, by his keeping, guarded in mind/soul. Turning to the 1970/2002 missal, in the logic of the collect of Sunday II, if God nourishes us interiorly with his word, we will rejoice in the vision of his glory with spiritual sight purified. In that of Sunday III it is that if God looks graciously upon the confession of our humility, we will be raised up by his mercy. The first looks ahead to eternal life in heaven; the second seeks relief in the present.

While there are common elements, the Lenten Sunday sets of the two missals are different. Below we speak about presence and absence in each set.

The way in which the 1962 Sunday collects emphasize the intimate relationship between body and soul, between corporeal ascesis and interior purification or spiritual progress, is not mirrored in the collects of Vatican II missals. A weaker version is found in just one 1970/2002 collect, that of Sunday III. Also, there is nothing in the new set of collects that is equivalent to the delicate presentation of the respective roles of God's grace and graced human effort found in the 1962 collect of Sunday I. In the 1962 collects there is an abiding awareness, on the one hand, of God's omnipotence and mercy and, on the other, of our frailty. Human frailty and the inner life are not so much emphasized in the revised collects. The only human movement in the 1962 missal is the striving by abstaining mentioned in the collect of Sunday I, and the only request to enter everlasting life (fellowship in his resurrection) is in the Palm Sunday collect that appears in both missals.

We turn now to the Lenten Sunday collects of the 1970/2002 missal. Using the language of mystery/sacrament, the collect of Sunday I explicitly roots Lenten observance in Christ's 40-day desert fast. There is nothing equivalent in the Lenten Sunday collects of the Tridentine missals. Also there is nothing equivalent in the Tridentine missals to the explicit mention of the three traditional means of doing penance in the post-Vatican collect of Sunday III. Two 1970/2002 collects, in contrast to just one in the 1962 set, ask that we may reach our heavenly goal.

---

[30] The petitions of the collects of Sunday II, III, IV of Lent and Passion Sunday, respectively.

New elements

There is a tone, a depiction of the faithful, and a type of petition in two of the1970/2002 Lenten Sunday collects that is new to the Sunday collects assigned to Lent in Roman Missals. The same new elements have also been introduced to Advent in the new missal.

The collect of Sunday IV of Lent asks that the Christian people may be able to hasten to the coming solemnity with prompt devotion and ready faith. Sunday IV is *Laetare* Sunday, and its collect is similar to the collect assigned to *Gaudete* Sunday in the same missal. The Advent prayer reads:

O God, who see your people faithfully awaiting the feast of the Lord's nativity, grant, we beseech you, that we may be able to arrive at the joys of such a great salvation, and ever to celebrate them with solemn prayers and ready rejoicing.[31]

The similarity lies in the petitions, both of which seek arrival at the approaching feast, and in the vocabulary, both use the unusual adjective *alacer*. In the Vatican II missals *alacer*, which is not found at all in the Tridentine missals, appears only in these two prayers.[32]

The second Lenten Sunday collect that is quite unlike any in the Lenten set of the Tridentine missals is assigned to Sunday V. It uses the adverbial form of the same word, *alacriter*, to ask that we, by God's help, may be found eagerly walking in that charity with which Christ handed himself over to death. *Alacriter* is found elsewhere in the Vatican II missals,[33] but not at all in the Tridentine missals. *Alacer* means lively, brisk, quick, eager; glad, happy, cheerful[34] – that is, it includes both quickness and gladness. It describes a wonderful spiritual disposition, but not one usually associated with Lent. The word is not found in the Vulgate, either in adjectival or adverbial form.

The collects of *Gaudete* and *Laetare* Sundays (Advent III and Lent IV respectively) in the new missal seem to have been selected/confected both to orient the faithful to the coming solemnity and to inspire or express an attendant gladness – the gladness to which we are exhorted by the traditional names of the days: *Gaudete*! *Laetare*! The essential difference between these two collects and the corresponding prayers of the Tridentine missals is that the Vatican II prayers do not speak of the interior person in

---

[31] Deus, qui conspicis populum tuum nativitatis dominicae festivitatem fideliter exspectare, praesta, quaesumus, ut valeamus ad tantae salutis gaudia pervenire, et ea votis sollemnibus alacri semper laetitia celebrare.

[32] *Alacer* appears in the prayer from *Rotulus of Ravenna* which was adapted for use on *Gaudete* Sunday. It was introduced by the revisers into the collect assigned to *Laetare* Sunday.

[33] *Alacriter* appears three times in all in the first and second typical editions of the Vatican II missals, and four times in the third.

[34] Charlton T. Lewis, *A Latin Dictionary* (Oxford: Clarendon Press, 1879) s.v., p. 79.

the way or to the extent that the Tridentine prayers do. These latter ask that God, by the grace of his visitation, illuminate the darkness of our mind (Advent) and refresh us with the consolation of his grace (Lent).

Paschaltide: the Culmination of Proper Time

A detailed discussion of likeness and difference in the two sets of Paschal collects is presented above.[35] Here we discuss the Paschal Sunday and holy day collects again, but this time our interest is the way in which each Paschal set completes the corpus of proper season Sunday collects in its respective missal.

1962 Missal

Advent
In three of the four Advent Sunday collects we await the Lord's coming expectantly and, to give the imperative verbs their due, demandingly, but otherwise – one might say passively if that word were not liable to misinterpretation. This "passivity" is an open, poised receptivity that longs for the Lord's merciful visitation. The remaining prayer, that assigned to Sunday II and the only one of the four addressed to the Father, asks him to rouse our hearts to prepare the way for his Son. The prayer recognizes that unless he rouses us we will not be able to prepare for the Son. Two further contingencies are presented as the prayer's other request unfolds. Unless we prepare the Son's way our minds will not be made pure through his coming, and unless they are made pure we will not be able to serve God which is what we ask to do. The wondrous relationship between divine grace and human freedom is flawlessly presented in this terse prayer of 18 words.

Christmas
If we begin with the night Mass of the Lord's Nativity and end with the Commemoration of the Lord's Baptism on the Octave Day of the Epiphany, there are nine Christmas collects in the 1962 missal. Five of these present us not as actors, but as grateful recipients of divine favor who await further favors. In the collect of the night Mass of the Nativity, we are those who have known the mysteries of Christ's light on earth and ask to enjoy his gladness in heaven; in that of the day Mass of the Nativity, that this new birth may free us from the yoke of sin; in that of the Octave day of the Nativity, that we may experience the Mother of the Lord interceding for us; in that of the Epiphany, that we may be led to heaven; in that of the Lord's Baptism, that we may be interiorly transformed.

---

[35] See pp. 201–5.

In addition to the collects of the night Mass of Christmas and the Epiphany, two other collects ask that we may gain heaven. Attached to these petitions is something about us. The collect of the Holy Name asks that we may one day see him in heaven whose name we venerate on earth, and that of the Holy Family that we may be instructed by the example of the members of the Holy Family and have fellowship with them in heaven.

Only in the two remaining Christmastide collects is there direct focus on our action. The collect assigned to the Dawn Mass of the Nativity asks that our deeds may reflect our faith in the Incarnate Word, and that assigned to Sunday within the Nativity Octave asks that God direct our actions so that, in the name of his beloved Son, we may be able to abound in good works. In this last there is, once again, a deft articulation of the relationship between divine grace and meritorious human action: only if God directs us according to his will are we able to perform good works in his Son's name.

Septuagesima

In the three collects of Septuagesima the human agents are, again, not acting or asking to act, but poised to receive: freedom from the afflictions of sin, defense against hostile forces, freedom from fetters and protection from misfortune.[1]

Lent

In five of the six Lenten Sunday collects we do not act, but attentively await protection, consolation, purification, and guidance from God. The collect of Sunday II, in which we confess that we are devoid of all strength, asks that God watch over us so that we may be protected and purified; that of Sunday III, that he stretch out his arm in our defense; that of Sunday IV that he revive us with the consolation of his grace; that of Sunday I of the Passion, that he look graciously upon us that we may be guided aright and guarded.

The collect of Palm Sunday anticipates a response from us in its request that we may be worthy of having the example of Christ's patience. The prayer also asks that we may attain heaven which is described as fellowship in Christ's resurrection.

Only the collect of Sunday I presents us as active: we are striving to obtain by abstaining. But here again our activity is a response to the prior action of God and its fruitfulness is conditioned upon his gift. It is God who purifies his family, the Church, through Lenten observance. We give ourselves to this observance by abstaining and pray that God may grant us two things: to be purified and, once purified, to do good works.

Paschaltide

We come now to the 1962 collects of Paschaltide. There are nine collects. Only two of these present us simply as recipients. The collect of Easter Sunday asks God to accompany the desires he inspires in us with his assistance. The collect of the second Sunday after Easter asks for everlasting happiness.

The seven remaining prayers all have petitions that ask God to grace us in a way which makes us act fittingly. The collect of the Octave Day of the Pasch asks that by God's generous granting we may hold fast in character and in life to all that the feast of the resurrection signifies; that of the third Sunday after Easter, that all who profess Christ may reject what is inimical to his name and pursue what befits it; that of the fourth Sunday, that God's people love what he commands and desire what he promises; that of the fifth Sunday, that we may think, by God's inspiration, those things which are right and, by his governance, do the same; that of the Ascension, that our minds may dwell in heaven with our ascended Lord; that of the Sunday after the Ascension, that we may bear a will devoted to the Lord and always serve his majesty with a sincere heart; that of Pentecost Sunday that God may grant us in his Spirit to be truly wise and ever to rejoice in the Spirit's consolation.

As is the case for Advent, Christmas, and Lent, there is one collect among those assigned to the Paschal Sundays that expresses the Catholic theology of grace with particular clarity. It is the collect assigned to the fifth Sunday after Easter which asks God, who is described as the one from whom all good things come, that we may think good things by his having breathed them in to us, and to do these same good things by his piloting or steering us.

Two paschal collects ask that we may attain heaven, those of the second Sunday after Easter (unending joy) and Pentecost (ever rejoice in his consolation).

Summary
Almost no activity at all is attributed to human beings in the 1962 Sunday and holy day collects of Advent, Septuagesima, and Lent. Only two of the nine Christmas collects pray that we actively respond to the Lord's birth – one that we live what we believe about the Incarnation and the other that we abound in good works done in the Son's name. It is quite a different matter with the Paschal collects – arrestingly so. Seven of the nine collects ask for graces that dispose us properly and/or bring us to act rightly. Further, cumulatively they ask for our every faculty to be fully and properly engaged. This arrangement of collects, or anyway of petitions, presents a concrete picture of a central Christian truth: transforming and enabling grace comes to us only through the death and resurrection of the Lord.

2002 Missal

For the sake of simplicity, in those cases where two collects are assigned to a single day and one of these is from the 1962 missal, we consider only the newly assigned prayer.

Advent

Three of the four collects ask that we may enter heaven. The fourth asks that we may arrive at the joys of the coming feast/of such a great salvation.[36] In collects of Sundays I and II we are hastening; in that of Sunday III, we are faithfully awaiting. Only in the collect assigned to Sunday IV do we ask simply to receive: the incarnation has been made known to us by the message of the angel and we ask to be brought to the glory of Christ's resurrection by his passion and cross.

The proportion of 2002 Advent collects that portray us as active (three) or poised to receive (one) is exactly the inverse of the proportion in the 1962 missal.

Christmas

There are ten Christmas collects to consider. Seven of the ten seem to present not as actors but as grateful recipients of divine favor who await further favors. In the collect of the vigil Mass of the Nativity, we ask that we may be fearless when we see Christ coming as judge; in that of the night Mass of the Nativity, that we may enjoy the gladness of Christ in heaven; in that of the day Mass of the Nativity, that we may be sharers of Christ's divinity; in that of the Octave day of the Nativity, that we may experience the Mother of the Lord interceding for us; in that of the second Sunday of the Nativity, that God fill the world with his glory and reveal himself to all people; in that of Epiphany, that we may be led to heaven; in that of the Baptism, that we persevere in the Father's good pleasure.

In addition to the collects of the night Mass of Christmas and the Epiphany, two other collects ask that we may gain heaven. In both of these certain behaviors attach to the petition. The collect of the feast of the Holy Family asks that, by imitating the Family's domestic virtues, we may one day have fellowship with them in heaven; and the collect of the vigil of the Epiphany asks that we may have the strength to pass by the darkness of the world and so arrive at our heavenly homeland. The last collect, that assigned to the Dawn Mass of the Nativity, asks that our deeds may reflect our faith in the Incarnate Word.

The proportion of 2002 Christmas collects portraying us as active or poised to receive is roughly the same as the proportion in the 1962 set. We are poised to receive in seven of ten in the Vatican II missals and in seven of nine in the Tridentine missals.

Lent

In two of the Lenten Sunday collects of the 2002 missal we do not act of ourselves. The collect of Sunday II asks that God nourish us with his word

---

[36] Advent Sunday III.

so that, with purified sight, we may come to a vision of his glory; that of Sunday III, that we may be raised by his mercy.

The collect of Palm Sunday, which is the same in both missals, anticipates a response from us in its request that we may be worthy of having the example of Christ's patience but does not have us acting. The prayer also asks that we may attain heaven, as does the collect of Sunday II.

The petitions of the collects of Sunday I, IV, and V present us, at least potentially, as active. The collect of Sunday I asks that we may understand the mystery of Christ and follow it with a worthy manner of life; that of Sunday IV that we may hasten to the coming feast with prompt devotion and ready faith; that of Sunday V, that we may found eagerly walking in the charity with which Christ gave himself up to death.

We are poised to receive in three of six 2002 Lenten Sunday collects, and in five of the six in the 1962 missal.

Paschaltide
There are eleven collects to consider. Six of the eleven present us simply as recipients. The collect of Easter asks that we may, through the renewal of the Holy Spirit, rise in the light of life; that of Sunday IV of the Pasch, that we may be led to the communion of heavenly joys; that of the Ascension vigil, that Christ will remain on earth with us and that we be with him in heaven; that of Sunday VII of the Pasch, that we may experience Christ remaining with us; that of the vigil of Pentecost, that the division of tongues may be gathered in a single confession of God's name; that of Pentecost, that God may do now in the hearts of believers what he did when the Gospel was first preached.

The five remaining collects all ask for a particular kind of engagement or action on our part. The collect of Sunday II asks that we may understand; that of Sunday III, that we may exult and await; that of Sunday V, that we may bear much fruit; that of Sunday VI, that we keep Paschaltide with earnest love; that of the Ascension that we may exult in holy joy and rejoice in devout thanksgiving.

Four collects ask that we may attain heaven, those of Sundays III, IV, V, and the vigil of the Ascension.

Summary
The change from being largely poised and waiting recipients in the preparatory seasons to enabled actors in Paschaltide that we note in the collects of the 1962 missal was not carried into the revised liturgy. These 1962 Paschal prayers, in which we ask for the right ordering of our minds, wills, thoughts, acts, desires and so forth, have been moved to the Sundays *per annum* in the Vatican II missals.

Paschaltide is the only proper season in the 2002 missal in which the number of collects that depict us simply as recipients of divine favor exceeds the number of collects that present us acting, six to five. The proper season collects of the new missal culminate in a resting in the joy of the Lord's resurrection and meditation upon it. Hence we find petitions such as may they grasp with worthy understanding by what bath, Spirit, and blood they have been washed, reborn, and redeemed (Sun III); may your people always rejoice (Sunday III); make those who celebrate these days of joy keep them with earnest love (Sunday VI); grant us to exult in holy joy and be glad in devout thanksgiving (Ascension). The Paschal collects of the 2002 missal are in large part devoted to a joy-filled and grateful savoring of the mysteries of the Lord's Resurrection and Ascension.

Lastly, in the Sunday and holy day collects of the proper seasons of the 2002 missal there are almost twice as many petitions for us to gain heaven as there are in those of the old missal, thirteen to the earlier seven.

Conclusion

We have carefully examined the collects assigned to the Sundays and holy days of proper seasons in the pre- and post-Vatican II missals, studying each collect in itself and in the light of its counterpart. We have also compared and contrasted the two sets of collects. In these final pages we explain why the two sets are equivalent, summarize their chief differences, and state what is and is not signified.

The two sets are equivalent and must be held to be such in every respect, for both have been given to us by the Church for worship. The case is similar to that of the oriental rites. The texts and ceremonials of the Divine Liturgy of the Byzantine Rite are very different from the Mass of the Roman Rite but in each the Paschal Mystery, the whole reality of our salvation that God has given to his Church to celebrate, is really and truly re-presented. The same must be said of the pre- and post-Vatican II missals. They arise from the same faith, celebrate the same saving mysteries, and are given to us by the Church. Moreover, the two missals have a significant number of common collects.

But as we have seen, to a considerable extent the collects of the respective sets do not approach God in the same way, seek the same things from him, present the same picture of the human situation, and so forth. The 1962 collects are more attentive to the interior person than are those of the post-Vatican II missals and, perhaps, more subtle in the way they draw their content from the mysteries being celebrated. In contrast, the Vatican II proper season collects are more explicit in the mention of feasts and the joy they occasion, less attentive to the inner aspects of spiritual transformation in Christ, and more likely to ask for the final attainment of heaven than for specific kinds of help on the way.

That there are significant changes in the theological and/or spiritual emphases of the collects of given seasons is clear. What is not clear, because we have not yet studied the collects assigned to *per annum* Sundays, is whether these changes in emphases are offset by the revisions in other parts of the missal. For example, we saw above that the 1962 missal assigns collects which, with only the fewest exceptions, present us as attentive and hopeful recipients of God's gracious action in the preparatory seasons of Advent and Lent, and assigns collects to Paschaltide that pray for godly dispositions and behaviors. Whether this is by design or a deep instinct of Christian faith, it does give eloquent if subtle witness to the truth that the grace which transforms us interiorly and gives us the strength to devote ourselves to God and his service comes to us through the death and resurrection of the Lord. The Paschal collects of the 2002 missal do not repeat this pattern but, rather, focus on the mysteries and joys of the season. The 1962 Paschal collects are assigned to *per annum* Sundays in the revised missals – that is, the erstwhile Paschal collects are included in the revised missals but appear in a different liturgical, theological, and spiritual context. Since we have not yet studied them in their new context, we are not able to say what the differences we note signify about the missal as a whole.

We close with a paradox. On the one hand, because of our incarnate nature, words and gestures matter. Each aspect and element of our prayers matters. For this reason, it is important to give very careful attention to the character, content, and aesthetic qualities of our prayers. Their value, which is inestimable, does not reside only in what they seek from God. It also, and perhaps more especially, resides in their truth, depth, beauty, and their capacity, by God's grace, to draw us into the saving mysteries and to God himself. On the other hand, human speech is always going to be inadequate; it will always fall short. But God is not limited by our limitations, and he knows what we need before we ask him.

BIBLIOGRAPHY

Ashworth, Henry. "The Prayers for the Dead in the Missal of Pope Paul VI," *Ephemerides Liturgicae* 85 (1971) 3–15.

Auer, Johann, and Hugh M. Riley. *A General Doctrine of the Sacraments and the Mystery of the Eucharist*. Washington, DC: Catholic University of America Press, 1995.

Augé, Matias. "Le Colletta del Proprio del Tempo nel Nuovo Messale," *Ephemerides Liturgicae* 84 (1970) 275–98.

Augustine, and D. W. Robertson. *On Christian Doctrine*. Upper Saddle River, NJ: Prentice Hall, 1997. 34, 15–122; 40, 309–48.

Augustine, and Joseph P. Christopher. *The First Catechetical Instruction: (de Catechizandis Rudibus)*. Westminster, MD: Newman Press, 1962.

Augustinus, Aurelius, Scholastica Hebgin, and Felicitas Corrigan. *St. Augustine on the Psalms*. New York, NY: Newman, 1974. 37, 33–1967.

Barba, Maurizio. "Il Temporale, L'« Ordo Missae » e il Santorale del Nuovo « Missale Romanum, »" *Ephemerides Liturgicae* 116 (2002) 320–66.

Braga, Carlo. "Il Nuovo Messale Romano," *Ephemerides Liturgicae* 84 (1970) 249–74.

—"Il 'Proprium de Sanctis,'" *Ephemerides Liturgicae* 84 (1970) 401–3.

Bruylants, P. *Les Oraisons Du Missel Romain: Texte Et Histoire*. Louvain: Centre de Documentation et d'Information Liturgiques, 1952.

Bugnini, Annibale. *La Riforma Liturgica, 1948–1975*. Roma: CLV-Edizioni liturgiche, 1983.

—*The Reform of the Liturgy, 1948–1975*. Collegeville, MN: Liturgical Press, 1990.

Cabrol, F. "Annonciation" (fête de L') *DACL* vol. 1.2 (Paris: Letouzey et Ané, 1913–53), col. 2244ff.

Callewaert, Camille. *Sacris Erudiri: fragmenta liturgica collecta* in *Sacris Erudiri*, Fragmenta Liturgica Collecta a Monachis Sancti Petri de Aldenbruggo in Steenbrugge ne Pereant (The Hague: Steenbrugis) (The Hague: Nijhoff, 1962).

Capelle, B, "La main de Saint Grégoire dans le sacramentaire grégorien," *Revue bénédictine* 49 (1937), 13–28.

Cassian, John. *Conferences* in Schaff, P, and Wace, H. (eds), *A select library of Nicene and Post-Nicene Fathers of the Christian Church*: second series, vol 11. Peabody, MA: Hendrickson, 1999.

Catholic Church. *Missale Romanum: Ex Decreto Sacrosancti Oecumenici Concilii Vaticani II Instauratum*. In Civitate Vaticano: Typis polyglottis Vaticanis, 1970.

—*Missale Romanum: Ex Decreto Sacrosancti Oecumenici Concilii Vaticani II Instauratum : Auctoritate Pauli Pp. [i.e. Papae] VI Promulgatum*. S.l: s.n., 1975.

—*Missale Romanum: Ex Decreto Sacrosancti Oecumenici Concilii Vaticani II
Instauratum : Auctoritate Pauli Pp. Vi Promulgatum : Ioannis Pauli Pp. II
Cura Recognitum.* Vatican City: Typis Vaticanis, 2002.

—*Missale Romanum: Ex Decreto Sacrosancti Oecumenici Concilii Vaticani II
Instauratum : Auctoritate Pauli Pp. VI Promulgatum : Ioannis Pauli Pp. II
Cura Recognitum.* Vatican City: Typis Vaticanis, 2008.

—Moeller, Eugenio, Jean-Marie Clément, and Bertrandus Coppieters 't Wallant.
Corpus Orationum, I-IX, Turnholti [Turnholt, Belgium] Brepols, 1992.

—*The Roman Missal: Renewed by Decree of the Most Holy Second Ecumenical
Council of the Vatican, Promulgated by Authority of Pope Paul Vi and Revised
at the Direction of Pope John Paul Ii.* Collegeville, MN: Liturgical Press, 2011.

—*The Voice of the Church: A Forum on Liturgical Translation.* Washington, D.C:
United States Catholic Conference, 2001.

Catholic Church, et al. *Sacrorum conciliorum: nova, et amplissima collectio:
in qua præter ea quæ Phil. Labbeus, et Gabr. Cossartius S.J. et novissime
Nicolaus Coleti in lucem edidere ea omnia insuper suis in locis optime disposita
exhibentur, quæ Joannes Dominicus Mansi, Lucensis, Congregationis Matris
Dei evulgavit.* Florentiæ: Expensis Antonii Zatta, 1759.

Catholic Church, and Leo Cunibert Mohlberg. *Missale Gothicum: (Vat. Reg. lat.
317).* Roma: Herder, 1961.

Catholic Church, and Leo Cunibert Mohlberg. *Liber Sacramentorum Romanae
Aeclesiae ordinis anni circuli (Cod. Vat. Reg. lat. 316/Paris bibl. Nat. 7193,
41/56) (Sacramentarium Gelasianum).* Roma: Herder, 1968.

Catholic Church, and Jean Deshusses. *Le sacramentaire grégorien, ses principales
formes d'après les plus anciens manuscrits.* Fribourg: Éditions universitaires,
1971.

Catholic Church, Alban Dold, and Leo Eizenhöfer. *Das Prager Sakramentar
(Cod. O. 83, Fol. 1–20, der Bibliothek des Metropolitankapitels).* Beuron in
Hohenzollern: Beuroner Kunstverlag, 1944.

Catholic Church, Alban Dold, and Klaus Gamber. *Das Sakramentar von Monza
(im Cod. F 1/101 der dortigen Kapitelsbibliothek): ein aus Einzel-Libelli
redigiertes Jahresmessbuch ; mit Anhang ein Scheyerer Sakramentar-Fragment
im Monza-Typ.* Beuron im Hohenzollern: Beuroner Kunstverlag, 1957.

Catholic Church, Antoine Dumas, and Jean Deshusses. *Liber sacramentorum
Gellonensis.* Turnholti: Brepols, 1981.

Catholic Church, Leo Eizenhöfer, Leo Cunibert Mohlberg, and Petrus Siffrin. *Liber
sacramentorum Romanae Aeclesiae ordinis anni circuli (Cod. Vat. Reg. Lat. 316/
Paris Bibl. nat. 7193, 41/56, Sacramentarium Gelasianum).* Roma: Herder, 1960.

Catholic Church and John XXIII, Pope. *Acta et Documenta Concilio Oecumenico
Vaticano II Apparando,* series 1, appendix volume I: (Typis Polyglottis
Vaticanis, 1960).

Catholic Church, Cuthbert Johnson, and Anthony Ward. *Missale romanum anno
1962 promulgatum.* Roma: CLV-Edizioni Liturgiche, 1994.

Catholic Church, and Angelo Paredi. *Sacramentarium bergomense: manoscritto
del secolo IX della Biblioteca di S. Alessandro in Colonna in Bergamo.*
Bergamo: Edizioni "Monumenta Bergomensia," 1962.

Catholic Church, and Patrick Saint-Roch. *Liber sacramentorum Engolismensis:
manuscrit B.N. Lat. 816, Le sacramentaire gélasien d'Angoulême.* Turnholti:
Brepols, 1987.

Catholic Church, Thaddäus A. Schnitker, and Wolfgang A. Slaby. *Concordantia verbalia Missalis Romani: partes euchologicae.* Münster: Aschendorff, 1983.

Chavasse, Antoine. "L'Avent Romain, du VIe au VIIIe Siècle," *Ephemerides Liturgicae* (1953) 297–308.

—*Le Sacramentaire Gélasien Du VIIe Siècle: Ses Deux Principales Formes.* s.l.: s.n., 1959.

Chupungco, Ansgar J. "The English Translation of the Latin Liturgy" *Notitiae* 18 (1982) 91–100.

Concilium Vaticanum II (1962–1965), and Johannes. *Acta et Documenta Concilio Oecumenico Vaticano II Apparando: Appendix II : Analyticus Conspectus Consiliorum Et Votorum Quae Ab Episcopis Et Praelatis Data Sunt.* Cittá del Vaticano: Typ. Polyglottis Vaticanis, 1961.

Consilium ad exsequendam Constitutionem de Sacra Liturgia. *Elenchus membrorum – consultorum – consiliariorum coetuum a studiis* (Vatican: Typis Polyglottis Vaticanis, 1964).

Consilium ad exsequendam Constitutionem de Sacra Liturgia. *Res Secretariae,* n. 12 (26 October 1964).*[1]

Consilium ad exsequendam Constitutionem de Sacra Liturgia. *Res Secretariae,* n. 19 (14 June 1965).*

Consilium ad exsequendam Constitutionem de Sacra Liturgia. Schema n. 61, *De Calendario,* 1 (12 February 1965).*

Consilium ad exsequendam Constitutionem de Sacra Liturgia. Schema n. 65, *De Calendario,* 2 (15 March 1965).*

Consilium ad exsequendam Constitutionem de Sacra Liturgia. Schema n. 75, *De Calendario,* 4 (10 April 1965).*

Consilium ad exsequendam Constitutionem de Sacra Liturgia. Schema n. 104, *De Anno Liturgico,* 5 (10 May 1965).*

Consilium ad exsequendam Constitutionem de Sacra Liturgia. Schema n. 132, *De Calendario,* 7 (3 December 1965).*

Consilium ad exsequendam Constitutionem de Sacra Liturgia. Schema n. 156, *De Missali* 20, (30 April 1966).*

Consilium ad exsequendam Constitutionem de Sacra Liturgia. Schema n. 186, *De Missali* 27 (19 September 1966).*

Consilium ad exsequendam Constitutionem de Sacra Liturgia. Schema n. 186, Addendum I, *De Missali* 27 (19 September 1966).*

Consilium ad exsequendam Constitutionem de Sacra Liturgia. Schema n. 188, *De Calendario,* 11 (22 September 1966).*

Consilium ad exsequendam Constitutionem de Sacra Liturgia. Schema n. 188, Addendum, *De Calendario,* 11 (22 September 1966).*

Deferrari, Roy J. *A Latin-English Dictionary of Saint Thomas Aquinas* (Boston: Saint Paul Editions, 1960).

Denzinger, Heinrich, and Adolf Schönmetzer. *Enchiridion Symbolorum: Definitionum Et Declarationum De Rebus Fidei Et Morum.* Barcinone: Herder, 1967.

---

[1] All the entries marked with an asterisk (*) are unpublished documents on file at the offices of the Secretariat of the International Commission on English in the Liturgy in Washington, D.C.

Deshusses, J. ed., *Le sacramentaire grégorien: Ses Principales Formes D'après Les Plus Anciens Manuscrits*, tome I, (= Spicilegium Friburgense, 16, Fribourg en Suisse, 1971).

Duffy, Eamon. "Rewriting the Liturgy: the Theological Issues of Translation" *New Blackfriars* 78 (January, 1997) 4–27 reprinted in Stratford Caldecott, ed., *Beyond the Prosaic* (Edinburgh: T&T Clark, 1998) 97–126.

Dumas, Antoine, and Jean Deshusses. *Liber Sacramentorum Gellonensis.* Turnholti: Brepols, 1981. The codex is Paris, Bibliothèque Nationale, lat. 12.048. The modern critical edition is A. Dumas, ed., Liber Sacramentorum Gellonensis (= CCSL CLIX), Turnholt, 1981.

Dumas, Antoine. "Les Oraisons du nouveau Missel Romain," *Liturgiques* 25 (1971): 263–70. English translation available in Lauren Pristas, "The Orations of the Vatican II Missal: Policies for Revision," *Communio: an International Catholic Review*, 30:4 (Winter, 2003): 629–39.

—"Les Sources du Nouveau Missel Romain," *Notitiae* 7 (1971): 37–42, 74–7, 94–5, 134–6, 276–80, 409–10.

Feltoe, Charles L. *Leo the Great* in Select library of Nicene and post-Nicene Fathers of the Christian Church, Second series, v. 12 (Grand Rapids, MI: Eerdmans, 1956).

Férotin, Marius, and Anthony Ward. *Le Liber Mozarabicus Sacramentorum et les manuscrits mozarabes.* Roma: CLV, Ed. Liturgiche, 1995.

Ferretti, Walter. "Le Orazioni 'Post Communionem' de Tempore nel Nuovo Messale Romano," *Ephemerides Liturgicae* 84 (1970) 323–41.

Gregory I, Pope. *Homiliae in evangelia* XIX. PL 76, 1153–59.

Gy, Pierre-Marie. *The Reception of Vatican II Liturgical Reforms in the Life of the Church.* Milwaukee, WI: Marquette University Press, 2003.

Haessly, Sister Mary Gonzaga. *Rhetoric in the Sunday Collects of the Roman Missal: with Introduction, Text, Commentary and Translation* (Saint Louis: Manufacturers Printery, 1938).

Heiming, Odilo. *Das Sacramentarium Triplex: die Handschrift C 43 der Zentralbibliothek Z Zürich. 1, Text.* Das Sacramentarium Triplex. Münster: Aschendorffsche Verlagsbuchhandlung, 1968.

Johnson, Cuthbert and Ward, Anthony. "The Sources of the Roman Missal (1975)," *Notitiae* 22 (1986): 445–747.

—and 32 (1996): 3–179. "The Sources of the Roman Missal (1975)," *Notitiae* 32 (1996).

Johnson, Cuthbert. "Prefaces: Shaping a New Translation" *Pastoral Music* 16 (April-May, 1992) 34–7.

Kiefer, Ralph A. "The Eucharistic Prayer" *Worship* 50 (1976) 316–23.

LeClerq, Henri. "Septuagesime" in *DACL* vol. 15.1 (1950), cols. 1262–66.

Leiva-Merikakis, Erasmo. "The Catechetical Role of the Liturgy and the Quality of Liturgical Texts: the Current ICEL Translation" *Communio* 20 (Spring, 1993) 63–83.

Lewis, Charlton T. *A Latin Dictionary* (Oxford: Clarendon Press, 1879).

Maertens, Th. "L'Avent: Genèse historique de ses thèmes bibliques et doctrinaux," *Mélanges de science religieuse* 18 (1961): 47–110.

Marini, Piero. "Elenco Degli 'Schemata' del 'Consilium' e della Congregazione per il Culto Divino (Marzo 1964 – Iuglio 1975)" *Notitiae* 18 (1982) 448–539.

Medina, Jorge A. "Cardinal Jorge A. Medina on the ICEL Controversy" *America* 182 (April 14, 2000) 17–19.

Mershman, Francis. "Ember Days," *The Catholic Encyclopedia* vol. 5 (New York: Robert Appleton Company, 1909) 399.

Migne, J.-P, and A.-G Hamman. *Patrologiae Cursus Completus: Sive Biblioteca Universalis, Integra, Uniformis, Commoda, Oeconomica, Omnium Ss. Patrum, Doctorum Scriptorumque Eccelesiasticorum Qui Ab Aevo Apostolico Ad Usque Innocentii Iii Tempora Floruerunt ... [series Latina, in Qua Prodeunt Patres, Doctores Scriptoresque Ecclesiae Latinae, a Tertulliano Ad Innocentium III].* Parisiis, 1844.

Mohlberg, Cunibert, Petrus Siffrin, and Leo Eizenhöfer. *Sacramentarium Veronense (Cod. Bibl. Capit. Veron. LXXXV [80]).* Roma: Herder, 1956.

Paul VI, Pope. "Sacram Liturgiam," *Acta Apostolicae Sedis* 56 (1964): 139–44.

—"Paenitemini," *Acta Apostolicae Sedis* 58 (1966): 177–98.

Pflieger, André. *Liturgicae Orationis Concordantia Verbalia. Pars Prima: Missale Romanum.* Freiburg/B.: Herder, 1964.

Pius XII, Pope. "Mediator Dei," *Acta Apostolicae Sedis* 39 (1947): 546–7.

Pristas, Lauren. " Missale Romanum 1962 and 1970: a Comparative Study of Two Collects," *Antiphon* 7:3 (2003): 29–33.

—"The Orations of the Vatican II Missal: Policies for Revision," *Communio: an International Catholic Review*, 30:4 (Winter, 2003): 621–53.

—"Theological Principles that Guided the Redaction of the Roman Missal (1970)," *The Thomist* 67 (April 2003): 157–95.

—"The Collects at Sunday Mass: An Examination of the Revisions of Vatican II." *Nova et Vetera* 3.1 (Winter 2005): 5–38.

—"The Pre- and Post-Vatican II Collects of the Dominican Doctors of the Church." *New Blackfriars* 86.1006 (Nov. 2005): 604–21.

—"Post Vatican II Revision of the Lenten Collects." *Ever Directed Towards the Lord: The Love of God in the Liturgy of the Eucharist Past, Present, and Hoped for.* Ed. Uwe Michael Lang and Society of St. Catherine of Siena. London: T & T Clark, 2007.·62–89.

—"Parachuted into Lent: The Suppression of Septuagesima," *Usus Antiquior* 1.2 (July 2010): 95–109.

Raffa, Vincenzo. "Le Orazioni Sulle Offerte del Tempo nel Nuovo Messale Romano," *Ephemerides Liturgicae* 84 (1970) 299–322.

Rose, André. "The Problems of the Liturgical Reform" in Alcuin Reid, ed., *Looking Again at the Question of the Liturgy with Cardinal Ratzinger* (Farnborough: Saint Michael's Abbey Press, 2002).

Sacrosanctum Oecumenicum Concilium Vaticanum II. "Sacrosanctum Concilium" in *Constitutiones Decreta Declarationes*, vol. 1 (Civitas Vaticana: Vaticanum Typographium, 1967), 3–54.

Speaight, Robert. "Liturgy and Language," *Theology: Monthly Review* 74 (October, 1971) 444–56.

Talley, Thomas J. *The Origins of the Liturgical Year*, (New York: Pueblo, 1986).

Thomas, *Sancti Thomae De Aquino. Summa Theologiae.* Alba [Italy], Editiones Paulinae, 1962.

Thurston, H. s.v. "Ash Wednesday," *The Catholic Encyclopedia* I, (New York, 1913) 775.

Toporoski, Richard. "The Language of Worship" *Communio* 4 (Fall, 1977)
    226–60.
Trautman, Donald. "Rome and ICEL" *America* 182 (March 4, 2000) 7–11.
Vacandard, E. "Carême," *DACL* vol. 2.2 (Paris: Letouzey et Ané, 1913–1953),
    col. 2139–58.
Vatican Council. *Acta Synodalia Sacrosancti Concilii Oecumenici Vatican II* vol.
    2.2 (Vatican: Typis Polyglottis, 1972).
Vogel, Cyrille. *Medieval Liturgy: An Introduction to the Sources,* revised and
    translated by William G. Storey and Niels Rasmussen, O.P. (Washington, DC:
    Pastoral Press, 1986).
Vogel, C. and Elze, R. *Le Pontifical Romano-Germanique du dixième siècle,* II
    (Città del Vaticano, 1963).
Wallant, Bertrandus Coppieters 't. *Corpus Orationum: Addenda et Corrigenda,
    Indices, Initia et Clavsvlae Orationum.* Tomu XI. Turnholti: Brepols, 1999.
Wilmart, A. "Le *Comes* de Murbach" *Revue Bénédictine* 30 (1913) 25–69.

INDEX OF PRAYERS

INDEX OF SCRIPTURE CITATIONS

GENERAL INDEX